Pelham Horse Year

Published in association with

Lloyds Bank

Pelham Horse Year

PAMELA MACGREGOR-MORRIS

PELHAM BOOKS
LONDON

First published in Great Britain by
Pelham Books Ltd
44 Bedford Square
London WC1B 3DU
1981

ISBN 0 7207 1329 3

Typeset by Cambrian Typesetters, Farnborough
Printed in Great Britain by
Hollen Street Press Ltd, Slough
and bound by Dorstel Press Ltd, Harlow

ACKNOWLEDGEMENT

Grateful thanks to Queen Anne Press for
permission to reproduce in Chapter 23 material
from *The Horse and Rider Yearbook 1980*.

Contents

1

The Alternative Olympics and the Reason for Them

By mid-April in 1980, most of the top British three-day event riders had let it be known that they had no intention of going to Moscow to ride in the Olympic Games, except in the extremely unlikely event that the Russians pulled their troops out of Afghanistan, which they clearly had not the smallest intention of doing.

The situation came to a head at the Birmingham International show at the National Exhibition Centre in March. The Horse Trials Committee of the British Horse Society announced that it intended to boycott the Moscow Olympic Games without waiting for a British Horse Society council meeting, and a meeting of showjumpers at Birmingham, hastily convened, was of a similar persuasion, by and large – even though the Secretary-General, Commander Jefferis, told journalists that the British Show Jumping Association was 'keeping its options open'.

There was a very strong feeling – quite rightly, in my view – that as the Soviet Union intended to make political capital out of the fact that they had been invited by the International Olympic Committee to stage the Olympic Games, in order to further their cause of world domination, it would be disloyal not only to one's country to go to Moscow, but also to those of our ancestors who fought and laid down their lives in two World Wars in the cause of freedom. The official Communist party booklet declaimed that the decision to hold the Olympics in Moscow was 'a convincing testimony to the general acknowledgement of the historical importance and rightness of the foreign policy of the Soviet Union, of the enormous services of the Soviet Union in the struggle for peace. . . . The wish of the Muscovites to organise the Olympic Games was an example of the high ideals of the peace programme consistently realised by the Communist Party of the Soviet Union. . . . The great social phenomenon of the Olympic Games . . . bears the stamp of the presence of two opposing political and class systems of the world – decadent capitalism and growing socialism – that becomes daily stronger.'

The former Sports Editor of *The Times* wrote, after the somewhat abortive Games had taken place, that yachting and equestrian sport, both of which had declined to support the Moscow meeting, had been disloyal to the Olympic movement and should perhaps be dropped from future Olympics. Perhaps our sailors and horsemen hold other loyalties, such as to their country and to the ideals with which they have been brought up. These principles are surely more important than allegiance to a now bogus sporting concept in which commercialism is rife and drugs are only one of the abuses to which athletes are prey.

The happiest equestrian Olympics were those which were held on their own, divorced from the main body of the Games which were held in Melbourne in 1956. Due to Australian regulations, horses were not allowed to be imported, so the horse events were held in Stockholm. With all the controversy which surrounds today's Games – concerning shamateurism, anabolic steroids and the rest – it seems to me that the further away from the modern Olympic concept one can get, the better.

The United States and West Germany had already decided to boycott the Olympics, so early in May the Western nations enlisted the blessing of the FEI (International Equestrian Federation) to hold Olympic alternative events under the title of Festival of Equestrian Sport, 1980.

Official recognition was given for a CDIO (Concours de Dressage International Officiel) at Goodwood from 7-11th August, for a CSIO (Concours Saute International Officiel) at Rotterdam from 13-17th August, and for a CCIO (Concours Complet International Officiel) at Fontainebleau, 37 miles south of Paris, from 21st-24st August. The British Government put up £20,000 as a reward for riders who boycotted Moscow, and Lord Inchcape made a substantial contribution towards the cost of putting on the dressage at Goodwood.

The NATO countries rallied around, and the American show-jumping team, which had not been in Europe for six years, since contesting the World Championships at Hickstead in 1974, jumped at the Paris International in June and then came to England, where they were based for Hickstead and the Royal International at Wembley before going to Dublin, where they won the Aga Khan Trophy, and then on to Rotterdam.

While no one would pretend that these Olympic alternatives bore the slightest similarity to the Olympic Games themselves, at least they provided a substitute for the real thing and a valid test of strength. It was not surprising that the dressage was dominated by the West Germans, but it was quite a turn-up for the book when Canada won the team gold medals for show-jumping, and equally unpredictable that the French won the team gold medals in the three-day event, even though they had the advantage of performing on their native heath.

It was inevitable that only the Russians, Bulgarians, Hungarians, Poles and Mexicans, plus some individuals from Rumania, Finland and Guatemala, contested the Olympic equestrian events, though Italy, strong though her Communist party is in the South, was a fairly unlikely member of an otherwise unholy alliance. The Russians won the team gold medals in all three disciplines.

Major Derek Allhusen, who helped to win a team gold medal for Britain in the 1968 Olympic three-day event in Mexico, and also won the individual silver medal, said at the time the boycott was being mooted:

'I feel that the equestrian world has every reason to be proud of the unselfish and responsible attitude adopted by our likely Olympic representatives in supporting the British Equestrian Federation's decision to stand by our Government's proposed boycott of the Olympic Games. From the very beginning Lucinda Prior-Palmer and Liz Edgar (to their eternal credit, as they were both strong candidates for inclusion in their teams) were in no doubt that it would be wrong to go to Moscow. Their determination to put their principles before their own self-interest has helped our BEF to present a united front on behalf of all sections of the British Horse Society and the British Show Jumping Association, and it is to be hoped that other representative bodies will follow suit.

'Meanwhile, Sir Denis Follows, pursuing his ridiculous argument that it is possible to divorce the 1980 Games from politics, continues to ignore the wishes of his country's Government, to the embarrassment of many of the sponsors on whom British sport so largely depends. Moreover, having stated publicly that he would take full account of the opinion of the House of Commons, he has evidently shown no willingness to recommend to his Olympic Committee that they should abide by the large majority vote in favour of a boycott.

'What he is really saying, and is so wrongly encouraging others to believe, is that the invasion and cruel subjugation of a small and non-aligned country by a world power is of secondary importance to the interests of sport.

'It is important to understand that everything in Russia, whether it is the success of their sportsmen or the artistry of their ballet dancers and gymnasts, is used for propaganda purposes to glorify the Soviet system. I remember being interviewed by a Radio Moscow reporter in my hired Volga car at the conclusion of the European Three-Day Event Championships in Moscow in 1965, when Britain sent her first equestrian team to Russia. I listened to the broadcast of this interview on my radio some two days later, as I was driving from the airport to my farm in Norfolk. Harmless as my remarks appeared to be in my praise for the organisation and the hospitality we had been shown, the script had been edited in such a way that I heard myself contributing, unwittingly, to the Russian propaganda machine.

'The presence in Moscow of Olympic teams from the Western nations will be used by the Kremlin to endorse their action in Afghanistan and to give it respectability in the eyes of the world. It will, moreover, deprive the Russian people of the opportunity to reflect upon the strong reaction of the Western nations to the hideous crimes of the Soviet leaders. A total boycott would pose a question which the Politburo would find very difficult to answer.

'The modern Russian is now much more susceptible to the views of the West and more sensitive to its strictures, and it is vital that he should be made aware of the world's condemnation of his country's brutal foreign policy and of the treatment of her dissidents. Quite one of the worst features of the preparation for the Games has been their wholesale removal from Moscow, probably never to return.

'I wonder whether our young people quite realise the extent to which they will be used by the Russians as puppets in a vast public relations exercise, the principal object of which will be to glorify one of the most evil and oppressive regimes the world has ever known. Of course, we are all intensely sympathetic to those who find themselves in their present dilemma, particularly the outstanding athletes who would have a good chance of winning medals, as the equestrian competitors would have done; but have they considered the possibility that a medal won in an unrepresentative field will be nothing but a hollow victory?

'I hope that all our likely Olympic representatives will reflect very seriously before they decide they are unable to follow the unselfish and patriotic example of our riders.'

2

Dressage at Goodwood

The International Dressage Festival at Goodwood marked a happy rapport between the Earl and Countess of March, Inchcape and Company Limited (the sponsors), and Mrs Margaret Thatcher, who arrived on the Sunday to indicate her approval of Britain's horsemen, who heeded her request to keep away from Moscow.

Predictably, West Germany won the team gold medals with 5067 marks. Switzerland took the silver with 4838, and Denmark the bronze with 4573. France (4521), the Netherlands (4500) and Great Britain (4354) followed behind. Britain was represented by Jennie Loriston-Clarke on Dutch Courage, Diana Mason on Special Edition and Patricia Gardiner on Manifesto.

For the second time (having also won the World Championship in 1978 at Goodwood) Christine Stückelberger and her coach, Georg Wahl, returned home to Switzerland with the individual gold medal. This was won by Miss Stückelberger on fifteen-year-old Granat, a Holstein horse which she bought very cheaply in Bavaria after he had been sold to an Italian and then developed a cough which prevented him being shipped. A multiple national champion in her own country, Miss Stückelberger travels with her trainer and her veterinary surgeon, Dr Joseph Loehrer, chief of the Army veterinary college in Bern, in constant attendance.

Dr Uwe Schulten-Baumer won the individual silver medal for West Germany on Slibovitz and his compatriot, Dr Reiner Klimke, won the bronze on Ahlerich, the scores being 1452 (Granat), 1373 (Slibovitz) and 1345 (Ahlerich). Dutch Courage finished sixth in this Grand Prix Special on the final morning.

Miss Stückelberger, who is aged thirty-three, not only claimed the individual gold (as she had done in Montreal four years earlier) but also won four of the five standard contests at the meeting. In addition to Granat, who has a lot of cold blood and must be quite exhausting to ride, she brought with her a

Uwe Shulten-Baumer, winner of the individual silver medal for West
Germany, on Slibovitz. (*Leslie Lane*)

seven-year-old, 17-hand, ex-steeplechaser called Turmalin, the
very antithesis of Granat and no more of a conventional
dressage type than he. Narrow and on the leg, he had only
eighteen months of training behind him, and has only been a
year in Miss Stückelberger's establishment. Nevertheless she
elected to ride him in preference to her nine-year-old international winner, Achat. Ridden with tact and sympathy, Turmalin
showed his flowing movement and charming temperament to
win the Prix St Georges and the Intermédiaire I with no

difficulty from Reiner Klimke on Feuerball and Uwe Sauer on Montevideo.

Three German horses took the first three prizes in the Intermédiaire II, Gabriela Grillo standing first and third with Galapagos and Ultimo, who were divided by Uwe Sauer's Hirtentraum. On the final afternoon, Miss Grillo, a musician, rode the ten-year-old Galapagos to win the Kür, or free-style to music, which was included in the Olympic programme for the first time in 1976 at the suggestion of Dr Josef Neckermann.

In the FEI Grand Prix test, Granat and Slibovitz were comparatively close. Granat made a few minor errors, his main fault being an almost absolute inability to show a collected walk. But he demonstrated his well-being and his ability to carry his years lightly with greatly improved mobility and suppleness of his hind joints in passage, where he was very hard to fault indeed.

Individual gold medallist, Christine Stückelberger, with Granat. (*Leslie Lane*)

His rival's mistakes were more serious, especially one disobedience, and in the Grand Prix Spécial he was far from being a match for Granat, being above the bit, unwilling or unable to use his hind legs sufficiently, and too much on his forehand.

Reiner Klimke's Ahlerich, the third of the top trio and recent winner of the Spécial at Aachen, showed his youth and inexperience in a couple of nervous explosions and in a modest passage and extensions, but he is very correct and regular. His predecessor, Mehmed, won his first Grand Prix when he was ten years old and went on to repeat the feat on forty-four occasions.

Jennie Loriston-Clarke and Dutch Courage, the leading British combination, seemed to have disimproved on their World Championship performance, which won them a bronze medal in 1978, whereas the first five in the Spécial had all upgraded their performances. This British pair's main strength lay in an excellent piaffe. Some experts are forced to conclude that a certain amount of retraining, and modifications to the rider's style, are necessary if horse and rider are to maintain their position in the face of all the young opposition that is on its way up from West Germany, the Netherlands and Denmark.

Results

FEI Grand Prix

1.	C. Stückelberger (SWI)	Granat	1749
2.	U. Schulten-Baumer (GER)	Slibovitz	1725
3.	G. Grillo (GER)	Ultimo	1654
4.	R. Klimke (GER)	Alherich	1633
5.	U. Sauer (GER)	Hirtentraum	1609
6.	J. Loriston-Clarke (GB)	Dutch Courage	1593

Grand-Prix Spécial

1.	C. Stückelberger (SWI)	Granat	1452
2.	U. Schulten-Baumer (GER)	Slibovitz	1373
3.	R. Klimke (GER)	Ahlerich	1345
4.	U. Sauer (GER)	Hirtentraum	1314

5. G. Grillo (GER)   Ultimo   1279
6. J. Loriston-Clarke (GB)   Dutch Courage   1252

Kür (Freestyle)

1. G. Grillo (GER)   Galapagos   557
2. G. Stockbrand (USA)   Bao   534
3. U. Schulten-Baumer (GER)   Feudal   525
4. C. Neale (CAN)   Martyr   510
5. T.J. Jorckston (DEN)   Lazuly   499
6. C. Neale (CAN)   Equus   491

Grand Prix Team

1. Germany   5067
2. Switzerland   4838
3. Denmark   4573
4. France   4521
5. Holland   4500
6. Great Britain   4354

FEI Prix St Georges

1. C. Stückelberger (SWI)   Turmalin   1344
2. R. Klimke (GER)   Feuerball   1321
3. U. Sauer (GER)   Montevideo   1260
4. M.O. Crepin (FRA)   Don Giovanni   1239
5. P. Cox (HOL)   Little Diamond   1227
6. S. Whitmore (GB)   Dutchman   1226

Intermédiaire II

1. G. Grillo (GER)   Galapagos   1496
2. U. Sauer (GER)   Hirtentraum   1494
3. G. Grillo (GER)   Ultimo   1460
4. A.G. Jensen (DEN)   Marzog   1420
5. A.M. Keyzer (HOL)   Amon   1408
6. T.J. Jorckston (DEN)   Lazuly   1407

Intermédiaire I

1.	C. Stückelberger (SWI)	Turmalin	1394
2.	U. Sauer (GER)	Montevideo	1376
3.	R. Klimke (GER)	Feuerball	1355
4.	M.O. Crepin (FRA)	Don Giovanni	1326
5.	U. Lehmann (SWI)	Werder	1305
6.	D. Stuyvers (HOL)	Gentil	1237

Team

1.	Germany	2731
2.	Switzerland	2699
3.	Holland	2573
4.	Great Britain	2351

3

Showjumping in Rotterdam

Incorporated within the framework of the thirty-third official international horse show, on the tree-lined showground of the Rotterdam Riding Club, this Olympic alternative attracted no fewer than thirteen international teams, and individual riders from five more nations, bringing a record total of eighteen nations to Rotterdam, where the European Championship had been held very successfully (especially for the British team, who won) in 1979.

Mrs Pamela Carruthers, who has become famous as a course-builder all over the world since she started building the courses at Douglas Bunn's All-England Jumping Course at Hickstead in 1961, was present as Technical Delegate, appointed by the FEI.

The first day was devoted to riding-in the horses in the strange arena, and the United States riders had a field day. Armand Leone from Franklin Lakes, New Jersey, a student at the New York school of medicine, jumped one of ten clear rounds in a field of fifty-two on Encore, a chesnut Throughbred former racehorse who won the last selection trial for the United States equestrian team. The baby of the team at twenty-two years of age, Armand pulled off a second clear round with Encore in 59.5 secs to win the Prix du Cercle Equestre de Rotterdam from Jimmy Elder, veteran of the Canadian team, on Candida (61.00 secs). Walther Gabathuler and Game Toy were third for Switzerland (61.4 secs) and John Whitaker fourth for Britain on Rushgreen (61.5 secs). These four were well clear of the field, though Tim Grubb was fifth, some 7 seconds behind his team-mate, on his American wife's dowry, the chesnut Turn on the Sun.

More thwarted Olympic combinations from the North American continent took the field in the Prix de Van Nelle, and this time Melanie Smith, the thirty-year-old rider from Connecticut, won by 1.5 seconds on the Dutch-bred seven-year-old Calypso, who carried her into second place in the

World Cup finals in Baltimore five months earlier. Once again, Walther Gabathuler was runner-up, this time on Harley, and Johan Heins, the European Champion in 1977, was third for the home side on Larramy, followed by three Frenchmen: Herve Godignon, Gilles Bertran de Balanda and Frederic Cottier.

No fewer than twenty-eight (nearly half the field of sixty) qualified for this barrage, which brought the day's labours to their end. In the meantime, Hugo Simon of Austria prevented an all-American grand slam when he won the accumulator, the Prix de Anker Kolen, on his bay mare, Sorry. His score of 1220 points comfortably beat the 1130 of Belgium's Eric Wauters on Rossantico and the 1100 of Britain's Nick Skelton on the Irish mare Barbarella, whose very fast time put him ahead of Jeff McVean of Australia on Autograph, who was equal on points. Best of the Americans was the twenty-nine-year-old Pennsylvania girl, Terry Rudd, who was seventh on Sandor.

Every one of the 170 horses on the ground was played-in on this opening day, when a wonderfully happy atmosphere prevailed, the sun shone, the facilities were excellent, and our hosts could not have been kinder. The only disadvantage became apparent later, when everyone returned to their hotels, threw open their hotel-room windows in true British fashion — and all the mosquitos of Rotterdam, which lies below sea-level and is full of water, made them their target for the night, dive-bombing with monotonous insistence; sleep was sought in vain.

John Whitaker, the twenty-five-year-old Yorkshire rider, turned out to be Britain's hero of the tour, and he first made his presence felt on the second day of the show when he rode Ryan's Son, who was short-listed for the Olympic team in 1976, to win the Prix Hanno. Ryan's Son, bred in County Wexford by Ozymandias, won the Irish Horse Board's special award for the most successful Irish horse in 1979, and his victory was a welcome morale booster for the British camp.

Of the fifteen clear rounds — over the sort of twisting course which just suited the Irish horse, who can turn and twist like a trout — only one was British, but that one was enough. Thomas Frühmann and Donau were leading for Austria on 42.3 secs when Ryan's Son leapt ahead with 38.4 secs, which could not be beaten. Paul Schockemöhle took El Paso into third place on

Austria's Hugo Simon, the leading individual rider at Rotterdam, seen here with Gladstone. (*Leslie Lane*)

44.2 secs, then Henk Nooren, Holland's sole professional rider, took Opstalan's Shoreline into second place in 41.5.

The British team needed a fillip to their morale, for they greatly missed the presence of Liz Edgar and the great Everest Double Glazing horse, Forever, from their number. Originally selected for the team, Liz and her husband, Ted, were resolutely determined not to overface their brilliant eight-year-old. Personally, I am sure that they were right, and that the hierarchy of the BSJA were exceeding their terms of reference in attempting to coerce them into going. Ted and Liz insisted that in the invariably heavy going of the Rotterdam showground Forever, who does not perform in the deep, would be more of a liability than an asset. Ironically, the going was firm and remained so throughout.

Ronnie Massarella, *chef d'équipe par excellence*, told me:

'I think we're all suffering from the loss of Liz and Forever. We all felt that here was one horse we could really rely on, to make a firm foundation upon which to build. We've all dropped a bit of morale without them, and Nick [Skelton]'s lost it doubly because he'll have to try to take their place. We've told all the other riders that it was our strategy to go badly on the first day, but I don't think they swallowed it, the performances were too realistic!

'There is no secret about it — both Graham Fletcher and Robert Smith are going badly — it's anybody's guess who is going the worse. Both Graham's horses arrived here with temperatures which they acquired on the boat journey from Hull, and Robert's Video hasn't really been himself since Aachen. Tim's and Nick's horses, who came via Harwich, are lucky to be all right as their captain wouldn't let them stay with their horses or go below and feed them, even though it was as calm as a millpond.

'I firmly believe that we ought to bring our own vets abroad with us for the major championships. However, John's victory may just have saved the day for us — the Americans weren't going so well until Calypso won, and inspired the other riders. I shall play John as banker at Number 4.'

After their performances on the first day, the Americans started favourites for the Grand Prix des Nations — it is doubtful

whether Britain would have been tipped so highly even if Liz
Edgar had decided to risk her once-in-a-lifetime horse — but in
the event, the results exceeded most people's wildest dreams. In
the meantime, Hugo Simon brought off a second victory, this
time in the Prix de Lake Kralingen. It is ironic that he
'discovered' an Austrian grandmother in 1972, having failed to
make the German shortlist, in order to ride for Austria in the
Munich Olympics. Now that the German team has lost Hans
Günter Winkler, Alwin Schockemöhle and Hartwig Steenken,
the Germans would no doubt be very glad to get him back again.

Nations Cup day dawned fair and bright and hope rose anew
in many hearts, including those of the ill-considered Canadians,
whose three-day event team had already sprung a surprise when
they won the World Championship in Lexington, Kentucky in
1978.

When all thirteen teams had completed the first round,
Britain and West Germany, as of old, were disputing the lead on
8 faults, from Canada with 8.25. At this juncture, Britain was
the only team to have two clear rounds, achieved by Nick
Skelton on Maybe and John Whitaker on Ryan's Son, while
Graham Fletcher's 8 faults on Preachan counted in preference
to Tim Grubb's 14.25 on Night Murmur, who stopped in the
treble and going into the double.

The treble, fence 13, proved to be unlucky for several shining
hopes, in particular its last element, which caused falls, refusals,
withdrawals and eliminations and reduced the home side to
three men. Mrs Pamela Carruthers had an interesting explanation
for the disasters, which was the middle element of white posts
and rails: 'Horses don't seem to look at white fences, and those
who didn't were in trouble.'

The breezy day became hot and humid during the second
round and the only team to improve on their first-round
performances were the Austrians, who pulled themselves up
into third place with 20 faults, behind Britain with 18.50 and
the jubilant Canadians with 16.50. Double clear rounds were
jumped by Nick Skelton on Maybe, by Mark Laskin, Canada's
No. 2, and by Thomas Frühmann on Donau for Austria. But as
far as the British were concerned, the real hero was Ronnie
Massarella, who tells a good team that they will win, and they
do, and tells a young and inexperienced team of amateurs, two

of whose horses are not going well, that they will win, and they come within two points of doing so in a world-class field.

For Michel Vaillancourt, Mark Laskin, Ian Millar and James Elder, this was their most prestigious victory since they won the World Championship in France in 1970. Mexico, who won the bronze medal in Moscow a month earlier, Sweden and Denmark all retired at the end of the first round. West Germany's weak link turned out, surprisingly, to be Gerd Wiltfang's Roman, whose promise when he won the World Championship as a seven-year-old in Aachen in 1978 and the European Championship here a year later caused him to be regarded as a truly remarkable horse.

The individual medals went to the three highest-placed combinations in the Grand Prix de Rotterdam International Gold Cup, a two-round, two-course competition with forty starters and a treble which caused innumerable falls and refusals. There was a very tight distance between the second and third elements. Mrs Carruthers told me afterwards: 'There were two non-jumping strides between the first two elements and only one between the second and third — we have always had one and two, and perhaps I should have insisted on its being altered by the course-builder, Sieto Mellema, when I inspected it. But they soon learned how to ride it.'

With heights ranging to 5ft 3ins and spreads to 7ft 2ins it was a real Olympic-type test, and at the end of the first round Bertran de Balanda, whose grandfather was an international rider, was in the lead on his gallant but sometimes erratic bay stallion, Galoubet A, with one time fault, followed by Jeff McVean with the grey Autograph on 2.25, while John Whitaker with Ryan's Son, Walther Gabathuler on Harley, Melanie Smith on Calypso, Hugo Simon on Gladstone, and Eric Wauters on Winnetou were level on 4 faults apiece, followed by Paul Schockemöhle on Deister with 4.25.

The twenty-five best-classified combinations went on to the second round, when John Whitaker, Melanie Smith and Hugo Simon went clear and had to jump off for the medals. Melanie Smith went first on Calypso and made a mistake at the second fence, Ryan's Son faulted at the same fence but was 2.4 secs faster, and finally Gladstone made sure of victory with a careful clear which earned him threequarters of a time fault.

The British team display their Nations Cup silver medals to the obvious
satisfaction of *chef d'équipe*, Ronnie Massarella (right). From left to
right: Tim Grubb, Nick Skelton, John Whitaker and Graham Fletcher.
(*Leslie Lane*)

He had already scored another second on Sorry and on
Landgräfin on Saturday and was without doubt the leading
individual of the show, with John Whitaker a worthy winner of
the silver medal.

The Canadians won the gold medals in Mexico City in 1968,
and twelve years later they proved themselves to be in the first
flight again. As for Britain – as Colonel Sir Harry Llewellyn
said proudly, choked with emotion, at half-time: 'We are
always at our best with our backs to the wall!'

Results

Prix du Cercle Equestre de Rotterdam

		points	secs
1. Armand Leone (USA)	Encore	0.00	59.5
2. James Elder (CAN)	Candida	0.00	61.0

		points	secs
3. Walther Gabathuler (SWI)	Game Toy	0.00	61.4
4. John Whitaker (GB)	Rushgreen	0.00	61.5
5. Tim Grubb (GB)	Turn on the Sun	0.00	68.1
6. Hugo Simon (AUT)	Gladstone	0.00	69.3

Prix de Anker Kolen

		points	secs
1. Hugo Simon (AUT)	Sorry	1220.00	92.1
2. Eric Wauters (BEL)	Rossantico	1130.00	70.4
3. Nick Skelton (GB)	Barbarella	1100.00	61.3
4. Jeff McVean (AUS)	Autograph	1100.00	68.6
5. Michel Vaillancourt (CAN)	Chivaz	1090.00	65.9
6. Edgar Cupper (BEL)	Symphatico	1090.00	66.2

Prix de Van Nelle

		Course		Jump-off	
		points	secs	points	secs
1. Melanie Smith (USA)	Calypso	0.00	78.2	0.00	40.4
2. Walther Gabathuler (SWI)	Harley	0.00	75.2	0.00	41.9
3. Johan Heins (HOL)	Larramy	0.00	74.7	0.00	42.0
4. Herve Godignon (FRA)	Faro de Biolay	0.00	70.1	0.00	42.7
5. Gilles Bertran de Balanda (FRA)	Galoubet A	0.00	75.5	0.00	44.5
6. Frederic Cottier (FRA)	Flambeau C	0.00	74.2	0.00	45.0

Prix Hanno

		Course		Jump-off	
		points	secs	points	secs
1. John Whitaker (GB)	Ryan's Son	0.00	95.9	0.00	38.4
2. Henk Nooren (HOL)	Opstalan's Shoreline	0.00	91.2	0.00	41.5
3. Thomas Frühmann (AUT)	Donau	0.00	93.5	0.00	42.3
4. Paul Schockemöhle (GER)	El Paso	0.00	91.8	0.00	44.2
5. Joaquin P. de Las Heras (MEX)	Alimony	0.00	90.0	0.00	47.1
6. Irma Smulders (HOL)	Stargazer	0.00	98.6	0.00	51.6

Prix de Lake Kralingen

		secs
1. Hugo Simon (AUT)	Sorry	80.2
2. Melanie Smith (USA)	Val de Loire	80.9
3. Armand Leone (USA)	Encore	85.6
4. Walther Gabathuler (SWI)	Harley	86.1
5. Henk Nooren (HOL)	Opstalan's Shoreline	88.8
6. Gerd Meier (HOL)	Piraat T	90.9

Prix d'Erasme

			points	secs	Jump-off points	secs
1.	Ian Millar (CAN)	Arnica	0.00	61.5	0.00	26.9
2.	Hugo Simon (AUT)	Landgräfin	0.00	61.5	0.00	28.0
3.	Herve Godignon (FRA)	Heur de Bratand	0.00	64.2		
4.	Johan Heins (HOL)	Socrates	0.00	66.2		
5.	Leif Nilsson (SWE)	Miss Larette	0.00	66.4		
6.	Stany van Paesschen (BEL)	Boulzicourt	0.00	67.9		

Nations Cup

			Course A points	Course B points	Total points
1.	Canada				
	Michel Vaillancourt	Chivaz	8.00	4.00	
	Mark Laskin	Damuraz	0.00	0.00	
	Ian Millar	Brother Sam	0.25	4.25	
	James Elder	Volunteer	8.00	8.00	
			8.25	8.25	16.50
2.	Great Britain				
	Graham Fletcher	Preachan	8.00	8.00	
	Nick Skelton	Maybe	0.00	0.00	
	Tim Grubb	Night Murmur	14.25	6.50	
	John Whitaker	Ryan's Son	0.00	4.00	
			8.00	10.50	18.50
3.	Austria				
	Roland Fischer	Icarus	12.00	20.00	
	Georg Riedl	Weekend	20.00	0.00	
	Thomas Frühmann	Donau	0.00	0.00	
	Hugo Simon	Gladstone	0.00	8.00	
			12.00	8.00	20.00

Prix de Supertrio

			points	secs
1.	Eric Wauters (BEL)	Rossantico	0.00	57.2
2.	Hugo Simon (AUT)	Sorry	0.00	57.6
3.	Gerd Wiltfang (GER)	Boyfriend	0.00	59.3
4.	Jorge Carneiro (BRA)	Bernar	0.00	60.0
5.	Kevin Bacon (AUS)	Tununda	0.00	62.2
6.	Walther Gabathuler (SWI)	Game Toy	0.00	64.9

Prix Pierson

		Course points	secs	Jump-off A points	secs	Jump-off B points	secs
1.	Henk Nooren (HOL)	0.00	83.6	0.00	47.9	0.00	33.2
2.	Hugo Simon (AUT)	0.00	83.1	0.00	46.8	0.00	33.8

	Course		Jump-off A		Jump-off B	
	points	*secs*	*points*	*secs*	*points*	*secs*
3. Nick Skelton (GB)	0.00	84.7	0.00	48.5	0.00	35.6
4. Eric Wauters (BEL)	0.00	86.1	0.00	48.1	0.00	35.8
5. Thomas Frühmann (AUT)	0.00	80.5	0.00	49.1	0.00	38.1
6. Anton Ebben (HOL)	0.00	87.6	0.50	52.7		

Prix Amro

		points	*secs*
1. François Mathy (BEL)	Grand Duc	0.00	59.4
2. Heinrich-W. Johannsmann (GER)	Sarto	0.00	61.3
3. Graham Fletcher (GB)	Double Brandy	0.00	61.6
4. Armand Leone (USA)	Wallenstein	0.00	61.8
5. Max Hauri (SWI)	Beethoven	0.00	62.0
6. Piet Raymakers (HOL)	Isocrates Eurotex	0.00	62.6

Prix BMW

		points	*secs*
1. Herve Godignon (FRA)	Faro de Biolay	32.00	78.9
2. Hugo Simon (AUT)	Landgräfin	32.00	79.2
3. Hugo Simon (AUT)	Sorry	31.00	80.6
4. Norman Dello Joio (USA)	Johnny's Pocket	30.00	75.7
5. Walther Gabathuler (SWI)	Game Toy	30.00	76.7
6. Rob Ehrens (HOL)	M Pascha	30.00	77.6

Grand Prix de Rotterdam International Gold Cup

		A	B		Total	Jump-off	
		points	*points*	*secs*	*points*	*points*	*secs*
1. Hugo Simon (AUT)	Gladstone	4.00	0.00	65.0	4.00	0.75	58.6
2. John Whitaker (GB)	Ryan's Son	4.00	0.00	64.8	4.00	4.00	40.0
3. Melanie Smith (USA)	Calypso	4.00	0.00	71.3	4.00	4.00	42.4
4. Paul Schockemöhle (GER)	Deister	4.25	0.00	72.0	4.25		
5. Jeff McVean (AUS)	Autograph	2.25	4.25	75.8	6.50		
6. Walther Gabathuler (SWI)	Harley	4.00	4.00	64.4	8.00		

4

The Three-Day Event at Fontainebleau

Most people found the journey to and from France somewhat tedious in that it involved, where possible, circumventing the French ports, which were blockaded and closed to shipping by a strike of French fishermen, who apparently decided that the best way to obtain better prices for their fish and a petrol subsidy from their Government was to inconvenience the Britons as much as possible. So Princess Anne set off two days early to the Ostend car ferry, entering France well inland at Lille and driving around Paris to Fontainebleau. Many others travelling out to support the team followed the same devious route, but the journey was by no means easy and included a lot of night-driving through France.

Fontainebleau itself is a delightful and historic town and it was here, in the Palace, that Napoleon Bonaparte spent his last days in France before being exiled to St Helena. It is also the home of equestrian sport in France, and I remember coming here for the official French International Show (CSIO) in 1971. The last senior official three-day-event championships to be held in France were those of the European Three-Day Event in 1969 at Haras du Pin in Normandy. Here the Normandy Bank first made its bow, and so many horses were killed (I believe the total was five) due to bad riding and the inability to get them sufficiently fit that in France the sport went into eclipse at this level for a decade.

At the end of the first day of dressage the West Germans, far from unpredictably, were in the lead, represented by Otto Ammermann, an unmarried insurance broker who has helped to win silver medals in the 1976 Olympic Games, at the European Championships at Burghley the following year, and at the World Championships in Lexington, Kentucky in 1978. Riding the Oldenburger, Volturno, he had scored 46.80 penalty points and his compatriot, Helmut Rethemeier on Santiago, was lying fifth with 50.80. In between were Jonas Hugosson of Sweden on

Collombey (48.60), Michael Huber of the United States on Gold Chip (49.60) and Britain's Helen Butler on Merganser II (50.00).

By the end of the second day's dressage the picture had undergone a radical change. The leader was now Britain's Rachel Bayliss with her young horse Mystic Minstrel, on 34.00 penalty points, followed for West Germany by Karl Schultz on Madrigal with 36.20 and by the captain of the United States team, Mike Plumb, on his Australian-bred Laurenson with 45.80, and thus one point better than Otto Ammermann and Volturno, the overnight leaders, who had slipped back to fourth.

As far as team places were concerned, the American position was strengthened by the fact that Torrance Watkins had come up into fifth place with the fiery little skewbald pony, Poltroon, who had finished second at Burghley a year earlier. In view of the eventual result it is interesting to note that disputing seventh place with Michael Huber and Gold Chip was Nils Haagensen of Denmark on Monaco, the horse on which he had won the European Championship in Luhmühlen the previous year.

Among those of the mighty to fall were Richard Meade with Kilcashel (23rd on 56.60), Captain Mark Phillips on Lincoln (31st on 63.40), and Lucinda Prior-Palmer on Village Gossip (65th on 83). During his test Gossip had been in one of his least co-operative moods, and his rider did not dare to put him on the bit lest he explode, so he went on a loose rein throughout. She had hoped to ride Killaire here, but when he went lame a week earlier she was very glad that the selectors had insisted on her riding Gossip too at the final trial at Dauntsey, for she had not been on his back for a year.

When they walked the cross-country course, the riders deemed it to be big but fair; it was the going — deep sand all over the course, which rides very dead — that bothered them most. 'Down in Normandy they have all grass, which rides like Leicestershire!' groaned a foxhunting lady from the Belvoir Vale. 'Why couldn't they have held it there?'

Lucinda Prior-Palmer thought that the course-builder, François Serrel, had been kind in that his difficult fences were followed by easy ones, and others noted that alternatives were

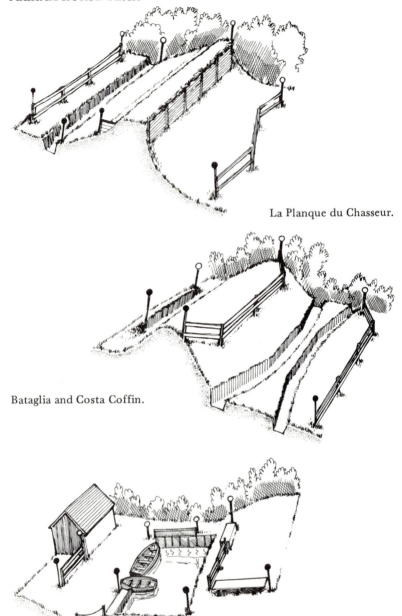

La Planque du Chasseur.

Bataglia and Costa Coffin.

France Cottage and
Ecluse Saint-Yves.

provided for the first time ever in France. The interest of Captain Mark Phillips and Richard Meade, however, became merely academic all too soon, for the former could not start on the speed and endurance phase because Lincoln had strained a muscle in a forearm. Worse was to come when Kilcashel returned to the 'box' after roads and tracks, seized up with azoturia, and had to be withdrawn.

Though the days were hot, the nights grew cool around dawn and the early starters had the best of conditions. The steeple-chase course, a traditional Continental figure-of-eight, was on the small side and caused no serious problems.

The box was hard to find among the trees, but to find it was to gain entry unchallenged by the gendarmes who guarded it. The British camp had set up their station on and around a bank, where Captain Martin Whiteley perched on a shooting stick. The Irish deployed themselves nearby, led by Brigadier and Mrs Friz Fowler. The Irish team included the Brigadier's daughter, Jessica Harrington, on Amoy which he bred himself.

Mervyn Bennett charted the course for Australia on Regal Reign with a clear round, which eventually put him sixth at the end of the speed and endurance phase. He was immediately followed by Siobhan Reeves-Smyth, late of the Irish Junior team, on Millicent Bridge, an honest hunter with a better turn of speed than would at first appear.

The bad news for Britain came on apace, the next being a fall for Chris Collins and Gamble at some white rails, after which Chris had to retire with concussion. Then Lucinda Prior-Palmer redressed the balance with a fast and brilliant round on Village Gossip which brought her up to tenth place (from lying 65th out of 69 starters!). 'If he goes like that across country,' she said happily afterwards, 'I'll forgive him any number of bad dressage tests!'

Helen Butler and Merganser got round with just one stop, going into the water, before Jimmy Wofford put the United States in front with a fast and faultless round on Carawich, followed by Torrance Watkins on Poltroon with much the same sort of performance, only just behind.

Opposite: A selection of Fontainebleau's most challenging cross-country fences.

Helen Butler and Merganser tackle 'La Planque du Chasseur' fence. (*Kit Houghton*)

Poltroon, only 15 h.h., has proved to be quite a remarkable little horse. She is out of a spotted hunter pony by the Thoroughbred Hopper's Pride. The dam was a show hunter pony and a considerable foxhunter. Poltroon finished second at Burghley in 1979, won Lexington and Ship's Quarters in 1980, and hopefully goes to Luhmühlen in 1982.

Nils Haagensen and Monaco, who had won the 1979 European Championship at Luhmühlen for Denmark, overtook Carawich with just as quick a clear round. German hopes slumped when

Karl Schultz and Madrigal, second in the dressage, had a fall at the Table and Drop. Then America's prospects likewise plummeted when Mike Plumb and Laurenson were eliminated (as they had been in Lexington two years earlier) at the water complex at 29 and 30, Ecluse Saint-Yves, which was more horrendous than it should have been because it came so late on the course — fifth from the end, in fact. When Mike Huber, the baby of the American team at twenty-two, had a fall with Gold Chip, that put paid to the United States team.

Now that the team was out of the hunt Britain's hopes rested on the chance of an individual medal, but these evaporated when Rachel Bayliss's Mystic Minstrel, like many another good dressage horse before him, fell twice — once at the Double Coffin and again at the Zig-Zag.

So at the end of the speed and endurance phase (unrelated to dressage marks) Nils Haagensen and Monaco led with 7.60 from Jimmy Wofford and Carawich with 8.40, and Lucinda Prior-

Safely out of the water jump, Nils Haagensen and Monaco. (*Kit Houghton*)

Palmer and Village Gossip disputed third place on 16 with Georges Serignac of the home side on Talcor. Adding the dressage scores, Monaco (57.20) still led from Carawich (66.60) with Poltroon third on 75.00. Village Gossip had leapfrogged from 65th place to 10th, with an alacrity remarkable even for this astonishingly individual young woman. Moreover, her clear round showjumping moved her up to a final seventh place, which is almost Biblical in its message.

Thus Nils Haagensen and Monaco proved that their European title had been no fluke, Jimmy Wofford proved that he was just as good as he was in the late 1960s, and Torrance Watkins' Poltroon proved once more that a good little 'un can hold her own in any company if her heart is stout and in the right place.

The French showed that they can take on the rest of the world again, the Germans that they can make their horses last. Only a quarter of the field failed to complete the cross-country, and a third jumped it clear. Yet Britain, Canada (the world champions) and the United States (the previous world champions) were all eliminated.

The most unpleasant sight of the meeting, which happily I was spared, was undoubtedly the incident involving the Argentine horse, Bravio, an eight-year-old chesnut stallion. After a fall and a refusal, the horse was obviously 'cooked', yet his rider, José Ortelli, beat him into a solid timber fence on a bank and broke his horse's leg so that the animal had to be put down on the spot. In another incident, again involving an Argentine horse, spectators intervened to prevent the rider remounting his exhausted horse after it had fallen. This sort of thing will kill the sport if it is allowed to continue.

The only remaining problem for the British team was that of getting home, as angry fishermen were still guarding closed docks. Most returned via Belgian ports, enjoying a homeward journey that was more pleasant and more restful than the journey out. Despite the travelling difficulties, Fontainebleau was still a good deal preferable to Moscow.

Results

Individual Championship

		Dressage	Steeplechase	Cross-country	Showjumping	Total
1. Nils Haagensen (DEN)	Monaco	49.60	—	8.40	1.50	59.50
2. James Wofford (USA)	Carawich	58.20	—	8.40	5.25	71.85
3. Torrance Watkins (USA)	Poltroon	48.20	—	26.80	0	75.00
4. Joel Pons (FRA)	Ensorcelleuse II	54.00	—	31.60	1.50	87.10
5. Pascal Morvillers (FRA)	En Douce II	54.40	—	35.20	0	89.60
6. Mervin Bennett (AUS)	Regal Reign	67.20	—	26.00	5.00	98.20
7. Lucinda Prior-Palmer (GB)	Village Gossip	83.00	—	16.00	0	99.00
8. Georges Serignac (FRA)	Talcor	78.20	—	16.00	5.00	99.20
9. Helmut Rethemeier (GER)	Santiago XXXI	50.80	—	47.60	5.00	103.40
10. Otto Ammermann (GER)	Volturno III	46.80	—	56.80	0	103.60
11. Rüdiger Schwarz (GER)	Power Game	50.40	—	54.40	0	104.80
12. Jean-Yves Touzaint (FRA)	Flipper 1	66.00	—	29.60	10.00	105.60
13. Thierry Touzaint (FRA)	Gribouille C	67.80	—	33.20	5.00	106.00
14. Paul Loiseau (FRA)	Elding Bleu	69.00	—	32.40	5.00	106.40
15. Armand Bigot (FRA)	Gamin du Bois	56.20	—	56.00	0	112.20
16. Patrick Marquebielle (FRA)	Flamenco III	68.60	6.40	37.20	1.75	113.95
17. Elizabeth Ashton (CAN)	Sunrise	62.60	—	58.80	0	121.40
18. Phillipa Glennen (AUS)	Range Finder	72.40	—	39.20	10.00	121.60
19. Siobhan Reeves-Smyth (IRE)	Millicent Bridge	88.80	—	36.00	0	124.80
20. Alain Lhuissier (FRA)	Luron II	79.40	—	48.80	0	128.20
21. Harry Klugmann (GER)	Veberot	55.80	—	67.20	5.75	128.75
22. Helen Butler (GB)	Merganser II	50.00	—	84.00	1.00	135.00
23. Jessica Harrington (IRE)	Amoy	63.80	—	85.60	0.50	149.90
24. Wayne Roycroft (AUS)	Clouseau	55.40	20.80	88.40	0	164.60

		Dressage	Steeplechase	Cross-country	Showjumping	Total
25. Andrew Hoy (AUS)	Davey	55.60	—	119.60	0	175.20
26. Dirk van Mieghem (BEL)	Nancledra	74.80	—	87.60	15.00	177.40
27. Herbert Blöcker (GER)	Contrast	51.80	—	136.00	0	187.80
28. Karl Schultz (GER)	Madrigal	36.20	—	152.80	0	189.00
29. Simon de Jonge (HOL)	Upper Church	57.80	10.40	114.80	15.75	198.75
30. Anna Casagrande (ITA)	Winsor Lodge	67.60	—	128.80	10.00	206.40
31. David Foster (IRE)	Inis Mean	68.40	—	136.00	10.00	214.40
32. Reni Pillot (FRA)	Farouk II	63.20	2.40	144.40	11.25	221.25
33. Mark Ishoy (CAN)	Law and Order	67.20	5.60	147.20	10.00	230.00
34. Karen Stives (USA)	The Saint	54.60	—	171.80	5.25	231.65
35. Peter Gray (BER)	Gunnar	75.80	2.40	142.00	15.00	235.20
36. Luc van Mieghem (BEL)	Domino	56.00	—	139.20	44.75	239.95
37. Gen Ueda (JAP)	Aisterking	59.80	—	182.40	0.25	242.45
38. Eddy Stibbe (HOL)	Autumn Haze	53.80	28.40	176.80	11.75	270.75
39. James Smart (CAN)	Jack the Lad	73.60	4.80	199.2	0	277.60
40. Pedro Mercado (ARG)	Cafayate	86.00	—	218.80	0	304.80
41. Gerrit Lozeman (HOL)	Herman Kroton	70.00	—	235.20	20.00	325.20
42. August Desmedt (BEL)	Haraudiere	99.00	—	354.00	21.75	474.75
C. Michael Huber (USA)	Gold Chip	49.60	—	100.40	wdr	
Rachel Bayliss (GB)	Mystic Minstrel	34.00	—	170.00	wdr	
Washington Bishop (USA)	Taxi	51.60	—	293.61	wdr	
Christopher Collins (GB)	Gamble VIII	71.40	10.40	ret		
José Ortelli (ARG)	Bravo	69.40	—	ret		
Giovanni Rossi (ITA)	Escort	70.40	—	ret		
François B. de Benque (BEL)	Oberon	107.00	—	ret		
Fernando M. Zuviria (ARG)	Ucase	79.00	—	ret		
Loraine Laframboise (CAN)	Krumbein	67.00	—	elim		
Albert Desmedt (BEL)	Proza	82.40	8.80	elim		
Jonas Hugosson (SWE)	Collombey	48.60	—	elim		

		Dressage	Steeplechase	Cross-country	Showjumping	Total
Frederico Castaing (ARG)	Eclipse	76.00	—	elim		
Nicholas Holmes-Smith (CAN)	Sinnerman	67.40	—	elim		
Ronnie MacMahon (IRE)	Parkhill	67.80	—	elim		
Martin Lips (HOL)	Baby Face	59.20	6.40	elim		
Helen Cantillon (IRE)	Wing Forward	80.20	—	elim		
Mark Todd (NZ)	Jocasta	76.20	—	elim		
Marina Sciocchetti (ITA)	Tristan	60.20	—	elim		
Mike Plumb (USA)	Laurenson	45.80	—	elim		
Yvan Scherer (FRA)	Harry	69.40	—	wdr		
Eduardo Zone (ARG)	Don Chicho	74.80	—	wdr		
Alberto Gonzales (ARG)	Frisio	80.80	13.60	wdr		
Neil Ishoy (CAN)	L'Esprit	70.20	—	wdr		
Richard Meade (GB)	Kilcashel	56.60	—	wdr		
Alessandro Miserocchi (ITA)	MacDonald	69.80	wdr			
Mark Phillips (GB)	Lincoln	63.40	wdr			
Mervin Bennett (AUS)	Regal Realm	77.00	wdr			

Team Championship

			Total
1. *France*			
Joel Pons	Ensorcelleuse II	87.10	
Jean-Yves Touzaint	Flipper I	105.60	
Thierry Touzaint	Gribouille C	106.00	
Armand Bigot	Gamin du Bois	(112,20)	298.70
2. *Germany*			
Otto Ammermann	Volturno III	103.60	
Rüdiger Schwarz	Power Game	104.80	
Harry Klugmann	Veberot	128.75	
Karl Schultz	Madrigal	(189.00)	337.15
3. *Australia*			
Mervin Bennett	Regal Reign	98.20	
Phillipa Glennen	Range Finder	121.60	
Wayne Roycroft	Clouseau	164.60	
Andrew Hoy	Davey	(175.20)	384.40
4. *Ireland*			
Siobhan Reeves-Smyth	Millicent Bridge	124.80	
Jessica Harrington	Amoy	149.90	
David Foster	Inis Mean	214.40	
Ronnie MacMahon	Parkhill	elim	489.10
5. *Holland*			
Simon de Jonge	Upper Church	198.75	
Eddy Stibbe	Autumn Haze	270.75	
Gerrit Lozeman	Herman Kroton	325.20	
Martin Lips	Baby Face	elim	794.70
6. *Belgium*			
Dirk van Mieghem	Nancledra	177.40	
Luc van Mieghem	Domino	239.95	
August Desmedt	Haraudiere	474.75	
Albert Desmedt	Proza	elim	892.10

Eliminated

USA		
Mike Plumb	Laurenson	elim
Torrance Watkins	Poltroon	75.00
C. Michael Huber	Gold Chip	elim
James Wofford	Carawich	71.85
Great Britain		
Helen Butler	Merganser II	135.00

Total

Richard Meade	Kilcashel	elim
Christopher Collins	Gamble VIII	elim
Lucinda Prior-Palmer	Village Gossip	99.00

Canada

Elizabeth Ashton	Sunrise	121.40
Mark Ishoy	Law and Order	230.00
Nicholas Holmes-Smith	Sinnerman	elim
Neil Ishoy	L'Esprit	elim

Italy

Marina Sciocchetti	Tristan	elim
Anna Casagrande	Winsor Lodge	206.40
Alessandro Miserocchi	MacDonald	elim
Giovanni Bossi	Escort	elim

Argentine

Frederico Castaing	Eclipse	elim
Fernando M. Zuviria	Ucase	elim
Alberto Gonzales	Frisio	elim
Pedro Mercado	Caffalate	304.80

5

The Moscow Olympic Games

Through two French colleagues, Paulette and Roger Levalleur, who travelled independently to Moscow 'for the record', as it were, I have been able to obtain some official results and some interesting photographs.

Though the Russians took all the team gold medals, the individual gold medals failed to be won by the host nation. That for dressage went to the Austrian Elisabeth Theurer (who won the 1979 European Championship at Aarhus, where she beat Christine Stückelberger). Miss Theurer, a twenty-two-year-old economics student, who won with 1623 points, was implored by the head of the Austrian Equestrian Federation not to travel to Moscow to compete. She insisted on going, he resigned in protest.

The individual gold in the three-day event went to Federico Roman on Rossinan, for Italy. He is well known but unsuccessful in European three-day events. The roads and tracks course was so hard, uneven and slippery that the Technical Delegate deemed it to be dangerous in parts and reduced it by 4 kilometres, so that it could not be said to be a true Olympic test.

The showjumping gold medal went to Jan Kowalczyk, who is also a reasonable second-ranker in Europe. The form of the teams who went to Moscow — Mexico and Italy — was not impressive in Rotterdam or Fontainebleau.

Results

Dressage — Grand Prix

Judges: E: Erich Heinrich (GER)
H: Jytte Lemkow (DEN)
C: Jaap Pot (HOL)
M: Col. Gustav Nyblaeus (SWE)
B: Tilo Koeppel (COL)

Mon Chérie and Elisabeth Theurer, winners of the Olympic dressage gold medal for an embarrassed and ungrateful Austria. (*Levalleur*)
'We have ways of making you jump' — cross-country Moscow-style. (*Levalleur*)

		E	H	C	M	B	Total	Individual place
1. USSR								
Yuri Kovshov	Igrok	313	312	311	333	319	1588	2
Viktor Ugriumov	Shkval	310	313	301	291	326	1541	3
Vera Misevich	Plot	239	252	263	231	269	1254	6
2. Bulgaria								
Petar Mandajiev	Chtchibor	236	262	244	254	248	1244	7
Svetoslav Ivanov	Aleko	228	232	239	240	251	1190	8
Guergui Gadjev	Unimatelen	241	209	223	216	257	1146	9
3. Rumania								
Anghelache Donescu	Dor	239	253	258	273	232	1255	5
Dumitru Velicu	Dezebal	225	194	225	208	224	1076	10
Petre Rosca	Derbist	228	179	224	191	193	1015	12
4. Poland								
Jozef Zagor	Helios	205	202	229	207	218	1061	11
Elke-Karin Morciniec	Sum	183	181	208	167	215	954	13
Wanda Wasowska	Damazy	173	174	193	184	206	930	14

Individual riders

		E	H	C	M	B	Total	
Elisabeth Theurer (AUT)	Mon Chérie	325	321	325	316	336	1623	1
Kyra Kyrklund (FIN)	Piccolo	297	303	296	276	286	1458	4

Dressage — Grand Prix Spécial

Judges: E: Jytte Lemkow (DEN)
H: Erich Heinrich (GER)
C: Col. Gustav Nyblaeus (SWE)
M: Tilo Koeppel (COL)
B: Jaap Pot (HOL)

			E	H	C	M	B	Total
1.	Elisabeth Theurer (AUT)	Mon Chérie	276	272	286	267	269	1370
2.	Yuri Kovshov (USSR)	Igrok	258	256	267	266	253	1300
3.	Viktor Ugriumov (USSR)	Shkval	253	259	241	240	241	1234
4.	Vera Misevich (USSR)	Plot	246	254	233	248	250	1231
5.	Kyra Kyrklund (FIN)	Piccolo	234	240	211	196	240	1121
6.	Anghelache Donescu (RUM)	Dor	196	204	185	166	209	960
7.	Guergui Gadjev (BUL)	Unimatelen	155	178	167	187	194	881
8.	Svetoslav Ivanov (BUL)	Aleko	171	167	161	170	181	850
9.	Petar Mandajiev (BUL)	Chtchibor	172	181	161	154	178	846
10.	Jozef Zagor (POL)	Helios	148	156	151	164	185	804
11.	Petre Rosca (RUM)	Derbist	136	158	155	133	159	741
12.	Dumitru Velicu (RUM)	Dezebal	131	161	130	137	161	720

Showjumping — Team Competition

					Total
1.	USSR				
	Nikolai Korolkov	Espadron	(8)	4	
	Viktor Poganovsky	Topky	8	0.25	
	Viktor Asmaev	Reis	4	(7.25)	
	Viatcheslav Chukanov	Gepatit	4	0	
			16	4.25	20.25
2.	Poland				
	Wieslaw Hartmann	Norton	12	12	
	Jan Kowalczyk	Artemor	4	8	
	Marian Kozicki	Bremen	(33.5)	4	
	Janusz Bobik	Szampan	16	(24)	
			32	24	56
3.	Mexico				
	Alberto Valdes Lacarra	Lady Mirka	8	(12.25)	
	Gerardo Tazzer Valencia	Karibe	23.25	8.5	
	Jesus Gomez Portugal	Massacre	(27.25)	8	
	Joaquin Perez de las Heras	Alymony	8	4	
			39.25	20.5	59.75
4.	Hungary				
	Andras Balogi	Artemis	(73.75)	28	
	Barnabas Hevesi	Bohem	16	12	
	Ferenc·Krucso	Vadroja	16	16	
	Jozsef Varro	Gambrinus	36	(61.75)	
			68	56	124
5.	Rumania				
	Dumitru Velea	Fudul	12	(61.75)	
	Alexandru Bozan	Prejmer	12	31.75	
	Ion Popa	Likurich	(53.75)	41.75	
	Dania Popescu	Sonor	20.25	32.75	
			44.25	106.25	150.5
6.	Bulgaria				
	Hristo Katchov	Povod	(45)	28	
	Nikola Dimitrov	Vals	17.75	29	
	Boris Pavlov	Monblan	28.75	(32)	
	Dimitar Guenov	Macbet	30	26	
			76.5	83	159.5

Showjumping — Individual

1.	Jan Kowalczyk (POL)	Artemor	4	4	8
2.	Nikolai Korolkov (USSR)	Espadron	4	5.5	9.5
3.	Joaquin Perez de las Heras (MEX)	Alymony	8	4	12 *
4.	Oswaldo Mendez Herbruger (GUA)	Pampa	8	4	12 *
5.	Viktor Poganovsky (USSR)	Topky	4	11.5	15.5
6.	Wieslaw Hartmann (POL)	Norton	4	13	16
7.	Barnabas Hevesi (HUN)	Bohem	16	8	24

*   Jump-off: P. de las Heras   4-43.23 secs
           Mendez Herbruger   4-43.59 secs

8.	Marian Kozicki (POL)	Bremen	12	12.5	24.5
9.	Viatcheslav Chukanov (USSR)	Gepatit	12	12.75	24.75
10.	Brois Pavlov (BUL)	Monblan	16	10.5	26.5
11.	Alberto Valdes Lacarra (MEX)	Lady Mirka	12	16	28
12.	Christopher Wegelius (FIN)	Monday Morning	16	14.25	30.25
13.	Nikola Dimitrov (BUL)	Vals	24	12.25	36.25
14.	Ferenc Krucso (HUN)	Vadrozsa	16	24.25	40.25

ret	Jesus Gomez Portugal (MEX)	Massacre
elim	Dimitar Guenov (BUL)	Macbet

Three-Day Event — Team

1. USSR

Yuri Salnikov	Pintset	151.6	
Valery Volkov	Tshetti	184.6	
Sergei Rogozhin	Gelespont	(338.8)	
Alexander Blinov	Galzun	120.8	457.0

2. Italy

Anna Casagrande	Daleye	266.2	
Euro Federico Roman	Rossinan	108.6	
Marina Sciocchetti	Rohan de Lechere	(308.4)	
Mauro Roman	Dourakine IV	281.4	656.2

3. Mexico

Fabian Vazquez Lopez	Cocaleco	elim	
David Barcena Rios	Bonbona	362.5	
Manuel Mendivil Yocupicio	Remember	319.75	
Jose Luis Soto Perez	Quelite	490.6	1172.85

4. Hungary

Zoltan Horvath	L'Amour	668.6	
Istvan Grozner	Biboros	498.6	
Laszlo Cseresnyes	Fapipa	436.2	
Mihaly Olah	Ados	elim	1603.4

Eliminated

Poland

Miroslaw Szlapka	Erywan	241.8
Jacek Wierzchowjecki	Bastion	411.8
Jacek Daniluk	Len	ret
Stanislaw Jasinki	Hangar	elim

Bulgaria

Tzvetan Dontchev	Medisson	185.8
Dimo Khristov	Boghez	ret
Trifon Datzinski	Mentor	elim
Djenko Sabev	Normativ	elim

India

Darya Singh	Bobby	elim
Mohammed-Khan Khan	I-AM-IT	elim
Hussain Khan	Radjdoot	ret
J.S. Ahluwalia	Shiwalik	elim

Three-Day Event — Individual

		Dressage	Steeplechase	Cross-Country Jumps	Cross-Country Time	Showjumping	Total
1. Euro Federico Roman (ITA)	Rossinan	54.4	0	0	49.2	5	108.60
2. Alexander Blinov (USSR)	Galzun	64.4	2.4	0	54.0	0	120.80
3. Yuri Salnikov (USSR)	Pintset	53.0	1.6	20	72.0	5	151.60
4. Valery Volkov (USSR)	Tzhetti	54.0	4.0	60	61.6	5	184.60
5. Tzvetan Dontchev (BUL)	Medisson	66.4	0	0	114.4	5	185.80
6. Miroslaw Szlapka (POL)	Eriwan	52.4	1.6	100	82.8	5	241.80
7. Anna Casagrande (ITA)	Daleye	61.2	0	100	90.0	15	266.20
8. Mauro Roman (ITA)	Dourakine	63.4	0	100	118.0	0	281.40
9. Marina Sciocchetti (ITA)	Rohan de Lechere	55.2	85.6	60	97.6	10	308.40
10. Manuel Mendivil Yocupicio (MEX)	Remember	53.0	3.2	120	140.8	2.75	319.75
11. Sergei Rogozhin (USSR)	Gelespont	57.0	0	120	146.8	15	338.80
12. David Barcena Rios (MEX)	Bonbona	54.4	38.4	80	147.2	42.5	362.50
13. Jacek Wierzchowiecki (POL)	Bastion	43.0	4.0	180	184.8	0	411.80
14. Laszlo Cseresnyes (HUN)	Fapipa	85.0	36.8	140	154.4	20	436.20
15. José Luis Soto Perez (MEX)	Quelite	64.0	23.2	200	192.4	11	490.60
16. Istvan Grozner (HUN)	Biboros	66.6	40.8	200	181.2	10	498.60
17. Zoltan Horvath (HUN)	Lamour	65.2	88.0	180	310.4	25	668.60
Dimo Khristov (BUL)	Boghez	68.8	3.2	120	142.4	wdr	
Darya Singh (IND)	Bobby	74.8	35.2	elim			
Fabian Vazquez Lopez (MEX)	Cocaleco	62.0	8.8	elim			
Mohammed-Khan Khan (IND)	I-AM-IT	74.0	146.4	elim			
Trifon Datzinski (BUL)	Mentor	65.8	12.0	elim			
Stanislaw Jasinksi (POL)	Hangar	55.8	1.6	elim			
Djenko Sabev (BUL)	Normativ	59.4	0	elim			
J.S. Ahluwalia (IND)	Shivalik	84.0	188.0	elim			
Mihaly Olah (HUN)	Ados	54.0	92.0	elim			
Jacek Daniluk (POL)	Len	49.2	0	elim after C			
Hussain Khan (IND)	Radjoot	81.8	44.8	elim after C			

6

The Unacceptable Face of the Three-Day Event

The unacceptable face of the three-day event first showed itself in Rome in 1960. One of the worst obstacles there consisted of concrete drainage pipes, about a foot in diameter, their open end inflicting frequent injuries to horses, who left hair and skin on them as they took off. Bertie Hill, who rode the Queen's horse Countryman III, felt for some years afterwards that he did not wish to know about horse trials any more.

The next horror that comes readily to mind was at the World Championships at Punchestown in 1970, where fence 29 broke all the unwritten rules by combining a spread with a drop. It took a heavy toll, and in the field of carnage which ensued, only

Richard Meade and The Poacher about to fall at the notorious fence 29 at Punchestown in the 1970 World Championships (*Clive Hiles*)

Lucinda Prior-Palmer and Be Fair bravely attempt Kiev's second fence, in the 1973 European Championships.

the luck of the Irish saw to it that there were neither equine nor human casualties. Mary Gordon-Watson won the individual title there on Cornishman V. She told me afterwards that the only fence she really enjoyed jumping was the last, because she knew that the rest were safely behind her.

Princess Anne was the most distinguished of many hapless victims claimed by the notorious second fence in the 1973 European Championships at Kiev in the Ukraine. Fence 2 was a big, square rustic oxer over a ditch in which several horses were trapped, and nearly buried.

There have been, on the credit side, several outstandingly successful courses, most notably the one built for the 1972 Olympic Games in Munich by Otto Pohlmann. Faced with enormous disparity in the field — which included Britain, who were then the best in the world and had been for the previous five years; the United States, who were knocking at the door; undermounted and inexperienced teams from behind the Iron Curtain; and a Mexican team mounted from a pool of European horses — he saw to it that no horses were hurt, let alone killed,

and no riders were injured. And he achieved the correct result, with the gold medal going to Great Britain, the silver to the United States and the bronze to West Germany.

The European Championships at Luhmühlen in 1975 followed the pattern of the World Championships at Burghley a year earlier. The watchword was moderation in all things and the three-day event not only won a lot of new friends among horse lovers around the world but also converted some of its former critics.

But the rot has set in again. It started at the Olympic Games in Montreal in 1976, where the combination of appalling going and a sequence of unnecessarily demanding fences caused a number of casualties, most notably Lucinda Prior-Palmer's Be Fair, who broke down as did Hugh Thomas's Playamar), slipping the ligament off a hock. Worse was to come two years later in the World Championships at Lexington, Kentucky, where too tough a complex of water fences and a high degree of humidity, caused by a decision to hold the trials in September rather than allowing them to clash with the October Sales to

Fontainebleau, 1980 — The Argentinian combination, Fernando Zuiviria and Ucase, fail to take off properly at the President's Accordion resulting in a fall . . . *Below*: Officials ran forward to help the winded horse, which struggled to its feet after lying on the ground for several minutes. Zuiviria wanted to finish the course and attempted to remount, much to the disgust of the French crowd whose vehement protestations forced him to retire. (*Kit Houghton*)

the detriment of each, resulted in the oxygen count being so low that several horses had to be given oxygen artificially after the cross-country. That night the stables resembled an old-time cavalry casualty clearing station, except that the drip-feeds and other recovery aids were a great deal more sophisticated than any enjoyed by horses exhausted in battle.

Even Luhmühlen in 1979 saw several horses finishing the speed and endurance phase with their tongues hanging out (which is not a sight best calculated to please) because the course-builder elected to follow the traditional water complex at fence 6 with a second one two from home.

The 1980 Fontainebleau course appeared to ride well, but it could only be negotiated safely by top horses in peak condition. Jack Le Goff, French-born coach to the American team, which he took to second place, told me: 'I don't think that there was anything wrong with this course — you just had to ride it and not make any mistakes, that's all.' He felt that Badminton was sometimes too testing but it varied from year to year.

Most people who ride horses and go to see them perform do so because they like them. Jimmy Wofford, who won a team silver medal on Kilkenny in 1972, told me then: 'I love this horse — when he dies I shall have him stuffed and keep him on my mantelpiece!' Kilkenny is still alive, twenty-two years young, shod, brought in at night in winter, and turned out by day with a shaggy grey pony for company. Carawich, who was bred in England, won Burghley in 1976 and a silver medal at Fontainebleau, is the nearest to Kilkenny he will ever have.

No one can prevent people entering unfit or inadequate horses or riding them badly, but stewarding can and must be rigidly enforced to prevent horses being abused. Two had to be put down at Fontainebleau; five died at Haras Du Pin during the European Championships that Britain won in 1969.

Accidents are unavoidable, but many can be prevented. Unless the sport is tightened up its unacceptable face will bring it into discredit and alienate many supporters.

7

New Zealander Wins Badminton

Mark Todd arrived from New Zealand at the end of February 1980 with two new horses. Less than two months later he had beaten all the top British combinations to win the Whitbread Trophy at Badminton, on Southern Comfort, who cost a mere £500 as a green station-horse.

Colonel Frank Weldon designed the course as an Olympic trial, the decision not to go to Moscow following the Russian invasion of Afghanistan having not yet been taken. Thus it was a stiff course, but neither riders nor spectators realised just how stiff it was for the simple reason that, apart from the fact that it went the opposite way round, it differed very little from the previous year's course. The Lexington Dog Kennels now involved an extra 'bounce' and had changed their name from Lexington to Badminton, and the Footbridge had acquired an extra dimension.

The field was a record one of eighty-eight and included Andrew Hoy from Australia with Davey, the Burghley Champions; David Green with the former bronco, Swift Deal; three Belgians; European Champion Nils Haagensen from Denmark with his Luhmühlen title winner Monaco; one Spanish and two American entries.

The dressage judges, all three of whom were due to officiate at the Olympic Games, were our old friend Marquis Fabio Mangilli from Italy, Comdt Michel Buret from France, and the little-known Mr Z. Teply-Widner from Czechoslovakia (the latter's markings, it transpired, were totally erratic and a source of wonder to all).

The first day of dressage is usually the one on which the 'rabbits' do their tests, but this year many of the top riders had two horses and appeared on their second horses early in the running. Thus Captain Mark Phillips and the Queen's home-bred Columbus, winners here in 1974, were first into the arena, followed by Lucinda Prior-Palmer, who had already won the

Whitbread Trophy four times. On this occasion she was riding her grey New Zealand horse, Mairangi Bay. They finished second at the end of the day, with 47.8 penalty points to the 46.2 of Jane Starkey and Topper Too, the Olympic and World Championship team reserves. By the end of the second day they had both been outstripped and pushed back to third and fourth places by Rachel Bayliss on Mystic Minstrel with 42.6 (with Gurgle the Greek, Rachel had won the European silver medal the previous year) and Judy Bradwell on her Punchestown winner Castlewellan with 44 penalty points.

Cross-country day dawned sunny, with a north-east wind, and it soon became evident that the going, which was known to be hard, was also poached and rutted. This applied even on the roads and tracks, where Lucinda retired her little grey horse, who had taken a fair old pasting in the humidity of Lexington's World Championships nineteen months earlier. Columbus collapsed at the Luckington Lane fences, and Gurgle the Greek, also fifteen years old, did the same three fences on, at the Footbridge, which caused a lot of grief. Then Richard Walker, holder of the Midland Bank Championship, had to pull out with John of Gaunt, and anxious spectators and relations waiting in or near the box to see the early finishers did not see one until Colin Wares came in on Bilbo Baggins II, the fifth to set out and the first to finish.

Then Nils Haagensen retired Camicorn, his second string, at the Bullfinch in the Centre Walk and the first to go clear was the triple Olympic gold medallist, Richard Meade, with his recently acquired Irish horse, Kilcashel. Only five others achieved this, one being Richard's other horse, Speculator.

Jane Holderness-Roddam's Warrior, who had won here two years earlier, fell at the Quarry (fence 27) but then, miraculously, after eight other horses had retired or incurred cricket scores, Helen Butler (Hugh Thomas's sister-in-law) and her little-known Merganser II, whose sole previous claims to fame had been to finish third at Wylye and Burghley, went clear in a very fast time. They finished the cross-country with nothing to add to their 57 dressage penalties and went gloriously into the lead. (Merganser II is a nine-year-old by that great Irish sire of jumpers, Chou Chin Chow.)

However, this fast, clear round did not give confidence to

those who followed. The next competitor, Ireland's Helen Cantillon, fell at the second fence, the Fallen Tree, with Wing Forward and fractured her wrist. The tale of misadventures continued until Goran Breisner, based with the expatriate Swede, Lars Sederholm, in Oxfordshire, went clear on Ultimus. The next to do so was Mark Todd, the eventual winner, on Southern Comfort, a former stock horse which he had owned for only a matter of weeks and for which he had paid just a few hundred pounds. (The going rate for a top-class international horse in Europe is £35,000–£40,000).

Davey was among the later defaulters, as was Monaco, the European Champion. Castlewellan dropped back in the placings with 80 penalties, but Lucinda Prior-Palmer went into second place with the holder of the Badminton title, Charles Cyzer's gallant Killaire, and Richard Meade brought Speculator into fourth place. But Jane Holderness-Roddam and the young Foxy Bubble got very wet indeed at the lake fences and Captain Mark Phillips on Lincoln, the last competitor, finished the speed and endurance phase in eighth place.

The showjumping phase is always the most tedious part of a three-day event until it is time for the last half-dozen or so competitors. The order of appearance is usually in reverse order to the placings, and so it was on this occasion. Merganser II, going last, demonstrated that he is not as good at showjumping as he is across country and he dropped from first to fourth place with four mistakes. Killaire with Lucinda took a dislike to the board in front of the water and gave it a clout that could have been a stop with any lesser rider. Could it have reminded him of the upturned punt at the lake, as some suggested somewhat fancifully? I think not, but in all events it cost him his second successive victory for Mark Todd and Southern Comfort went clear to win with nothing to add to their dressage score of 64.6. Killaire had collected 7.6 cross-country time penalties and 5 showjumping penalties to add to his 53.8 dressage score, giving him a total of 66.4. Ultimus and Breisner for Sweden had nothing to add to their dressage score of 74.6, and Merganser II was fourth with 77. Jayne Wilson was fifth with Flying Solo, an eight-year-old Irish horse whose rider was in the junior European team two years earlier, and Captain Mark Phillips scraped home on Lincoln despite a stop at the

Zig-Zag and the Quarry. Mark finished with 97.4 points which put him fractionally ahead of the European Champions, Haagensen and Monaco, whose score of 99 included 20 penalties incurred for a stop at the Slide — thus confirming the opinion of those who found their European victory a flash in the pan.

Richard Meade and Kilcashel finished eighth with 100.4, including 44.4 time penalties, but Speculator had been withdrawn before the veterinary inspection on Sunday morning. Richard and Lucinda proved yet again that they are out on their own. Each has passed the acid test of succeeding with a variety of different horses, which so very few do. They must without a doubt be the best riders in the world in this all-embracing sphere.

Every Badminton produces a post-mortem, and this one more than most. After all, two horses were withdrawn after the dressage, two more on phase C (roads and tracks), and one before the cross-country; eleven were eliminated on the cross-country and nineteen retired; two more were withdrawn before the third day — thirty-seven defaulters, for various reasons, from a field of eighty-eight.

The going was unquestionably the worst aspect of all, but the drop fences at Badminton have always come under fire, and this time was no exception. 'Horses are forever having to drop onto the hard, or land halfway up a bank,' one former rider and Badminton winner remarked. 'They get sick of being asked the question.'

After winning this great victory, Mark Todd confessed that he had been really worried about the course and that he had had an anxious moment at the Footbridge when Southern Comfort landed in the ditch, but recovered. And several riders made it plain that they would not ride at Badminton again. Joanna Winter (daughter of the celebrated former champion National Hunt trainer, Fred Winter) remarked: 'I have a couple of good young horses at home, and I'd like to take them abroad with a team, but if I have to take them to Badminton to prove themselves — no way.'

Lord Hugh Russell was the course inspector, and he went round it with Captain Michael Naylor-Leyland and Captain Martin Whiteley, a very experienced international rider:

'We felt that, as always, it was big, but that there were no bad fences — and this was proved by the fact that the faults were well spread around the course. But because the roping-off, which is necessary to keep back the crowds, had not then been done it made a difference to the impression we received. Horses unaccustomed to these crowds of some ¹00,000 people had to be led through them and only saw the fence within the last few strides. This restricted view could have had a distorting effect upon the approach and in some cases they had to jump after a sharp turn, as at the Pardubice Taxis. It is possible, too, in the light of hindsight, that the balance was not quite right in the middle of the course — there were not sufficient fences where a rider could kick on and say 'This is fun', building up his own and his horse's confidence before being faced with another problem, such as the drops. By the time they had reached the Sunken Road, horses were sick of them.'

Jane Holderness-Roddam felt that the going had been compacted by the thousands of pairs of feet that had walked the course in the three preceding days:

'The course itself was not that difficult, but the going was too hard. Badminton is usually more difficult than the Olympic Games, it asks the question over and over again, but the strain should be on the rider's brain and not on the horses. I much prefer to jump the course the other way round. On Wednesday it looked nice and green, but on Saturday it was not the same at all after people had climbed on the bank, slid down the Slide and removed most of the grass. The steeple-chase, however, was a great improvement as a figure of eight, and horses finished fresh because they were not on the same rein all the time.'

Mark Todd added: 'You had to ride every fence — you could never let up.'

Badminton had been intended, of course, as an Olympic trial, but the previous week the British Equestrian Federation had announced that Britain would not be going to the Olympic Games in Moscow because of the Russian presence in Afghanistan. Virtually all the three-day event riders had already made it known that they had no intention of going.

The new Badminton champions, Mark Todd and Southern Comfort, the former station-horse from New Zealand. (*Leslie Lane*)

RESULTS

		Dressage	Roads & Tracks/Steeplechase	Cross-Country Jumps	Cross-Country Time	Showjumping	Total
1. Mark Todd (NZ)	Southern Comfort	64.6	—	—	—	—	64.6
2. Lucinda Prior-Palmer	Killaire	53.8	—	—	7.6	5	66.4
3. Goran Breisner (SWE)	Ultimus	74.6	—	—	—	—	74.6
4. Helen Butler	Merganser II	57	—	—	—	20	77
5. Jayne Wilson	Flying Solo	63.8	—	20	4	—	87.8
6. Mark Phillips	Lincoln	57.4	—	40	—	—	97.4
7. Nils Haagensen (DEN)	Monaco	53.2	7.2	20	13.6	5	99
8. Richard Meade	Kilcashel	56	—	—	44.4	—	100.4
9. Tessa Martin-Bird	The Mountaineer	73.2	—	20	12	5	110.2
10. Colin Wares	Bilbo Baggins II	71.4	—	20	11.2	10	112.6
11. Charles Micklem	Village Gossip	72.8	18	20	—	5	115.8
12. Gillian Fleming-Williams	Rescator	54.8	—	40	19.6	5	119.4
13. Clarissa Strachan	Merry Sovereign	52.2	—	40	27.2	5	124.4
14. Jessica Harrington (IRE)	Amoy	61.2	—	40	33.2	—	134.4
15. Jane Starkey	The Baptist	47.8	—	20	70.8	—	138.6
16. Sandy Pflueger (USA)	Free Scot	62.4	—	60	4.8	17.25	144.45
17. Rachel Bayliss	Mystic Minstrel	42.6	8	60	39.6	—	150.2
18. Vincent Jones	Bleak Hills	68.2	—	20	55.2	15.75	159.15
19. Jane Starkey	Topper Too	46.2	—	60	43.2	15	164.4
20. Beverley Thomas	Divine Intervention	68.6	—	60	29.6	20	178.2
21. Bridget Clarke	Harper's Bazaar	77.8	—	80	26.8	10	194.6
22. Jane Holderness-Roddam	Warrior	53.2	—	120	20	5	198.2
23. Diana Clapham	Windjammer	62.4	—	120	11.2	5	198.6
24. Janet Brookes	Script	77.6	—	60	36.8	32.5	206.9
25. Jane Louise Graham	Pikestone	60.6	—	80	57.2	15.25	213.05
26. Richard Walker	John of Gaunt	55	—	120	37.6	10	222.6
27. Elizabeth Purbrick	Felday Farmer	68.8	7.2	80	76.4	5	237.4
28. Dirk van Mieghem (BEL)	Nancledra	69.4	22.4	20	118	30	259.8
29. Sue Willcock	Touch of Gold	65.6	11.2	100	86	25	287.8

Withdrawn after dressage

David Green (AUS) — Swift Deal
Hugh Thomas — Quality Scope

Retired on Phase C

Lucinda Prior-Palmer — Mairangi Bay

Withdrawn after Phase C

Richard Walker — Seko Jimi

Eliminated on cross-country

Hugh Thomas — Mythic Light
Luc van Mieghem (BEL) — Domino
Ernie Fenwick — Knight Valliant
Wendy White — Soldier Blue
Anne Thomas — Campanario
Valerie Wofford (USA) — Touch and Go
Ruth Mackenzie (SPA) — Gitana
August Desmedt (BEL) — Haraudiére
Mark Cursham — Shanagarry
Albert Desmedt (BEL) — Proza

Retired on cross-country

Mark Phillips — Columbus
Nils Haagensen (DEN) — Camicorn
Rachel Bayliss — Gurgle the Greek
Christopher Collins — Gamble VIII
Julian Scott — Felday Folklore
Moira Donaldson — Little News
Hugh Suffern (IRE) — Madrigal
Lucinda Moir — Tilly Davins
Helen Cantillon (IRE) — Wing Forward
Anna Lamberly — Papa Gaetano
Pollyann Lochore — Loch Maree
Duncan Douglas — Our Mr Twink
Julian Seaman — The Reverend
Sandy Brookes — Welton Lightfoot
Andrew Hoy (AUS) — Davey
Tom Coates (CAN) — Dark Challenger
Sue Benson — Monacle II
Jane Holderness-Roddam — Foxy Bubble

Withdrawn after speed and endurance

John Conifey — Toreador
Judy Bradwell — Castlewellan
Richard Meade — Speculator III

Eliminated on showjumping

Michael Moffett — Red Fred

8

The Hunters' Improvement Society Shows at Newmarket, Shrewsbury and the Royal

The Stallion Show – 'Tub' Ivens Pulls Off Dramatic Double
Newmarket, 6 March 1980

The National Stallion Show of 1980, held at Park Paddocks, Newmarket, by kind permission of Messrs Tattersalls, was a resounding success for 'Tub' Ivens. He brought with him the winner of not only the King George V Cup for the supreme champion – Osiris – but also the Macdonald-Buchanan Cup for the best young stallion new to the premium stallion scheme – Lord of Arabia. In doing so Ivens accomplished a feat approaching Charlie Mumford proportions: it will be remembered that Mumford's Tea Caddy Stud in Northamptonshire won the Macdonald-Buchanan trophy on eleven occasions since the war and the King's Cup on a further fifteen.

The judges were Mrs Hugh Gingell, Master of the Cambridgeshire Harriers and only the second woman to officiate at Newmarket, and Mr Thady Ryan from County Limerick, Master of the Scarteen Hounds (the Black and Tans), which have been in his family for over 200 years.

This year, five officials, including a veterinary surgeon on the panel of the Hunters' Improvement Society, inspected the total entry of seventy on the day before the show and did some judicious culling, finding six stallions who did not merit final judging. This same panel later awarded the premiums.

Traditionally, proceedings started with Class A, the young horse class, which always packs the stands, even at 9 a.m. Bob Matson, former Master of the Wynstay, is always one of the early birds ('eccentrics', he terms them) who line the ringside at this hour on a cold morning in early March, when the wind is

often blowing straight across from Siberia. It is more than
encouraging that the attendance figures are increasing annually.

It was in 1975 that L.S. Ivens, whose father had also farmed
and dealt in the Grafton country, first brought a stallion to
Newmarket and won the Macdonald-Buchanan Cup. This he
achieved with Hay-Chas, a chestnut with a thickened hind leg
which it had caught under a gate while trying to get to a mare
which had been turned out in the next field. Now 'Tub' Ivens
brought seven stallions, five of them entered in this class.
Some strong competition came from Ernie Smith, another
hunting farmer from the Grafton country, whose home-bred
Evening All, by the premium stallion Evening Trial (sire of
Princess Anne's Goodwill) had been a good winner in-hand as a
youngster. Now he gave the winning Lord of Arabia (by the
American sire Home Guard) a run for his money before slotting
in between him and his stable companion Casino Boy, by the Le
Levanstell horse Levanter.

District Class 1, which covers Scotland and the North, was
won by Graham Heal's good horse Hubble Bubble. This stallion
stands in North Devon at the Vauterhill Stud which used to be
owned by Graham's late father, Frank Heal who for many years
was master of the Torrington Farmers' Hounds. By Gazing Star,
by Star Gazer, Hubble Bubble traces back on his dam's side to
a mare by that great 'chasing sire, Foroughi. Max Abram, a
stalwart supporter of the scheme who took four horses to the
show from his Busk Hill Stud near York, was second and third
with Bunny Boy, by Right Boy, and Amboise, by the Ballymoss
horse Royal Palace, both of which stood three seasons' training,
the former under both codes.

In the Midlands class the ubiquitous Massarella family had a
winner in the bay nine-year-old Rapid Pass, by Ribero, owned
by Louis Massarella from Leicestershire. (Louis' uncle, the late
Andrew Massarella, stood a related stallion, Riberio, by Ribot,
in County Cork during the last years of his life.) Evening All
was a good second, beating both the veteran BP, now based in
Hertfordshire with John Rawding, and Rough Lad who hails
from the same stud as Rapid Pass.

The class for stallions from Wales and the North-West had the
best racing record. It was led initially by the bay Big Ivor, bred
in the United States, by Sir Ivor out of a mare by Set Fair, and

owned by Mr and Mrs David Gethin. But Big Ivor eventually went down to third place, being deposed by Lloyd Evans's The Tystan, by Typhoon, and by the winner, Graham Lloyd's Current Magic, one of the best young horses in the premium scheme and, as holder of the King George V Cup, the defending champion. He has outstandingly good limbs with hard, flinty bone, and stands well over at the knee. This latter feature is sorely needed for the countless Irish draught mares that are back at the knee, an all-too-common failing which entails much weakness and strain on the tendons.

Current Magic, bought at Ascot for only £600, won three times as a six-year-old over hurdles, so he has done it all. He went on to stand third in a super-premium line-up.

It was interesting to see that My Eagle, who won the Macdonald-Buchanan Cup in 1979 for Mr 'Dewi' Lewis, had disimproved and was only eighth in the class.

District Class 4, for the Cotswolds and its environs, went to

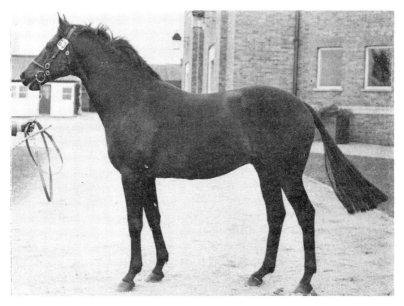

Osiris, owned by L.S. Ivens, not only claimed the King George V Champion Challenge Cup, but also won District Class 6. Newmarket, 1980.
(*Kit Houghton*)

H.R.H. The Princess Anne presents the Macdonald-Buchanan Cup to 'Tub'
Ivens whose Lord of Arabia was judged the best young stallion new to
the premium stallion scheme. Newmarket, 1980. (*Leslie Lane*)

Jimmy Snell from Cornwall with Supergrey, beating another
occupant of the Breage Stud, Abergwiffy, and 'Tub' Ivens's
Weatherbird – all three of them greys and all endowed with
quality and toughness which they proved on the flat and over
hurdles.

The Eastern Counties class went to the young champion,
Lord of Arabia who saw off such of his elders as Bill Wharton's
Garnered, Jimmy Snell's Zipperdi Doo Dah and River Poaching.

Finally, Osiris, who is very correct, not to say classically
conformed, proved his worth by winning what is traditionally
the best class of the day, that for the West Country (District
Class 6). Osiris, who is by Crepello out of Magic Flute by Tudor
Melody, was bred by Lord Howard de Walden and won over
nine furlongs at Newcastle as a three-year-old, after which he
was sold to Mr Ivens. Fourth for the Macdonald-Buchanan Cup
the previous year, he then served around ninety mares at Jimmy
Tamplin's stud near Minehead, where he returned for a second

season. He beat a rare lot of class stallions, including Saunter (winner of the King's Cup for Jimmy Snell in 1978), Max Abram's Better by Far, Graham Heal's Bold as Brass, 'Boss' Masters's Arthur Sullivan (winner of the King's Cup in 1974) and Graham Heal's The Ditton.

Princess Anne, who had watched much of the judging, presented the King's Cup to Mr Ivens. Thady Ryan, who had also judged here in 1979 with Captain George Rich, considered the standard to have improved and that the classes had less tail than in former years. 'We still need more bone, but not at the expense of quality and movement, as we saw in one or two horses today.'

Max Abram's stud swept the board in the Henry Tudor Cup for fertility, which they won with Ascertain, the big American-bred horse led by Don Chambers. Ascertain covered 146 mares for a percentage of 80.71 foals. Runner-up was Better By Far, who served 99 mares for a foaling percentage of 76.53. Saunter (89 for 71.79) was third for Jimmy Snell.

National Hunter Show
Shrewsbury, 25 June 1980

From an entry of 250 young horses that were judged by Captain George Rich and Mr Vivian Bishop (deputising for Mr Leslie Scott, who had been ill), the former judged the non-Thoroughbreds and Mr Bishop the Thoroughbreds, and the Edward Prince of Wales Cup for the champion young horse was won by the three-year-old brown Thoroughbred, Keyston Kelly, by Netherkelly out of Verona's Choice by Lord of Verona.

Produced by Raymond Allman near Evesham, Keyston Kelly is owned by Creative Television Workshops. It is perhaps a sign of the times that we now occasionally see ownership credited to a company and not to an individual. What a sadly anonymous follow-up to all the splendid, traditional names of owners of previous winners: Mrs Vaughan, Mr Reg Hindley, Mr Norman Crow, Mr Frank Furness, Mr 'Gino' Henson, Mrs Molly Cail — all great foxhunters and stalwart supporters of the Society. Perhaps Creative Television Workshops are too, and financial pressures force them to hide behind their firm's name.

The reserve champion, who also won the Harry Jarrett Cup

Sam Luxton's The Doper, reserve champion at Shrewsbury, 1980. (*Leslie Lane*)

for the best non-Thoroughbred, was the improved The Doper, by Cannabis, dam by Spiritus, who had a very successful season in the West Country for North Devon farmer Sam Luxton. The Walker-Okeover Cup for the best filly went to the non-Thoroughbred Daisy Hill, by Hill Farmer out of Llanarth Nerissa by Nerium, a Welsh cob. Daisy Hill is owned by Mr and Mrs Trembath, who bought her from her breeder, Mrs Bigley.

It would be true to say that this was not a vintage year for young hunters, though the standard was level and good. The most consistent champion was Miss Jeanes's chestnut two-year-old Royal Fiddler, by The Dane out of the showjumping mare Ruby Queen, by Ilbury, shown by Robert Oliver, who won his non-Thoroughbred class but was too naughty to figure in the championship judging. Indeed, he gave many an anxious moment to friends of Colonel Dick Spencer, recovered from his appalling fall hunting on Dartmoor but still very unsound, who was very nearly in receipt of both barrels when leading the runner-up to the winner, his own Second Chance, a real hunter by Quality Fair out of a Game Rights mare.

Sam Luxton had another victory with his two-year-old Thoroughbred Midnight Saunter, a grand sort of bay by Saunter out of a Solon Morn mare, bred in Cornwall, and Mr Ian Thomas, the Queen's dressmaker, had a good winner in his home-bred yearling, Lucky Dip, by Don't Look, whose dam, Lucky Strike, by Lucky Leprechaun, won the Edward Prince of Wales Cup and the Walker-Okeover Cup for the best filly here in 1973 for the late Mrs Molly Cail.

Another interesting winner was 'Dewi' Lewis's bay yearling filly, Alice XI, by Harvest Sun out of H4 Suzi by Lohengrin, one of the Holstein mares that was presented to the Society by the late Mr Geoffrey Palmer, and given to farmers who would breed from them. Alice was champion foal here the previous year.

When the produce groups were judged at the end of the day, Quality Fair and Ascertain were the best represented, numerically, but I did not hear the sire of the winning group announced and it was quite a shock to learn, at this of all shows, that it was the Hanoverian stallion Harvest Sun, who stands at the Trago Hanoverian Stud near Bodmin.

Mrs George Gibson judged the brood mares and foals with Peter Tozer, and Mrs Block's small hunter mare Remember Me, a full sister to the late Nat Galway-Greer's last Dublin champion, Never Forget, headed eighteen opponents. Sam Luxton had his third success of the day when his mare, Cheal Rose, won the Thoroughbred mares class from Mr and Mrs Reg Burrington's Bally Autry, also from Devon.

When the judges failed to agree in the championship judging, Colonel John Chamberlayne was called upon to arbitrate. He cast his vote in favour of Cheal Rose at the expense of the Hon. Mrs R.N. Crossley's Cuillin Hills — an odd decision at a Hunter Show. Home-bred, Cuillin Hills (who is by Count Albany out of Loch Ness by Water Serpent) has often carried Colonel Crossley hunting the Derwent Hounds, and Sam Luxton made her supreme at the Royal Highland, telling me that he would have liked to take her home to Devon.

The champion foal, winner of the Kadir Cup trophy, was a triumph for Mrs F.E. Wigley, better known perhaps as Ann

Martin, the journalist. She won it with the dark brown Meltem, by Hopton Lane out of Fiddler's Ferry by Ilbury.

The Royal Show
Stoneleigh, 30 June–3 June 1980

The ridden hunter classes at the Royal, which constitute the Ridden Hunter Show of the Hunters' Improvement Society, were judged by two men operating separately, as is usual here. Richard Meade, who had judged them previously four years earlier, handled the novices and four-year-olds, and the best of twenty-one novices was unquestionably Mrs Charles Cope's Worth Waiting, who was bred by June Stevens, Joint-Master of the Cotswold, out of a mare she hunted for seven seasons. He was sent to Mrs Cope to break and she was able to buy him subsequently.

In the four-year-old class, Mrs Peter Hobbs's Hilly Leys, winner of the Edward Prince of Wales Cup at Shrewsbury in 1979, hid his light under a bushel and slipped back from third to fourth, having won as he pleased at the Three Counties. In a moderate class, lacking any really outstanding contender, the winner was Miss Joanna Vardon's chesnut mare Crown Aquamarine, the latest in the remarkable dynasty she has bred up from a pony mare, using generations of premium stallions.

The weight classes were handled by Mr Tony Martyn, Master of the Glamorgan, who became yet another supporter of Lady Zinnia Pollock's great pattern of a lightweight hunter, Whaddon Way, the black son of Crosby Don. Whaddon Way is equally convincing as a ladies' horse and was duly awarded the accolade here by the Hon. Mrs David Rhys. Allister Hood was runner-up in the lightweight hunter class on Mr Tom Hunnable's Glenstawl, by Sunny Light, a winner at Dublin as a four-year-old.

In the middleweight class, Robert Oliver and Silversmith stood top from start to finish, and the only interest lay in determining who should dance attendance on him. This role was filled by David Tatlow with the 1979 Dublin champion, Zatopek, with Roy Trigg third on the brown Yeoman, by Kalimnos, a horse he owns jointly with his son-in-law, Mike Gibson, who had hunted him with the Cottesmore.

Lady Zinnia Pollock's Whaddon Way ridden by David Barker, Joint Master of the Whaddon Hunt. Whaddon Way was runner-up for the hunter title at Wembley, 1980. (*Kit Houghton*)

Thirteen heavyweights, who had the worst of the weather on a catastrophically wet day, were led initially by Robert Oliver on Flashman, but he knocked himself and was not going quite level behind, leaving Roy Trigg to win the day on Daks Harvest Light, from Allister Hood on Mr Hunnable's Super Coin, and Vin Toulson on Assurance, by Crawter.

It was Zatopek, however, who was reserve champion to Silversmith when the latter won the *Horse and Hound* Cup without the smallest difficulty.

Under Miss Peggy Pacey, a judge of the old school, Nigel Oliver, Robert's nephew, showed Miss Jeanes's Royal Fiddler to win the led championship and he then went on to win the

Robert Oliver and Mrs A.P. Bamford's Silversmith, winner of the *Horse and Hound* Championship Trophy at the Royal, 1980. (*Kit Houghton*)

Lloyds Bank qualifier from a star-studded field, judged by Mrs George Gibson. Reserve for this championship was Ian Thomas's lovely yearling, Lucky Dip, who won at the hunter show on his only previous outing.

It was eminently fitting that the champion filly should have been Lt. Col. and Mrs Neil Foster's home-bred brown filly, Mermaid, a three-year-old with great bone and substance which was bred by Royal Clipper out of a Game Rights mare that was bought from the late Bert Cleminson. The mare died foaling, and two foster mothers from the National Foaling Bank rejected Mermaid before she was accepted by a third. After weaning, her 'nanny' was (and still is) Jack Snowdon, a septuagenarian who has been stud groom to Colonel Foster since the latter was eighteen, and who showed her here.

Colonel Foster, who was Master of the Grafton for so many years, is president of the HIS and chairman of the Stallion Committee.

(For results of the shows featured in this article, see pages 131–40.)

9

Conrad Homfeld Wins Second Running of World Cup

The first World Cup was held in Gothenberg in the spring of 1979 and was won for Austria by Hugo Simon. The second, sponsored by Volvo and by the Netherlands Ministry of Agriculture, was held at the end of April 1980 in Baltimore, Maryland, and was won for the United States by Conrad Homfeld. This twenty-nine-year-old rider from Texas, well-known as a hunter judge on the North American circuit, rode Balbuco to victory by virtue of a consistent performance over the three legs of the final.

The FEI World Cup was inaugurated for the purpose, to put it bluntly, of providing occupational therapy, and a means of livelihood, for the professional riders of Europe during the winter. As all the meetings are held indoors, in a season that starts with Dublin in November and ends in April, it lacks the atmosphere of the summer international season, but it has a certain appeal and suits the Continental horses and riders and also, it would appear, the Americans. Whether it is quite what is needed for British and Irish horses and riders has yet to be established. Eddie Macken did not compete in the final as he was short of an experienced horse; David Broome, who had led throughout the preliminary phases in Europe, picked up a gastric infection in Maryland and his horses were off form; while the reigning World and European champion, Gerd Wiltfang, scorned to attend the final in view of the poor prize money put up by the local sponsors, Carte Blanche.

The competition has certainly brought cohesion into a series of totally unrelated indoor shows throughout the world, and it promises to go from strength to strength. In the first year there were the European League and the North American League, to which was added the Pacific League the following year, and then a fourth league in South America, comprising five events in five different countries. The Pacific League now comprises eight events, while the North American League has increased its fixtures to the maximum of twelve. The European League remains at eleven events. Though the Concours Saute International of Paris was added, the CSIO Birmingham is not holding a preliminary competition in 1981 as it is staging the final, which will be called the FEI Volvo World Cup Holland.

The field for the final in Baltimore consisted of John Fahey and Marianne Gilchrist from Australia, ten riders from North America, one from Venezuela and fifteen from Europe, who were flown over from Dusseldorf after competing at Gothenberg. The courses were built by the Hungarian-born coach of the American team, Bertalan de Nemethy. The cups he used were so shallow that the fences had too little knock-resistance and demanded super-clean jumping, so by popular request they were changed after the opening day.

The first preliminary competition was won by the American professional, Rodney Jenkins, on Third Man, and the second by Ian Millar of Canada on Year of the Cat. On the second day, the final warm-up competition, the Seiko Speed Stakes, also went to Rodney Jenkins.

The first leg of the World Cup was a two-round Grand Prix, but so few people bothered to go and watch it that it lacked atmosphere, especially as it was staged in a vast and deserted civic centre in the middle of downtown Baltimore, an incongruously unequestrian setting.

Six double clear rounds were recorded, three from the home side and three from West Germany. The winner was Melanie Smith, the Connecticut rider, on her brilliant seven-year-old Dutch-bred horse, Calypso, who was clear again in a fast time of 32.33 secs. Lutz Merkel was runner-up on Salvaro in 37.66 secs, and in third place, with the fastest 4 faults in the optimum time of 31.18 secs, was Mike Matz on Jet Run.

The second leg produced ten original clear rounds from a field of twenty-eight, and five double clears. In the final, however, only the youngest rider, twenty-three-year-old Piet Raymakers from the Netherlands, retained a clean slate, on Isocratus, who had joined his string only a few weeks earlier. Melanie Smith was runner-up on Calypso with the fastest 4 faults, going into the double, and Conrad Homfeld on Balbuco had the last fence down, 1.24 secs. behind Calypso.

Melanie Smith was now ahead with 37 points, Matz was second on 26, Homfeld third on 25 and Paul Schockemöhle fourth for West Germany on 24.

For the last leg, competitors went in reverse order of merit, and Melanie Smith and Calypso failed to join the six clear rounds when they hit the planks. In the second round seven went clear, but Calypso hit the upright going into the treble. The only two with double clear rounds were Leslie Burr, George Morris's pupil, on the clean-bred Chase the Clouds, and Hugo Simon of Austria on Gladstone. When the American girl made two mistakes in a fast time in the jump-off, Simon won this leg with only one down in nearly twice the time.

But Homfeld, third for the second day running, had the last word and probably the last laugh too, for his placings earned him the World Cup with 47½ points from Melanie Smith with 44½ and Paul Schockemöhle with 42. Hugo Simon, the defending champion, was fourth with 39, Michael Matz was fifth for the US on Jet Run (38) and Rodney Jenkins came sixth for the home side (29½). Best of the British entry (which consisted of Caroline Bradley, David Broome, Derek Ricketts, John Whitaker and Paddy McMahon) — was John Whitaker who came twelfth on Ryan's Son with 20½.

10

British Team Wins World
Driving Championship

If anyone had suggested, even weeks before the World Driving
Championship was due to take place in Windsor Great Park,
that Britain would win the team title from the redoubtable
Hungarians and the Poles, he would have been laughed to scorn
by any who happened to hear him. Yet this is exactly what
happened. HRH The Prince Philip, Duke of Edinburgh, with the
Queen's team of mixed bays, George Bowman with his active
Cumberland cobs, and Alwyn Holder with his team of Welsh
cobs finished the three days with a score of 229 penalty points,
Hungary was second with 262, and Poland won the bronze
medals with 374. The Netherlands wound up fourth with
493.5, Sweden were fifth with 534, Switzerland sixth with
540, while the Danish, West German and American teams were
all eliminated.

The individual gold medal was won for Hungary by the reigning world and European champion, Gyorgy Bardos, with the
very low score of 79. Thirty-four years old, he took over the
mantle of greatness from Imre Abonyi when the latter retired
in 1977. Bardos won the world title at Kecskemet in Hungary
in 1978 and the European title at Haras du Pin in Normandy in
1979. Successful in the defence of his world title here at Windsor,
he has remained unbeaten for three years with his team of wiry
grey Hungarian Lipizzaners.

George Bowman, who farms in Cumbria, took up driving while
recovering from an accident that crushed his hips. He was a
member of the Cumberland Farmers' branch of the Pony Club
as a boy, just after the war, and in 1956 he spent a season in
Canada as a rodeo rider, where he learned many of the timing
techniques that are so crucial to combined driving. Having
dominated the national events for years, and helped to win the
team silver medals in 1979, at Windsor he won the individual
silver medal with 105 penalty points, beating the 115.5 of the

bronze medal winner, Tjeerd Velstra of the Netherlands, formerly an international showjumper and now director of the Dutch Equestrian Centre at Deurne. Driving is his hobby, and he won the Royal Windsor Horse Show's Barclays Bank Grand Prix in 1978 and 1979 with a team of Friesians, who went well in the dressage phase, all stepping out well together. But he sold them after they were fourth at Haras du Pin where, on the sandy going, he discovered that as well as all stepping out together, they 'all got tired together'.

Fourth place, with 124 points, went to Alwyn Holder, a plant hire contractor from Surrey who won the British National Championship in 1977 at Goodwood, less than a year after hitching up his first team of Welsh cobs. He took up the sport because his daughters were very keen on riding and he got tired of walking or riding a bicycle when accompanying them. He has taught himself the very considerable art of driving a single, a pair and team and has turned the single and its equipage upside down in a ditch, happily without harm to himself or the horse.

In all, forty-two drivers took part, and on the day before the start, the competitors paraded behind Prince Philip through Windsor, down the Long Walk to the Copper Horse and thence to Smith's Lawn. As in the ridden three-day event, dressage and presentation occupy the first day. Gyorgy Bardos was the winner on 45 penalties, followed by George Bowman on 49 and by Prince Philip on 50. Close behind on 51 was the redoubtable Sandor Fülöp, a very experienced competitor from Hungary who is now director of his country's national stud at Kiskunsag.

The second day was devoted to the marathon, which took place over 32 kilometres and took approximately three hours to complete. The object of the marathon is to test the standard of fitness of the horses, and their stamina, and the horsemanship and judgement of pace of the competitors.

The marathon course was divided into five sections, A, C and E being completed at the trot except in difficult terrain, where walking is permitted, and B and D at the walk. In A, C and E natural or artificial obstacles, such as gates, sharp turns, water and steep hills, had to be negotiated. Section C, the obstacle section, was laid out adjacent to Smith's Lawn, and consisted of eight obstacles. Three competitors retired and a further six were eliminated over the toughest course yet seen. The obstacles

Prince Philip drives through the water obstacle. (*Jim Bennett*)

George Bowman negotiates the Sandpit. (*Leslie Lane*)

were so very tight that the bigger horses, such as Prince Philip's, were at a great disadvantage and had to be assisted by grooms through the Sandpit and the Maize (obstacles 7 and 8). This put them out of contention, for if anyone leaves the vehicle 20 penalties are incurred, disconnecting the traces also incurs 20 penalties.

The best performance was that of Gyorgy Bardos, for 34 penalties, followed by George Bowman on 36 and Tjeerd Velstra on 37, while Alwyn Holder had 42.

There were five clear rounds in the final obstacle driving phase, and after a drive-off the winner was the well-known and experienced Pole, Antoni Musial. He finished just ahead of Bardos, who was followed by Jan-Erik Pahlsson from Sweden, Wladislaw Adamczak from Poland and Ernst Fauth from Germany.

Former competitor Philip Hoffman from the United States, chairman of the baby powder firm of Johnson & Johnson, presented the prizes. Hoffman is famed for his grey bowler hat,

Opposite page: A selection of cross-country obstacles.

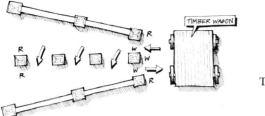

The Wood Yard

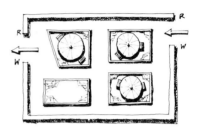

The Garden Pens

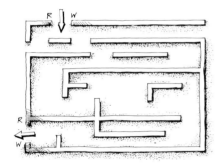

The Maize

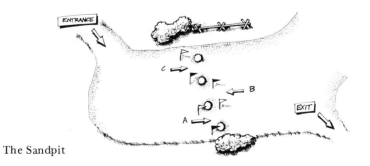

The Sandpit

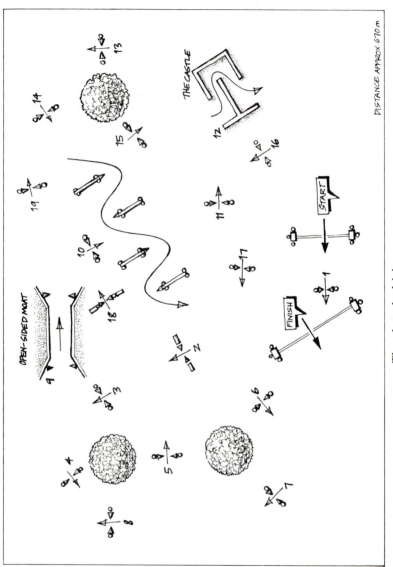

The obstacle driving course.

burgundy-coloured coat, constant cigar, and for the fact that he once encountered a lady driving a car down part of the marathon course at Windsor — indeed, collided with her, for she was going in the opposite direction. Happily, no such incident marred the very successful 1980 World Championships.

Results

Individual

1.	Gyorgy Bardos (HUN)	79
2.	George Bowman (GB)	105
3.	T.R. Velstra (HOL)	115.5
4.	Alwyn Holder (GB)	124
5.	Garbor Fintha (HUN)	136
6.	Antoni Musial (POL)	173
	Nenno Janssen (GER)	173
8.	Ferenc Muity (HUN)	183
9.	Zygmunt Waliszewski (POL)	201
10.	Jan-Erik Pahlsson (SWE)	205.5
11.	Helmut Kolouch (AUT)	210
12.	Ernst Fauth (GER)	231
13.	Wladyslaw Adamczak (POL)	239
14.	Mrs Christine Dick (GB)	240
15.	Georg Knell (GER)	246.5
16.	John Parker (GB)	248.5
17.	Rolf Kellenberger (SWI)	249
18.	Sandor Fülöp (HUN)	250
19.	Peter Munt (GB)	251
20.	Christian Lippuner (SWI)	291
21.	H.R.H. The Prince Philip (GB)	303
22.	A. Chardon (HOL)	316.5
23.	Christer Pahlsson (SWE)	318.5
24.	Jacques Jourdanne (FRA)	332.5
25.	Lt. Col. Sir John Miller (GB)	356
26.	S. Groenewoud (HOL)	378
27.	Mrs Robert Pirie (USA)	389.5
28.	L. Kraayenbrink (HOL)	415.5
29.	Mats Allvilk (SWE)	443
30.	Michael Gilbey (GB)	559
31.	C.A.P. van Opstal (HOL)	567
32.	John Richards (GB)	639
33.	James Fairclough (USA)	459.5 elim
34.	Christian Iseli (SWI)	671 elim
35.	Michael Freund (GER)	677 elim
36.	E. Palm Greisen (DEN)	734.5 elim

37. Nils Gyllensvaan (SWE)   775.5 elim
38. John Fairclough (USA)   779   elim
39. Bernd Duen (GER)   673   ret
40. L. Clay Camp (USA)   774.5 ret
41. James O'Rourke (USA)   792   ret
42. Niels Giversen (DEN)   796   ret

Team

	Presentation and Dressage	Marathon	Obstacle Driving	Indiv. Totals	Team Total
1. *Great Britain*					
HRH The Prince Philip					
Duke of Edinburgh	50	243	10	303	
G. Bowman	49	36	20	105	
A. Holder	72	42	10	124	229
2. *Hungary*					
G. Bardos	45	34	—	79	
S. Fülöp	51	179	20	250	
F. Muity	57	116	10	183	262
3. *Poland*					
W. Adamczak	73	166	—	239	
A. Musial	61	112	—	173	
Z. Waliszewski	53	112	36	201	374
4. *Holland*					
T.R. Velstra	55	37	23.5	115.5	
S. Groenewoud	68	260	50	378	
C.A.P. van Opstal	75	439	53	567	493.5
5. *Sweden*					
J.E. Pahlsson	65	140.5	—	205.5	
N. Gyllensvaan	91	elim			
C. Pahlsson	61	248	9.5	318.5	534
6. *Switzerland*					
C. Iseli	61	elim			
R. Kellenberger	53	186	10	249	
C. Lippuner	61	220	10	291	540

Eliminated
Denmark
West Germany
USA

11

Spring Horse Trials

Crookham (14–16 March 1980)
This year Sally Bullen, the organiser of the Crookham Horse Trials, was more ambitious than ever in that she catered for no fewer than 450 competitors. This large entry was split up into fifteen sections and the competition took place over three days on Tweseldown racecourse, near Aldershot.

Held in mid-March, Crookham is traditionally the curtain-raiser to the horse trials season and in 1980 it marked the start of a season that was looking towards the Olympics. Ironically, both sections of the Open/Intermediate class were won by foreign riders – the first going to an Irish 'cousin', Eric Horgan with Pontoon, who first came to fame by winning Punchestown; the second to Jens Mumme, who hails from West Germany but works in London, on the virtual novice, Credo.

Runner-up to Pontoon in the first Midland Bank Open/Intermediate section was Julian Scott on Barbara Hammond's evergreen veteran, Eagle Rock, and behind Credo in the second section came Wendy White on Soldier Blue and Julian Seaman on The Reverend.

Diana and Susan Clapham virtually farmed the two Midland Bank Intermediate sections, Diana winning the first on Beacon Light while Sue, riding Kalambu, finished second to Petrina Philpott on Hill Climb.

One of the most celebrated veterans of all time won the Veterans class – Mary Gordon-Watson's Cornishman V, who won Olympic team gold medals in Mexico and Munich, the European Championship in 1969 at Haras du Pin, and at Punchestown a year later captured the World title over an horrendous course. Twenty-one years young, and having hunted several seasons with the Cottesmore since his 'retirement', Corny was followed home by the modern pentathlete gold medallist, Captain Jim Fox, on Hugh Thomas's veteran of the Montreal Olympics, Playamar, and by Jennie Loriston-Clarke on Warrior, the horse usually ridden by her sister Jane Holderness-Roddam. Jim Fox also won a section of the Novice class on his own horse, Finisterre II.

Corbridge (22–23 March 1980)
Meanwhile, in the north, the Corbridge Trials were in doubt even after they started, and they were taking place for only the second time in four years. Nick Straker won the first Open/ Intermediate section comfortably on Barclay II and the second went to Ruth Williams on Lanson, 20 points behind. Karen Straker brought off a family double in the Junior Novice on Peppercorn.

Shelswell (22–23 March 1980)
In its second year, Shelswell Horse Trials, held on Baroness Maltzahn's parkland, brought out the reigning European champion, Nils Haagensen of Denmark, with Monaco, warming up for their attack on Badminton. They ran out easy winners, after a consummate dressage. Three points behind them in the dressage was young Ricenda Lord and Milton Bella, whose cross-country round was fractionally faster than that of Lucinda Prior-Palmer on Mairangi Bay. Next in line came the Novice and Open Midland Bank champions, Katrina Finlayson on Late Look and Richard Walker on John of Gaunt.

Jane Cooper and Bert won the other Advanced section, some 25 points behind Haagensen but still ahead of the more experienced combinations, including Charlie Micklem on Overseas Containers Ltd's Village Gossip.

Another notable partnership now in its infancy was that of Lucinda Moir on Mrs T. Pond's former hurdler, Queen Hill, who won an Intermediate section. Hugh Thomas on Ebony Green, a former show hunter, won a Novice section.

Downlands (26–27 March 1980)
Liphook's Downlands trials, over Mrs Kenneth Poland's land, was the next major engagement. The best score in the two sections of Midland Bank Advanced class was achieved by Judy Bradwell's Punchestown (1979) winner, Castlewellan. Until the cross-country phase, he was level with Captain Mark Phillips on the Queen's Columbus, but the veteran lost his footing

through his once-troublesome hind leg, just as they were coming out of the ditch at the penultimate Marsh's Steps fence. They incurred 20 penalties for a technical refusal which relegated them to fifth place.

Clarissa Strachan's Delphy Kingfisher finished second, 11 points behind the winner, with Diana Henderson on The King-maker and Colin Wares on Mrs Olive Jackson's Cricket III (late of the Irish junior team) well up in third and fourth places respectively.

Jayne Wilson won the other Advanced section on Flying Solo with 5 points in hand from Goran Breisner of Sweden on Ultimus. Breisner was level on points with Clarissa Strachan on Merry Sovereign, the horse she rode in the European Champion-ship team of 1979 in Luhmühlen, but the Swede went slightly slower across country. Hard on their heels came Virginia Holgate on Priceless, and then Nils Haagensen from Denmark with Camicorn. Haagensen had the misfortune to lose his other horse, Mr Kimple, when it broke its offside forearm in a collision, at speed, with the Ajax Insurance Wall, at which some half dozen horses came to grief.

Judy Bradwell had her second success of the day in the first Intermediate section on Derby House. Captain Mark Phillips was another Intermediate winner on the Range Rover Team's Town and County, who finished 6 points ahead of Lucinda Moir's Shelswell winner, Queen Hill.

Rushall (29 March 1980)

At Mr Barry Wookey's Rushall meeting on Salisbury Plain, a favourite pre-Badminton work-out for many in the south-west, the wet going was the biggest hazard that horses and riders had to face. Nils Haagensen took a narrow lead in the Advanced class on Monaco, but close behind them were Richard Walker on John of Gaunt and Seko Jimi, and Rachel Bayliss with Gurgle the Greek, the European silver medallist, and Mystic Minstrel.

In the end, they were all at the mercy of Sarah Bouët and Maytime III, who went clear in the showjumping and kept out of trouble at the river crossings, the first of which upset Captain Mark Phillips with Rough and Tough. Richard Meade retired Speculator III after a fall at the Hayracks, and Nils Haagensen had a refusal with Monaco coming off Badgers Bank. Charlie

Micklem had a disastrous dressage with Village Gossip, and in an attempt to write off his score put up the fastest cross-country round, though to no avail.

Following Maytime home were Richard Walker's two rides, Seko Jimi and John of Gaunt, then came Gurgle the Greek, Jane Cooper's Bert and, in sixth place, the then unknown New Zealand rider, Mark Todd, with Southern Comfort, destined to become the 1980 Badminton winner.

Ermington (1 April 1980)
Ermington Horse Trials, on the late Lord Mildmay's Flete estate, near Ivybridge, fell victim once again to the weather and did not take place as planned.

Brigstock (6–7 April 1980)
After his bad luck at Downlands, Mark Phillips' star was in the ascendant at Diana Maxwell's popular Brigstock meeting a week later. He won the first Midland Bank Advanced section on Lincoln, beating Liz Purbrick on Felday Farmer and Colin Wares on Yukon Melody. On Columbus, Mark then walked away with the second section as well. Columbus had broken a bone in his knee when it made contact with the wall at Liphook but miraculously he was now sound again. He proved his well-being by beating Seko Jimi, Gurgle the Greek, Flying Solo and Andrew Hoy's Burghley winner, Davey.

The third Advanced section went to Judy Bradwell's Castle-wellan, and her most doughty opponents were probably Nils Haagensen's European champion, Monaco, who finished third, 8 points behind, and Chris Collins's Gamble, who finished fifth. Fallers were Richard Meade on Kilcashel, Richard Walker on John of Gaunt and Janet Norton (née Hodgson) on Gretna Green.

Belton Park (12–13 April 1980)
At Belton Park, the seat of Lord Brownlow, Robin Cayzer and Fighting Fifth won the Midland Bank Open/Intermediate Section A from a high-class field which included John Marsden on Claughton. Judy Bradwell won the second section on William Hickling and the third went to Rosemary Anderson on Wells Fargo.

Bicton (26–27 April 1980)

Held on Lord Clinton's estate near Budleigh Salterton, this event enjoyed 439 entries. The Midland Bank Advanced class was won by Alison Hough with Sprackcliff from Phoebe Alderson on Mrs Welman's April's Dancer, Mark Todd on Jocasta, Eric Horgan on Pontoon, Miss C. Calloway on Bassanio and Jane Starkey on Acrobat. The Novice Regional Final was won by Captain Mark Phillips on Town and County, who performed a far better dressage test than did Ann Backhouse, the former showjumper, on Grain Fair.

Wramplingham (27 April 1980)

Debbie Saffell and Jacaranda triumphed at Wramplingham, in Norfolk, where another winner was Bridget Ensten on Miss Ruth McMullen's Carbrooke Charles. In the Novice sections, Judy Bradwell on Derby House and Richard Walker on Ryan's Cross were also well on the way to the Intermediate category.

South of England (1 May 1980)

In the South of England meeting at Ardingly, Sussex, Colin Wares and Cricket III won an Open/Intermediate class from Phoebe Alderson on April's Dancer, who later went on to win at Wylye.

Llanfechain (2–3 May 1980)

Gillian Fleming-Williams' Rescator and Miss S. Jackson's Major Tom were the winners of the two sections of the Intermediate two-day event.

Earl Soham (3 May 1980)

Earl Soham Lodge, in Suffolk, again ran a very successful meeting, where the winners included Debbie Saffell once more on Jacaranda.

Wellesbourne (10–11 May 1980)

Captain Mark Phillips won one of the ten Midland Bank Novice classes on the Range Rover Team's Fieldsman and Diana Clapham took another on Welton Mermaid.

Sherborne (11 May 1980)

At Sherborne Castle Horse Trials, the oldest one-day event in England, Sally Ann Singleton won the Midland Bank Open/ Intermediate class on Nubian. One of the Intermediate classes was won by Clarissa Strachan with Chevalier Noir, a horse that had been bought — as all her horses have been — by putting an advertisement in the *Western Morning News*. In second place, by 14 points, was Petrina Phillpot's Hill Climb, followed by the sixteen-year-old May Fox.

Chris Collins won the Midland Bank Novice Regional Final on Kinallen, with a 5-point lead, gained by virtue of a fast cross-country round, over Liz Purbrick on Peter the Great.

Windsor (16–18 May 1980)

At the Windsor Horse Trials two young riders, Hilary Meadows on Mr W.N. Newbery's Last Chance X and Lucinda Moir with Queen Hill upset the odds by beating Andrew Hoy and Davey, and Captain Mark Phillips with Town and County into third and fourth places respectively. The girls had scores of 70.5 (Last Chance) and 71.4 (Queen Hill) against 75.7 and 76.5 for the men.

In 1979 the going at Windsor had been appallingly wet. Now it was in complete contrast, and several horses were scratched in preference to running them on the sun-baked clay, which was fissured in places.

Jens Mumme and Credo, who had won at Crookham two months earlier, were clear leaders in the dressage. Sue Benson's Monacle was not going level behind and was subsequently withdrawn. Hilary Meadows and Lucinda Moir were in the ruck at this stage. The steeplechase course had been well rotovated and presented no difficulties, but there were several problems posed by the cross-country course, such as in the new complex of rails below the Copper Horse, where the two bounces were too tight. Both girls rode the course with great dash and verve, and were the only riders to finish within the time, but Town and County was still in front by virtue of a better dressage mark. Neither looked like making a mistake in the showjumping, but Town and County made a mess of the last two parts of the final treble and dropped back three places in the order. Event horses who can tackle coffins with equanimity often fail at combination showjumps.

Rufford (18 May 1980)

On account of the going, the Rufford Trials in Nottinghamshire suffered many withdrawals despite extensive rotovating and putting down sand on the landings. The Advanced class (Midland Bank, of course) was won by John Marsden on Claughton.

Bramham (29 May–1 June 1980)

At the Bramham Three-Day Event, John Marsden won the Advanced Midland Bank Standard section on the Newark Equestrian Centre's Claughton. Overcoming elimination on the previous day (an objection was overruled by the ground jury but later upheld by the jury of appeal) and lying second at the start of the showjumping, he went clear while the leader had a fence down.

Exactly the same fate had befallen Robin Cayzer on Fighting Fifth in the Sterling section, down to the minutest detail, and both riders must certainly have counted themselves fortunate and felt that luck, this time at least, was on their side. Fighting

En route to victory, John Marsden and Claughton at the
Bramham Three-Day Event. (*Leslie Lane*)

Fifth was followed home by Susie Brooke from Northern Ireland on Superstar IV, owned by her mother, Lady Brookborough. (Susie later competed in the British team for the Junior European Championships.) Runner-up to Claughton was Debbie Saffell on her little palamino stallion, Jacaranda. Each girl was between 4 and 5 points behind the winner.

Chepstow (6–7 June 1980)

Finally, the spring season came to a close at Chepstow, where among the winners were Pammy Mansfield on Odds Against II (owned by her father, Colonel Sivewright) and Miranda Frank on The Dark Imp.

*   *   *

As the foregoing horse trials reports suggest, it is not difficult to foresee a time when combined training takes over from show-jumping as the most popular competitive horse sport. Quite possibly, with the commercialism that is rife in showjumping, it has already done so.

12

International Three-Day Events

Punchestown (24–26 May 1980)
Lt David Foster of the Irish Army rode Inis Meain (better
known, perhaps, as Gralla, by Go Tobann, Fiona Kinnear's
double champion hunter at Dublin) to win the Punchestown
International Championship in May. Competing at this event
was an obligatory exercise for all candidates of the Irish team
aiming (then) for the Olympic Games. As it turned out, their
destination was to be the alternative Olympics at Fontainebleau.

Inis Meain did well in the dressage for 54.8 penalty points
and put up the best time of the day across country. He was
slightly over the time allowed in the showjumping, incurring a
mere three-quarter time fault, and won by more than 20 points.

Only 2 points divided the next three in the line-up, who were
all clear in the showjumping. Mark Todd of New Zealand, only
recently supreme at Badminton, was runner-up on Jocasta, and
Jessica Harrington, riding her father's home-bred Amoy, finished
third with a score identical to that of Eric Horgan on Pontoon
but faster across country.

Eric and Pontoon were fourth and in fifth place was Jane
Starkey, the best-placed British entrant, riding her young horse,
Rock Pipit, in his first three-day event. Clear in every phase, he
edged in front of Ronnie McMahon riding his own and Miss
Emily Parkhill's Parkhill, who was lightweight champion at
Dublin for three successive years.

Katrina Finlayson did well to finish seventh on her Midland
Bank novice champion Late Look, by Bill Manning's Don't
Look. Pollyann Lochore was eighth on Loch Maree, with two
showjumps down and only fractionally ahead of Siobhan
Reeves-Smyth's plebeian but eminently worthy Millicent Bridge,
who was one of the mainstays of the Irish team at Fontainebleau two months later.

John Watson withdrew Cambridge Blue, hero of the World
Championships in Lexington two years earlier and a member of

the winning European Championship team at Luhmühlen in 1970. The horse was just getting over a virus infection and was not one hundred per cent fit. Alan Lillington also decided to withdraw Seven Up in view of the firm going. Poor Helen Cantillon had the bad luck to break her arm just days before the competition, so Van de Vater, who helped to train Wing Forward, rode him for her and completed the event.

The cross-country course was virtually the same as it was in 1979, with the addition of the T-junction built for the Junior European Championships the previous August and a new Foot-bridge, very like that at Badminton — it hardly needs to be added that these two obstacles were responsible for most of the trouble on the second day.

The T-junction caused a number of refusals while the Foot-bridge, whose escape hatch was time-consuming, was the scene of several falls, among them Maureen Piggott with Barney II and David Foster's Ferrymaster. But only four retired from their encounter with Billy McLernon's course, which produced a logical result without eliminating any of the sixty-three starters. Such an outcome is quite a rarity in the annals of the three-day event.

Results

			points
1.	David Foster (IRE)	Inis Meain	63.95
2.	Mark Todd (NZ)	Jocasta	84
3.	Jessica Harrington (IRE)	Amoy	86
4.	Eric Horgan (IRE)	Pontoon	86
5.	Jane Starkey (GB)	Rock Pipit	94
6.	Ronnie McMahon (IRE)	Parkhill	97.2

Kalmthout (27–29 June 1980)

The next international engagement was Kalmthout, in Belgium. The weather was abominable and otherwise ambitious riders who regard international engagements as a challenge, were none the less glad that only Captain Mark Phillips was there to carry the flag. Riding the British Equestrian Federation's Rough and Tough, a horse which lost caste progressively with each public outing, he did well indeed to finish the dressage phase in seventh place out of thirty starters, just 18 points behind the winner.

While dressage tests were punctuated by heavy showers and outbreaks of thunder, the speed and endurance phase had to be undertaken in a non-stop downpour which worsened progressively as the day wore on, the going becoming more and more holding.

Despite having switched off his stop-watch instead of turning it on, while persuading his recalcitrant horse to enter the 'box', Captain Phillips nevertheless gauged the time sufficiently accurately to incur only 2.4 time penalties. In doing so he put up the best overall performance though Helmut Rethemeier from West Germany on Agazu had a better cross-country time. At the end of the day, Rough and Tough had gone up into second place, only 3 points behind Jan Lypczinski on Elektron for Poland, who had a fence down in the showjumping. A clear round for Captain Phillips would have signified a British victory, but the second element of the treble fell and, as at Boekelo the previous autumn, he finished in second place.

Results

1.	Jan Lypczinski (POL)	Elektron	84.2
2.	Captain Mark Phillips (GB)	Rough and Tough	87.0
3.	Helmut Rethemeier (GER)	Agazu	90.6
4.	Rudiger Schwarz (GER)	Sugril	108.4
5.	Luc van Mieghem (BEL)	Domino	111.2
6.	K. eras von Wengersky (GER)	Kobold III	115.6

Luhmühlen (28–31 August 1980)
German horse trials are always very happy engagements, and none more so than Luhmühlen. Here veteran captain of the American team, Mike Plumb, gained consolation for being eliminated with Laurenson at Fontainebleau the previous week, winning this international three-day event on his Montreal Olympic partner, Better and Better with 41.4 penalty points. Dieter Baumgart of the home side was runner-up on Kurfurst with 42 penalty points and Judy Bradwell was third for Britain on Castlewellan with 46.2. Wendy White finished twelfth on

Soldier Blue and Tessa Martin-Bird and The Mountaineer were placed thirteenth.

The United States won the team event with 183.6 points from Great Britain's 200.2. The West German team was third and Switzerland came fourth.

Results

Individual

1.	Mike Plumb (USA)	Better and Better	41.4
2.	Dieter Baumgart (GER)	Kurfurst	42
3.	Judy Bradwell (GB)	Castlewellan	46.2
4.	Guntager Lauge (GER)	Welfen Prinz	51.8
5.	Derek Dei Grazia (USA)	Thriller II	54.6
6.	Harry Klugmann (GER)	Knockboy	59

Team

1.	USA	183.6
2.	Great Britain	200.2
3.	Germany	219.2
4.	Switzerland	456.6

Boekelo (22–25 October 1980)

Boekelo, the Dutch three-day event which always invites a large field of young riders and up-and-coming horses from England, ran true to form this year. A sizeable proportion of the field of seventy came from the British Isles, in addition to a team from the United States, France and the USSR.

Clarissa Strachan, from Devonshire, and her European Championship horse Merry Sovereign, on whom she had finished fourth here in 1978, were the leaders after the completion of the dressage phase. But a hair's breadth separated the scores of the top competitors and Merry Sovereign was only 0.6 of a point better than the two who were disputing second place: Sandy Pflueger of the United States, but based in Surrey, with her English Thoroughbred Free Scot, by Free Boy; and Eddie Stibbe of the home side on Autumn Haze.

The American team led a field of seven in the dressage, but here again the scores were so close that placings at this stage meant very little. Britain was fourth, her second-best rider being Captain Mark Phillips on the Range Rover Team's Town and County in twelfth place, 5.2 points behind the leader. Princess Anne on the Queen's Stevie B, lying thirty-first, was only 13 points behind Merry Sovereign.

It all hinged, of course, on the cross-country, which exposed inadequacy as relentlessly as ever and, with the field so close together, also put a premium on speed. Sandy Pflueger with Free Scot lost no time in taking up the running when Clarissa Strachan and Merry Sovereign had a refusal and a fall. Colin Wares was even faster on Mrs Olive Jackson's Irish-bred Cricket III, performing in his first three-day event, and this ten-year-old put up the optimum time and went from fifteenth to second place.

Judy Bradwell on Derby House was fast and clear, and so was Angela Tucker on Willow Pattern — indeed, if these three had been in the team Britain would have been unbeatable, but Captain Phillips and Princess Anne were naturally reluctant to push their young horses. Stevie B, another horse savouring his first three-day event, accrued a number of time penalties over the steeplechase course before going convincingly clear across country, while Town and County is still immature but appears to have a bright future.

Maureen Piggott, daughter of champion jockey Lester, fell with Barney II when he attempted to jump, rather than ford, the water splash.

Only one fence separated the first four combinations when it came to the showjumping, and when Colin Wares and Cricket III went clear, it behoved Sandy Pflueger and Free Scot to emulate them. But they came within an ace of stopping at the water, in which they touched down, and a second mistake pegged them back to fifth.

Assisting France to win the team prize, Jean-Paul Lagrassiere and the French Anglo-Arab Darius finished in second place, just ahead of Nils Haagensen, Denmark's European champion and gold medallist at the alternative Olympic three-day event, on his young, green Cheers Danheat.

Britain finished third of the seven teams, behind the USSR,

after Princess Anne had to retire Stevie B with some heat in a foreleg.

Results

Individual

1.	Colin Wares (GB)	Cricket III	55.4
2.	Jean-Paul Lagrassiere (FRA)	Darius	58
3.	Nils Haagensen (DEN)	Cheers Danheat	62.2
4.	Eddie Stibbe (HOL)	Autumn Haze	64
5.	Sandy Pflueger (USA)	Free Scot	64.8
6.	Judy Bradwell (GB)	Derby House	68.8

Team

1.	France	237
2.	USSR	271.2
3.	Great Britain	301.05

13

Autumn Horse Trials

Heckfield (2–3 August 1980)

The autumn season had opened the previous week at Heckfield in Hampshire. Rachel Bayliss won both Midland Bank Open/ Intermediate sections: the first on Gurgle the Greek, who did a better dressage than Judy Bradwell's Castlewellan and then went faster across country; and the second on Mystic Minstrel, who had a showjumping fence down, putting them behind Jane Holderness-Roddam with Warrior, but they caught up and overtook Warrior across country.

Nicola May, the reigning European Junior Champion, took the first Intermediate section on Commodore IV and the other went to David Stride on The Merchant.

Dauntsey (2–3 August 1980)

Over Toby Sturgis's land at Dauntsey, in the heart of the Duke of Beaufort's country, the team trial for the alternative Olympics was held as the third section of the Advanced class. It was perhaps an omen that it was won not by one of our own contenders, but by Andrew Hoy of Australia, on Davey, the winner of the Raleigh Trophy at Burghley a year before. After finishing third in the dressage, with 25 points to the 24 of Captain Mark Phillips on Lincoln and the 21 of Rachel Bayliss with Mystic Minstrel, they put up the fastest time across country to win with 37 penalty points, followed by Miss Bayliss with 41 and Lucinda Prior-Palmer on Killaire with 51.

Miss Prior-Palmer also rode Village Gossip for the first time in a year to finish ninth with one refusal — and was very glad that the selectors had insisted on her doing so, as Killaire went lame a week before he was due to go to France and Gossip had to travel in his place. But for the stop, he would have been third overall. Liz Purbrick was fourth on Felday Farmer, Richard Walker was fifth on John of Gaunt with the same score but a

Jane Cooper and Bert, an up-and-coming combination.
Dauntsey, 1980. (*Kit Houghton*)

slower cross-country, Helen Butler came sixth on Merganser and
Richard Meade tenth after taking the cross-country very easily
on Kilcashel. Mark Phillips had two refusals at the Wishing Well
on Lincoln, which cost him his place in the team, but he went
to France to compete as an individual.

Virginia Holgate won the Advanced II section on Nightcap,
beating Jane Holderness-Roddam on Warrior, who was being
prepared for Burghley, Jane's favourite event. The first section
went to Rachel Bayliss on her fifteen-year-old veteran, Gurgle
the Greek, and she was also second on the Argentinian-bred
Trenque Lauquen. Katy Hill won the second Intermediate class
on Hard Times, and the other section went to Chris Collins on
Kinallen.

Eglinton (2 August 1980)
The Clydesdale Bank Advanced class at Eglinton was well won
by Jennifer Caley on Chili con Carne, who vanquished a high-

class field including Captain Mark Phillips on Town and County, who stopped at the Zig-Zag. Wendy White was second and fifth with the young Woodland Rights and Soldier Blue, by Kadir Cup, and Pollyann Lochore finished third on Loch Maree. Captain Phillips gained recompense when the Range Rover Team's Classic Lines (by Armagnac Monarch out of a mare by Arctic Slave, and Fieldsman, by Helluva Fella) finished first and third in the Novice regional final.

Susan Hendry won the Intermediate class on Count Rostov, which was a Scottish victory over Belinda Norton on Zeppelin II.

Annick (6 August 1980)

Rosemary Anderson and Wells Fargo, by Pony Express, won the Clydesdale Bank class at Annick, Ayrshire, on a day when over-night rain had made the cross-country going treacherous and several riders, chief among them Captain Mark Phillips with Persian Holiday, who was destined for Burghley, withdrew after the dressage rather than put their horses at risk. Yet two hours later, after the sun had shone warm and bright, the going was excellent.

Wells Fargo, who started the showjumping with a two-fence margin for error, went clear, but his owner's other horse, West-way, who had been lying second, hit five fences. The eventual runner-up was Janet Norton on Volant, 13 points behind the winner.

Lesley Kidd and Top Notch were winners in an Intermediate class here.

Dumfriesshire (9 August 1980)

Pollyann Lochore and Loch Maree were another combination which withdrew from the Advanced class at Annick. But three days later, at the Dumfriesshire meeting, they were in the lead after the dressage phase by one point from Sally Eldred on Hamlet IV and Janet Norton on Gretna Green.

Loch Maree also emerged unscathed from the cross-country round, and avoided trouble at the bogey hay rack which put paid to Hamlet, Script and Shanagarry. Only 10 time penalties put Loch Maree well in contention, though Wendy White's Soldier Blue fared better still, with only 5 time penalties to add to his dressage score of 33. But his luck did not hold in the showjumping, where he felled the planks. Loch Maree won with 41 penalties, while on 43 points Soldier Blue and stable companion Woodland Rights disputed second place for twenty-one-year-old Wendy White, winner of the Dutch event at Hooge Mierde.

Captain Mark Phillips won an Intermediate section on the Range Rover Team's Fieldsman, and the other went to Shirley Jackson on Ground Control.

Iping (9 August 1980)

Hugh Thomas, a strong administrator in embryo and a convincing commentator who wields a formidable pen, won the Midland Bank Open/Intermediate section A class at Iping, West Sussex, on Mythic Light.

Molland (10 August 1980)

Molland was to have been used as the final work-out for the Olympic team, had there been one. The Australians made use of this early August event as a pre-Fontainebleau schooling ground, so too did Mark Todd from New Zealand on his second string, Jocasta.

Andrew Hoy and Davey, who had already won at Dauntsey earlier in the week, brought off a double over this undulating course on Tom Stevens' land, which extends out over Exmoor to an altitude of 1000 feet. Jane Cooper was second, 6 points behind, on Fairy, and Lucinda Moir just one point behind her on Queen Hill. The Intermediate class went, by virtue of a good dressage, to Sue Benson on Radley Slim.

Locko Park (14–16 August 1980)

So to the Midland Bank Championships at Locko Park, Derbyshire, where, thanks to its owner, Patrick Drury-Lowe, the sponsors who underwrite this great sport year after year get some small reward in the way of publicity, which they never seek.

For the second year running, Richard Walker won the Open Championship on Kent Leather Distributors' John of Gaunt, beating last year's Novice Champion, Katrina Finlayson on Late Look, by 9 points.

Torrential rain on the night before the start had its usual devastating effect upon the going. The dressage leaders were

Captain Mark Phillips with Persian Holiday (35 points) Rachel Bayliss with Trenque Lauquen (36 points) and Richard Walker with John of Gaunt (37 points).

The most influential obstacles were the steps into and out of the water, which claimed among their victims Captain Mark Phillips with Rough and Tough and Liz Purbrick's Felday Farmer, who stopped at both elements. Lucinda Prior-Palmer had a stop there too, coming out with Foxy Bubble (he had stopped at the Badminton Lake with Jane Holderness-Roddam four months earlier). Lucinda also had a fall at the wall with Botany Bay.

Katrina Finlayson took Late Look into an early lead, with only 11 time penalties, and maintained this lead to the end of the day, though Richard Walker and John of Gaunt had 16 time penalties and were only one point behind due to their better dressage. Next came Rachel Bayliss on Trenque Lauquen, and then Captain Phillips on Persian Holiday, who had been given an easy run as Burghley was only two weeks away.

Captain Mark Phillips on the Range Rover Team's Town and County at Locko Park, 1980. (*Kit Houghton*)

Rachel Bayliss and the Argentinian-bred Trenque Lauquen.
Locko Park, 1980. (*Kit Houghton*)

The showjumping arena had been levelled and newly grassed, and as it had not yet settled the heavy rain had made it very deep. Virginia Holgate and Priceless jumped the first clear round, which moved them up two rungs to third place. When Richard Walker and John of Gaunt also went clear the pressure was certainly on Katrina Finlayson, as just one mistake would deprive her of the lead. Alas, Late Look touched a couple of poles and dropped back to second place behind John of Gaunt. Alex Hough and Sprackcliff, with the joint fastest cross-country time, came up into fourth place above Persian Holiday.

Captain Mark Phillips had qualified three of the Range Rover Team horses for the Novice Championship, and he won it with the six-year-old Classic Lines, who produced the second best dressage test and the fastest novice cross-country time for a total of 49 points — 13 points better than Judy Bradwell on Derby House. Captain Phillips was also third on Town and County, with 56 points.

Claughton (23 August 1980)

Jane Perera won the Midland Bank Advanced class at the Claughton horse trials in Lancashire with Queen's Counsel III, by dint of a clear round in the showjumping which gave her a one-point advantage over Liz Kershaw, on Three Cups, who felled the gate. John Marsden finished third on Claughton, who incurred 16 time penalties over the cross-country course, which did not suit him.

Sue Platt from Cheshire won the first Intermediate section on Merlin Fox, whose dressage was good enough to withstand the cross-country challenge of Robin Donaldson's Conundrum. The second section went to Andrew Brown from Berwick-on-Tweed, with Leroy, who again scored by virtue of his dressage mark, Madeleine Fielder's Persuasion having identical time penalties across country. Andrew Fielder, previously well known for his successful showjumping partnership with Vibart, won the second novice section on his wife's horse, Sharna.

Hampton Lodge (25 August 1980)

A field with several far-flung entries competed in the Warwickshire Hunt's trials at Hampton Lodge, where Polly Schwerdt on Dylan II was a clear Intermediate winner from John Marsden on Black Monk and Richard Walker on Ryan's Cross. Marjorie Comerford won the other Open/Intermediate section on Mrs Jewson's Barty, from John Mansfield on Kenneth Beeston's Farmer Kojak and Princess Anne on the Queen's Stevie B.

Bucklebury (30–31 August 1980)

David Hancock rode Maria Comacho's Klammer to win the first Open/Intermediate section at Bucklebury, whose course was designed by Lorna Clarke and featured a downhill start. Ten points behind in second place was Goran Breisner of Sweden and his and Lars Sederholm's Ultimus. Virginia Holgate won the next section on Night Cap from Debbie Saffell's Jacaranda and Julian Scott on Barbara Hammond's Eagle Rock. The third section went to Joan Marsh-Smith's Tudor Court, at the expense of Joanna Winter's Houdini.

Rudding Park (30–31 August 1980)

Captain Mark Phillips rode Town and County to win the

Advanced class at Rudding Park in Yorkshire. The first Intermediate class went to Marjorie Comerford on Barty and the
second to Elizabeth Firth on Capricorn VI, both wins due to
speedy progress across country.

Dalmahoy (31 August 1980)
At Dalmahoy, Edinburgh, Lesley Kidd, aged eighteen, and Top
Notch achieved their third consecutive victory, to add to their
wins at Annick and Devonshaw.

Kyre (3 September 1980)
Peter Gleave and Klipspringer, respectively the sons of Margaret
Hough and of Bambi V who together won Badminton in 1954,
were the winners of the first Intermediate section at Kyre before
going on to bigger things in the Osberton three-day event.

Burghley (4–7 September 1980)
After the traumas of Fontainebleau, and with the memory of
Badminton still fresh in the mind, many people went to Burghley
distinctly half-heartedly, wondering perhaps just what was
coming next.

They need not have worried, for Charles Stratton, the director
of this splended meeting in Lord Exeter's lovely park, and Bill
Thomson, who has always built the course here (except for one
year when Colonel Henry Nicol took it on), were only too
acutely aware that the onus was on Burghley to restore the
public's confidence in the three-day event, and that if they
failed to do so, the sport would have been dealt an irreparable
blow from which conceivably it could never recover.

Bill Thomson is an excellent fence builder. He built the first
course at Burghley twenty years ago and, as course-builder to
the Combined Training Group, as it used to be called, of the
British Horse Society, he has built courses, great and small, for
all manner of three- and one-day events, from Badminton down-
wards, all over England. Burghley's 1980 course was a testing
one, as it always is, and there were horses who could not make
the spread, for instance, of the Tiger Trap which suddenly
appeared over the open water — but there was no grief and no
injured horses, and we could all breathe a sigh of relief and say

to ourselves: 'This is what horse trials used to be like, should be like and *must* become like again!'

In the lead at the end of the first day of dressage was Virginia Holgate on Priceless, whom the judges — Major Lawrence Rook, Colonel G. Nyblaeus of Sweden and Major Eddie Boylan from Ireland — awarded 44.2 penalty points. Towards the end of the following day Rachel Bayliss had come up to equalise on Trenque Lauquen but both were overtaken by Captain Mark Phillips on Persian Holiday, with 43.6 points. Richard Walker took John of Gaunt into fourth place with 45.2. Thus was the scene set with all the predicted principals nicely placed, among them Jane Holderness-Roddam with Warrior, lying ninth on 55 points. Mrs Suzy Howard, the nice American lady from Far Hills, New Jersey, who so sportingly gave Jane a half-share in Warrior so that she might ride him in the *British* team for the European Championships of 1977 here, told me: 'Warrior is retiring from the three-day event and I've given her [Jane] the other half — it must be the most expensive present anyone's ever had, for now Tim [Holderness-Roddam] has got to spend £150,000 or so on a farm, in order to keep Warrior in the manner to which he is accustomed!'

In his last three-day event Warrior started as number 10 and went clear round the cross-country course in the optimum time, picking up only 0.8 of a time fault on the steeplechase to add to his dressage score. This kept him in the lead until fifty-four of the field of seventy-five had gone, when Richard Walker and John of Gaunt, the eventual winners, took up the running. Fourth in dressage, with 45.2, they went clear but collected 1.2 time faults across country, giving them a total of 46.4 penalties.

But Captain Mark Phillips and Persian Holiday were still to come, and they made no mistake, incurring only 0.8 time penalties across country to retain a slim lead with 44.4 penalty points from John of Gaunt. Rachel Bayliss and Trenque Lauquen slipped out of contention with 8.8 steeplechase time penalties and 37.2 cross-country time penalties.

The showjumping phase, run off according to the British system in reverse order of merit (which usually means one need only watch the last three in this less exciting phase), went according to plan for Warrior, whose clear round meant that he retained third place. John of Gaunt made one mistake but sadly Persian Holiday, whose forte showjumping is not, went lolloping into the first fence and took it by the roots, and had another fence down as well. Thus victory went to Richard Walker and John of Gaunt, who well deserved it. Persian Holiday was runner-up.

Poor Percy — he has not always been sound, he had the misfortune to break a rein at Badminton and he failed to make the 1976 Olympic team when at the height of his powers. He is now to retire to the hunting field, Mark having given him to his mother, so let us wish him a long and happy career in the finest sport of all.

After receiving the Raleigh Trophy, Richard Walker announced that John of Gaunt, too, is to retire, aged twelve — so Burghley '80 did not exactly produce any shining hopes for the future, though Priceless, Gemma Jay (Sue Benson), Foxy Bubble (Lucinda Prior-Palmer), Peter the Great (Elizabeth Purbrick) and Trenque Lauquen were all in the final shake-up.

Most importantly, thirty-one went clear across country, though six were eliminated, nine retired, and three were withdrawn. Alan Lillingston from Ireland on Seven Up distinguished himself by being the only competitor to finish the steeplechase and cross-country courses completely unpenalised.

Markyate (10 September 1980)
Sue Benson and Rip-Rap were victorious at Markyate, where they were followed home in the first Intermediate class by Marjorie Comerford on Barty. Richard Walker was another winner with Ryan's Cross, and Sue Benson finished second on H. Neill's Radley Slim.

Suckley (13 September 1980)
Peter Gleave and Klipspringer won again at Suckley, the other Intermediate class going to Sue Clapham on her mother's and Miss Rothbarth's Final Edition.

Taunton Vale (13–14 September 1980)
Peter Copland, aged eighteen, won the first Advanced class at the Taunton Vale meeting. Riding his mother's Langton Gold, by the Somerset stallion Langton Heath, and taking time off

from his A-level studies, he went deceptively fast to beat the field, nearest of whom was Mary Hunter on Primore Hill, by Ben Faerie.

The other Advanced class was a great triumph for Clarissa Strachan and Radjel for the latter had dislocated a fetlock joint in a road accident and had to spend several months in plaster. His dressage was so good, however, that he was able to repel all comers who went faster across country, nearest of whom was Sally Harmer on Banc Foli Mead.

Captain Mark Phillips hurt his left hand when Rough and Tough, trying to stop but being frustrated in the attempt, jumped awkwardly.

Central Scotland (16 September 1980)
Shirley Jackson and Ground Control ran out the winners of the Open/Intermediate class at the Central Scotland trials at Dunsinnen in Perthshire from Diana Niven and Gortwella, one point behind in second place, after putting up the best cross-country performance. Sue Hendry and Count Rostov, who finished third, were also impeded by a high dressage mark.

Tetbury (20 September 1980)
Michael Tucker's Tetbury horse trials were completely bedevilled by the weather, but no one allowed that small consideration to spoil the day and Liz Purbrick won the first Advanced section on Felday Farmer and was third in the second on Peter the Great.

The second section was won by eighteen-year-old Lucinda Moir, who brought off a notable double when she won a section of a very strong Novice class on Rabble before putting up the fastest time of the day to win on Mrs Pond's Queen Hill from Marion Pascoe's Sunny Intervals. Lucinda, who has been properly brought up (and not only concerning things equestrian) to hunt and show, and whose mother, now Mrs Bryer, and grandmother, Mrs Skelton, are consummate horsewomen, won the training voucher, which she intends to use in Holland.

Captain Mark Phillips rode with torn ligaments in his left hand and had the misfortune to fall on that arm again when Town and County slipped. Tuffy Tilly, Wendy White and Hugh Thomas were other fallers.

Rotherfield Park (21 September 1980)

On the following day the weather was perfect for the new Rotherfield Park event, organised by Hopper Cavendish and held on Sir James Scott's land and in his park near Alton. With the course designed by Hugh Thomas using all the natural features and undulations, it was designed to cater for the Intermediate horses preparing for Wylye and Osberton, and fulfils a real need.

The first Intermediate section was won by Mrs Liz Tyley's May Fox, who did well to receive, at the age of sixteen, the award for the fastest cross-country round. Sue Benson won the second section with Dr Lawson-Baker's Rip-Rap, and the third went to the Queen's Stevie B, ridden by Princess Anne, who was so delighted with him and the way he went that she patted him repeatedly as they circled after finishing. Later she scanned the score board with incredulity, and observing that she had won exclaimed: 'I don't believe it!' What a three-day horse he will make.

The Open/Intermediate was won by Jane Holderness-Roddam's Warrior, as if in celebration of his retirement from three-day events. Warrior led by 17 points from Richard Walker on Atlas Express Group's Ryan's Cross.

Wylye (25–28 August 1980)

At Lord and Lady Hugh Russell's Wylye fixture in late September, now an international three-day event, Phoebe Alderson, formerly a highly successful point-to-point rider, was the undisputed heroine. On two mares, April's Dancer and Turbulence, both bought as yearling fillies by Mrs Welman as breeding prospects, she finished first and third.

Virginia Holgate performed an outstanding dressage test on Night Cap.

On the steeplechase, Lady Cottenham was the only casualty, when Touch of Class fell and she sustained concussion. The cross-country course, particularly the Double Coffin, caused a number of falls. Count von Wengersky approached the Double Coffin too fast on My Melodi and had to retire, which was disappointing for West Germany as he was their sole representative. The upright leading into the bank in front of the members' tent proved to be as prevalent a source of penalty as ever. Robin

Cayzer with Mr D possibly merits the dubious distinction of achieving the most spectacular fall here. The new Bow Steps, a variation on the Helsinki original, with parallel bars replacing single rails, set as usual on the side of a hill, caused several falls, all happily innocuous.

Captain Mark Phillips was in trouble at the water with the British Equestrian Federation's sadly ungenuine Rough and Tough (who, in all conscience, advises them on their purchases?) and was penalised as for a stop.

Virginia Holgate on Night Cap had a 10-point lead and may have felt that she was home and dry, but as it turned out, Phoebe Alderson was fractionally faster on April's Dancer and Turbulence leapfrogged no fewer than fourteen places into third place behind Ginny Holgate. Lucy Bywater and The Countryman won the International Junior event by 6 points from Elizabeth Firth's Capricorn VII and Lesley Kidd's Top Notch. The National Novice two-day event went to Jane Starkey with Buckley.

Jan Jonsson from Sweden, who won the Olympic Bronze in Munich in 1972, and now rode Karabinjar, was clear in every department and had nothing to add to his dressage score. Hugh Thomas on Ebony Green and David Stride on The Merchant were similarly free of penalty other than the mill-stone of dressage, which hung least heavily from the neck of David Stride, who finished fifth.

Royal Deeside (27 September 1980)
Sue Hendry and Count Rostov won the Open/Intermediate at Royal Deeside, Aboyne, near Aberdeen, to take the Scottish Points Championship from her runner-up here, Pollyann Lochore's Loch Maree, as the Scottish season drew to a close.

Batsford (28 September 1980)
Batsford (Moreton-in-Marsh) clashed with Wylye, but it still produced a ding-dong finish to the Midland Bank Advanced class, which was won by one point by Richard Walker on Ryan's Cross from John Marsden on Claughton. Ryan's Cross did an excellent dressage for 34 penalties and then totted up 34 time penalties over the country, but still contrived to win. John Marsden won an Intermediate class on Black Monk II and Richard Walker won another on Freeway.

Osberton (3–5 October 1980)

Michael Foljambe first ran a three-day event on his land and in his park at Osberton, near Retford, in 1971. It became a one-day event thereafter until this year, when its owner generously responded to the appeal for additional three-day events, and it fulfilled its purpose admirably. A really friendly meeting, it had an excellent, straightforward course built by Tony Dobson, who looks after Mr Foljambe's stud of Cleveland Bays (the Queen sent three mares to Osberton David, who runs with his ten permanent wives, this year) and served a two-year apprenticeship with the late Major Peter Cazalet, who trained the Queen Mother's 'chasers, before spending a further season and a half as second horseman with the Belvoir.

With its peacock-inhabited stable yard and its old-established Guernsey herd, Osberton is a delightful place for a three-day event. The Midland Bank Golden Griffin section was won by Josephine Marsh-Smith on Tudor Court, by Tudor Treasure. Ninth after the dressage, Tudor Court had nothing to add to his dressage penalties, a performance emulated only by Duncan Douglas's Our Mr Twink, who finished sixth. Vincent Jones's Precision II, in the lead after the dressage, lacked the speed to hold his place and dropped to ninth.

Lorna Clarke was runner-up on Swapshop, 10 points behind the winner, and Clarissa Strachan was third on Radjel, whose dislocated fetlock, having stood up to the Taunton Vale, also proved able to stand up to a three-day event, much to the delight of his owner. Wendy White's Woodland Rights went a good gallop for only 2.4 penalties and finished fourth with a show-jump down.

Peter Gleave and Klipspringer, who are seventeen and fourteen years old respectively, scored a hard-fought victory in the Scofton section by 0.4 of a point from John Tulloch on Bower Grit, one of a sizeable Scottish contingent. The final Rayton section was won by John Marsden, who withdrew Claughton after the steeplechase, having been invited to take him to Boekelo, but went into the lead with Black Monk with the fastest cross-country. When Shirley Jackson's Ground Control had three showjumps down Marsden was able to stay in front. Ground Control had led in dressage and Miss Jackson lodged a successful appeal against 50 time penalties, which were reduced to 26. Sue Benson took Rip-Rap into second place with 74 points to the winner's 72.95. Ground Control had 83, followed by David Hancock on Miss Comacho's Klammer.

Powderham Castle (4 October 1980)

Polly Schwerdt and Dylan II won the Open/Intermediate at Lord and Lady Courtenay's Powderham Castle fixture by 7 points from Captain Charles Lane's Royal Hadleigh. In the Novice division, Lucinda Moir rounded off a highly successful season by winning on Rabble, who also scored at Tetbury for Mr Martelli.

Chatsworth (11–12 October 1980)

Chatsworth has yielded its Advanced class to Rachel Bayliss on no less than six occasions – she won it five times on Gurgle the Greek and this year it was the turn of the young Mystic Minstrel, who fell twice at Fontainebleau after leading in the dressage. Now he was being taken slowly to restore his confidence. Despite 36 time penalties, his low dressage mark of 22 still gave him 6 points in hand over John Marsden with Claughton. Ruth Williams finished third on Lanson.

Sue Platt, the twenty-two-year-old Cheshire rider, won the first Intermediate section on Merlin Fox, while eighteen-year-old Gay Birtwistle won section III on The Barrister, owned by her father, Major J.N.D. Birtwistle, himself a well-known competitor.

Goodwood (19 October 1980)

At Goodwood, where the course includes the gentle undulations of the South Downs, fitness and speed were of the essence. By virtue of their performance across country, Goran Breisner with his own and Lars Sederholm's Ultimus ran out the winner, one point ahead of Josephine Marsh-Smith's Tudor Court, fresh from his Osberton triumph.

Rachel Bayliss and Mystic Minstrel led after the dressage, as at Fontainebleau, and were still in the lead after the showjumping, in which clear rounds were few and far between, but a corrected error and a stop across country proved their downfall.

Colin Wares, on the eve of his departure for Boekelo, won the first Intermediate section on Mrs Olive Jackson's Mr Wiseguy.

Her ambition is to bring off the double of the Cheltenham Gold Cup and Badminton. She has already won the former with Midnight Court, and is building up a string of event horses which may well achieve the second leg of this unique double.

Polly Schwerdt, recently the winner at Powderham, won the second Intermediate section and the trophy for the best rider under twenty-one. The Wylye winner, April's Dancer, was eliminated at the splash.

*   *   *

Horse Trials Points Championships Awards 1980

The Calcutta Light Horse Challenge Trophy, awarded to the owner of the horse gaining the most points at horse trials and three-day events during the current year:

CLAUGHTON   141 points

Owners: Miss A.L. Daybell and Miss M.E. Way, Proprietors of The Newark Equestrian Centre.

The Tony Collings Memorial Challenge Trophy, awarded to the rider gaining the most points on any horse or horses at horse trials and three-day events during the current year:

RICHARD WALKER   179 points

The Edy Goldman Trophy, awarded to the rider under twenty-one for the whole of the current year, gaining the most points at horse trials and three-day events:

DUNCAN DOUGLAS   198 points

The Wide Awake Trophy, awarded to the breeder of the most successful horse which is sired by a Hunters' Improvement Society Premium Stallion:

CLAUGHTON   17 hh, bay gelding, 1973. Dam: Harmazelle, Sire: Sweet Ration

Breeder: Mr J.H. Scott

14

International Showjumping (CSIOs)

Each country is permitted by the FEI to hold one official international horse show and to stage a Nations Cup, a two-round competition over the same course for teams of four riders, the scores of the three best counting in each round. The European season of outdoor meetings usually starts in Rome, which is arguably the most entrancing of all fixtures because it has such a beautiful showground, the Piazza di Siena in the Borghese Gardens, just outside the ancient city wall at the top of the Via Venito.

The ground, which is guarded by *carabinieri* in their unique Napoleonic hats, is bounded by umbrella pines and profusely decorated with azaleas in pots. There is a gracious leisureliness here too — mornings are free to spend walking in the eternal city; after lunch one arrives at the horse show to sit in the sun (usually) for two competitions, a speed and a Table A class; and by dusk it is all over. How civilised!

In 1980 the going was too hard for many riders to risk their horses' legs, so Britain was not represented in Rome, where the French team initiated their season of superiority by winning the first Nations Cup of the year.

But at Lucerne the following week, Ronnie Massarella and his merry men (Lionel Dunning with Jungle Bunny, Graham Fletcher with Preachan, Tim Grubb with Night Murmur and Malcolm Pyrah with Charles Fox) fought back and won the Nations Cup to keep the French *amour propre* within bounds — though the result remained in doubt until the last horse had jumped.

Rowland Fernyhough and Bouncer, the grey Irish horse which Judy Crago owns, cleared 7 feet 2 inches to win their third puissance on the trot. Graham Fletcher was only narrowly beaten in the Grand Prix on Preachan.

A week later came Hickstead, where a substantially different team with the exception of Dunning and Jungle Bunny who were not on form, kept the French at bay again — but only just. Liz Edgar on Forever, John Whitaker on Ryan's Son and Robert Smith on Video had not ridden as a team before but they were in the lead at half time with just 4 faults (by Video). France was second on 12, the Netherlands third on 19, Australia (fielding a man short) had 20, while Ireland (32) and West Germany (28) — how are the mighty fallen, after the German dominance of the past decade — were already struggling, with Sweden (52.25) already hopelessly outclassed.

In the second round a straight fight developed between Britain and France. Frederic Cottier and Flambeau C challenged with a clear, Jungle Bunny had 4 at the water, Michel Robert and Belle Bleu had 4, Liz Edgar and Forever achieved a magnificent double clear. Twenty-two-year-old Etienne Laboute and Fidelité, and Robert Smith and Video both knocked up 8, so it was all up to the number 4s, the fullbacks. Gilles Bertran de Balanda and the explosive stallion Galoubet achieved their second clear and so, providentially, did that coolest of customers, John Whitaker on Ryan's Son.

Liz Edgar's Forever, who is by a German stallion out of a mare by the great French jumping sire Furioso, by Precipitation, won the £5,000 first prize in the £15,000 Grand Prix. There were seven double clears over Pamela Carruthers' course to go against the clock, and the young Dutchman, Rob Ehrens, set the target, clear in 42.3 seconds, on Koh-I-Noor. Jungle Bunny went clear in 43.1; Harvey Smith on Sanyo San Mar had the last part of the treble down; Nick Skelton and Maybe were close on 42.4 secs. Marianne Gilchrist and Goldray for Australia were too slow in 43.3, John Whitaker on Ryan's Son had a pole down, but Forever, last in the draw, ran out the winner in 41.1 secs.

Following Britain's safe retention of the Edward Prince of Wales Cup at Hickstead for the fourth successive year, France were the victors in the Nations Cup at Aachen over 'Mickey' Brinckmann's demanding course.

Herr Brinckmann was in the German cavalry when the last World War broke out. The son of a cavalry officer and an officer and a gentleman in every sense, he hates to see horses taken advantage of by artificial problems. He believes that show-jumping should approximate to natural conditions as nearly

Liz Edgar on Forever during the Grand Prix at Aachen, 1980. Liz became the first woman ever to win the German Grand Prix. (*Findlay Davidson*)

as possible. For this reason he likes a big, open course with natural obstacles included in it, as at Hickstead, Dublin and Aachen. While the Aachen course is always the toughest in Europe, probably in the world, it remains popular because it is also the most scrupulously fair.

Brinckmann's courses often include big square oxers which are, of course, eaten up by the powerful German showjumpers and give them an advantage. But out of the twelve visiting nations — a total of thirteen teams, including the home side — it was France who won on Friday the 13th, drawn at No. 13.

At the halfway stage Germany led on 4 faults from Britain, France and Switzerland with 8 and Ireland and the Netherlands still in the hunt on 12. But, such is the importance of luck in showjumping, even at the highest level, Mexico would have been in the lead with only 1.25 faults had not Jesus Portugal been jumped off by Massacre over the parallels.

The Dutch team all made mistakes in the first round and

were clear second time. Britain's amateurs scored 4 and 4 (Tim
Grubb on Night Murmur), 0 and 4 (Liz Edgar and Forever, who
got under the last part of the treble), 4 and 0 (Robert Smith
and Video), and 4 and 4 (John Whitaker's Ryan's Son) totalling
16 for fifth place. Switzerland and Germany disputed second
place with 12, and France had to fight out the finish with the
last ditch being defended by Gilles Bertrand de Balanda on
Galoubet, the volatile stallion whose characteristic kick-back
automatically makes him a favourite with the crowds. He had
to go clear to keep France on a winning total of 8, and he did,
which gave France a total of 24 points for the President's Cup
(the world team championship, first presented by Prince Philip,
the President of the International Equestrian Federation, in
1965) against Britain's 17.

The winning French team at Aachen consisted of Frederic
Cottier with Flambeau (0,0) Herve Godignon and Faola d'Escla
(4,0) Jean-Marc Nicolas with Mador (4,4) and Gilles Bertrand
de Balanda with Galoubet (4,0).

Liz Edgar and Forever had earlier in the week won the Grand
Prix — Mrs Edgar being the first woman ever to do so at Aachen.
Five horses survived for the final encounter, the second barrage,
over six fences, and Forever was clear again, going first, in 46.6
seconds. John Whitaker was runner-up on Ryan's Son in 50.3
and Alfonso Segovia was third for Spain on Agamemnon in 51.6.

When Forever first arrived in Ted Edgar's yard as a young
horse among a load of others from Germany, Liz asked Ted
disapprovingly: 'What have you bought this little runt for?' But
the little runt grew and developed into a magnificent big, deep
chestnut horse, almost Irish in appearance. The £3,000 he won
here put him second on the winners' list with £3,562, behind
the £3,875 of Paul Schockemöhle; John Whitaker was lying
third with £2,775.

Schockemöhle rode El Paso to share the Nordrhein-Westfalen
prize with Henk Nooren on Opstalan. On Deister he was runner-
up to Ulrich Meyer zu Bexten on Magister in the German
International Championship, in which Tim Grubb finished third
on Night Murmur. Deister also won the International Casino
prize, over a cup and a puissance course, from Malcolm Pyrah
and Towerlands Chelsea Girl, whose Waterloo was a 6 feet
6 inches wall.

The next engagement was in Paris, where the French CSIO was held for the second year at Longchamp and the home team added the Nations Cup to those they had already collected in Rome, Aachen and Liege. France's score was 12½ faults, Switzerland finished second with 16¼, while the US team, competing at its first European show in six years, was third with 18 faults. Belgium finished fourth on 19½, and Italy disputed fifth place with West Germany on 24 faults. Britain brought up the rear with an inglorious 24¾ faults.

Lionel Dunning and Jungle Bunny (13,8) Pam Dunning on Roscoe (4¾,4) Caroline Bradley and Tigre (0,0) and Tim Grubb and Night Murmur (8,8) were the individual scorers. Tim and Night Murmur won the Chanel Prize, and became Britain's only winners in Paris. Melanie Smith, runner-up for the World Cup in Baltimore, had the only clear round in the barrage for the Grand Prix de Paris to win on her Dutch-bred seven-year-old, Calypso.

The scene moved on to Dublin, where the Americans triumphed in the sixth Aga Khan Cup, and their distinguished trainer, Bertalan de Nemethy, received it from the Aga Khan himself.

Made in Ireland and valued at £8,000, the cup's predecessor was first presented by the present Aga Khan's grandfather in 1926 and has been won outright by Switzerland in 1930, Ireland in 1939 and 1979 and Britain in 1953 and 1975.

Coming as it did, only a week before the alternative Olympic confrontation in Rotterdam, the American victory enhanced their status and they started virtual favourites. Their victory in Dublin was not achieved, however, over a course that even approached Olympic dimensions, but they did beat the victorious French into fourth place.

At the end of the first round the US team of Norman Dello Joio on Allegro, Armand Leone on Wallenstein, Katie Monahan on Silver Exchange and Melanie Smith on Calypso had but a single time fault, incurred, unhappily, by Allegro (with apologies). Ireland were second with 4, Britain third with 4¼, France fourth on 8, knocked up by de Balanda, their best rider, on Galoubet, and West Germany and Australia brought up the rear on 19¾ and 21¾ faults respectively.

In the second innings the Americans improved their position

with three double clears, so that their fourth rider was not required to pull out again. Britain needed the second clear round of David Broome and Philco for a no-fault second round score, to total 4½ and take second place from Ireland and France, who were equal third on 8 faults. West Germany were fifth on 29¾ and Australia lagged in sixth place with 53¼.

Ronnie Massarella left Harvey Smith out of the team and went into battle with the quartet who had won the World and European Championship in 1978 and 1979 respectively — Caroline Bradley, Malcolm Pyrah, Derek Ricketts and David Broome.

Harvey has never been much of a team man and his sights were set, as always, on the money, specifically the £3,000 first prize of the Irish Trophy, the Grand Prix of Ireland. He had won it in 1976 on Olympic Star, and this year he won it on the same horse, who now goes by the name of Sanyo San Mar.

Six went clear in the first round but Harvey was the only survivor in the first, untimed, jump-off — albeit with a time fault which did not, in fact, have any bearing on the result. Calypso had an upright down, Tigre was retired after stopping twice at the double, Chainbridge (who won in 1978 and was runner-up in 1979) and Silver Exchange both hit the upright leading into the double, and the Australian Autograph with Jeff McVean retired. So Silver Exchange (Katie Monahan) and Calypso (Melanie Smith) followed Harvey home. Having also won the Guinness International on Sanyo Music Centre, as well as the Jamieson Whiskey Match International, Harvey captured the Guinness Gold Tankard for the leading rider of the show. Eddie Macken on Carrolls Royal Lion cleared 7 feet to win the Shell Puissance.

Calgary, held in mid-September at the Spruce Meadows ground, has always been a happy hunting ground for the British team. For the third successive year they won the Nations Cup, finishing with 8 faults to beat the Netherlands with 16 and Canada with 32. John Whitaker pulled off a double clear on Ryan's Son and was the leading rider of the show.

In the first round of the Nations Cup, Malcolm Pyrah was also clear for Britain on Charles Fox. Graham Fletcher and Preachan, with 4 fences down, had the discard score, but Jean Germany, riding Whistling Song in her first adult team, had

Malcolm Pyrah and Charles Fox competing at Calgary, 1980.
(*Bob Langrish*)

only one down. At half-time Britain and the Netherlands were joint leaders on 4 faults.

Whistling Song had 4 again in the second round but worse had befallen Holland, despite a double clear for Johan Heins on Laramy. Switzerland (36) finished fourth behind Canada, and the United States (40) were fifth.

Rob Ehrens and Koh-I-Noor won the Rothmans Grand Prix for the Netherlands from Alan Brand on Sibulation for Canada and Graham Fletcher on Sowerby Parks, who was third for Britain.

15

The Showing Scene in 1980

In England and Ireland the hunter classes, both ridden and led, are the most important aspects of any horse show in that they reflect the standard of the horses that are being bred. With the Thoroughbred, the hunter-type is the best riding horse in the world, capable not only of doing the job for which it has evolved over nearly three hundred years — that of carrying its rider following hounds over our countryside throughout our wet winters, which demands great stamina and stoutness of heart — but also of making first-class three-day event horses.

The attraction of the show classes may be the prerogative of the specialist, but the proportions and symmetry of the well-made — or rather, correctly made — horse are discernible by anyone with an eye for beauty, and the finer points of conformation and movement are assimilated with experience. For the enthusiast and the stockman alike, the fascination of the hunter classes never palls, and it is encouraging indeed that the type in general has remained constant over the years, though inevitably, with more and more infusions of Thoroughbred blood, it gets finer and finer, too often at the expense of bone and substance. It seems there are not enough heavyweight brood mares about to produce sufficient weight-carrying horses. Ireland, however, has done a useful job in resuscitating its Irish Draught breed, which before the last war was an admirable clean-legged all-purpose horse which would work on the land, pull a trap and carry a saddle to take the farmer hunting on Sundays.

Ridden Hunters
The overall pattern was one of a fairly moderate middleweight division with one or two notable exceptions and an encouraging number of heavyweights — and true heavyweights, up to fifteen stone or more — though none was so outstanding that it could

be declaimed the definitive hunter of the year. One cannot help but make the comparison to the days of Mighty Fine and Mighty Atom in the late forties and early fifties respectively, when each of these horses won the Dublin championship for the late Nat Galway-Greer and then arrived in England to rule the roost for two and four seasons respectively, monarchs of all they surveyed.

There was, however, one ridden hunter which was undisputedly the most consistent in 1980, and was awarded the Waterford Crystal Points Championship trophy. This was the South Essex Insurance Group's chesnut five-year-old Assurance, by Crawter, who was produced by Vin Toulson, who had bought him as a four-year-old at the Horse of the Year show. Vin was thrilled with this animal's bone and movement at Wembley and was determined to buy him, which he did. Assurance won his first championship at Hertfordshire County, which was followed by the South of England and Great Northern titles, but his consistency was perhaps most notable in the number of times he stood reserve champion — Royal Windsor to Silversmith; Devon County to David Tatlow on Zatopek; the Royal Bath and West to Robert Oliver on Mobility Ltd's The Consort; Royal Norfolk to Allister Hood on Mr Tom Hunnable's Grenadier; City of Leicester to Zatopek; and Bucks County to David Barker on Lady Zinnia Pollock's Whaddon Way. He was not produced at the Horse of the Year show, having nothing more to prove.

Assurance was bred by Maxie Jones on the Elton estate, near Peterborough. He is out of a mare who is a direct descendant of a Thoroughbred mare who was a full sister to Grudon, who won the 'snowstorm' Grand National in 1902, his feet packed with butter to prevent the snow from balling. A shy breeder, she was eventually turned out with a Shire colt, who duly got her in foal. The line has been breeding heavyweights from that day, and a half-brother by Quality Fair, Fair Spark, won several championships for Norman Crow in 1974.

Flashman, owned by Mrs Peter White, wife of a London bookmaker, was Show Hunter of the Year for Robert Oliver in 1979, but this time he was not so successful and did not appear until the South of England in mid-June. There he was overfresh and stood down to Assurance. At the Three Counties show he won the championship from his stable companion, The Consort,

South Essex Insurance Group's ridden hunter, Assurance — a consistent winner in 1980. (*Kit Houghton*)

who had already stood supreme at the Royal Bath and West and Royal Cornwall shows.

At the Royal, Flashman was pulled in first in the heavyweight class but was found to have knocked himself, so was withdrawn. Roy Trigg took his place on Daks Harvest Light, who was followed by Mr Hunnable's Super Coin, another Irishman, with Assurance third. The last time we saw Flashman was at the Royal International at Wembley, where he was beaten by The Consort — and where Assurance wound up seventh under Colonel Neil Foster, who loves quality horses, and David Howie from Yorkshire, son of a notable hunter judge and MFH, Major John Howie.

Flashman went to the Horse of the Year show but was not going quite level and Robert Oliver declined to show him.

Success at the early shows, notably Newark and Royal Windsor, often sets in train a run of subsequent victories, and Vin Toulson seemed set for a triumphant year when he won the championship at Newark early in May with the brown middleweight Fleet Street, by Pele's sire Go Tobann, who stood in Co. Cork. But Fleet Street was beaten at Windsor by Silversmith, where he was patently unhappy in his mouth, and then, as Daphne Toulson recalls, everything happened to him: he put up a splint, developed a virus and, though all right at home, proved to have a 'screw loose' when he got to a show, and so he was diverted to other channels as he seemed unlikely to settle.

Luckily for Vin, he had another string to his bow in the chesnut Spring Close, a heavyweight five-year-old by Cantab, whom they found six miles up the road. He was very backward, like so many young heavyweights, and had done nothing but hunt with the Cottesmore, but Vin produced him to win the novice championship at Peterborough, after which he won his class at Oakham and was second to the eventual champion at the Horse of the Year show, of which more anon.

Robert Oliver, who had swept all before him for the two previous years, started in similar style when he won the championship at Royal Windsor with Mrs Bamford's Silversmith, who had come out of training to be the top novice of 1979, when owned by Lady Zinnia Pollock and ridden by David Barker.

Silversmith won his class at the Shropshire and West Midland show at Shrewsbury, but in the championship he was overcome by Vin Toulson having his first and last ride on Rosalind Dudley's grey heavyweight, Freckles. At the Royal, Silversmith reproduced his Royal Windsor form to win his class and the championship *Horse and Hound* Cup, but after this an accident to his near-fore fetlock kept him out of the ring for the rest of the season.

He was the quality middleweight, and in a non-vintage year for what is usually the most prolific source of champions, the only other one to make his mark was the reigning Dublin champion, Zatopek (by Sunny Light), who had been shown there by George Chapman, Master of the Island Hounds in Co. Wexford, but was now owned by Mr Rodford and ridden by David Tatlow. Zatopek was champion at Devon County and Great Yorkshire shows and won the Champion of All England Gold Cup at Peterborough, which once again coincided with the Royal International at Wembley. He also won his class at the Royal and the Horse of the Year shows and finished third in the title fight.

Thomas Hunnable has two admirable middleweights in the former Dublin champion, Foggy Wood, who won at Ballsbridge for Michael Hickey, and George Chapman's 1979 reserve, Grenadier (by Ozymandias), who had to be ridden in the championship by the kennel huntsman. 'I could not put him on Zatopek, who's a bit of a boyo,' he told me at the time – though assuredly Grenadier would have won the championship had he been better shown.

Foggy Wood was champion, produced by Paul Rackham and ridden by Allister Hood, at the Essex show, where his owner was president, and also at the Lincolnshire. Grenadier was champion at the Royal Norfolk, while the lightweight Glenstawl, another Dublin winner, was champion at Oakham.

The lightweights were dominated at all the major shows, however, by Lady Zinnia Pollock's beautiful pattern of a top quality thirteen-stone horse, Whaddon Way, by Crosby Don, who always gave of his best for David Barker. Black horses are said to be either very good or the complete reverse, and this one surely comes into the former category, for he consistently won ladies' classes too with great aplomb, ridden by Rachel King, and often pulled off the double of the lightweight and ladies' classes.

This used to be almost a commonplace occurrence in the days of such lightweights as Mrs Alec Wood's Prince's Grace but now, in these times of sliding standards, it is the exception rather than the rule. All the lightweights produced by Count Robert Orssich, Harry Bonner and Jack Gittins, of course, went as well side-saddle as they did astride – Robert's ridden by Ann Davy, Harry's by Mrs Tollit and Jack's schooled at home by the maestro himself!

Ridden again by Vin Toulson, the top small hunter of the year was Col. and Mrs Guy Wathen's chesnut four-year-old Baritone (by Barolo) who ruled supreme until the Royal International, winning at Newark and Royal Windsor, and finishing second at the Royal to the Scottish invader, the McCowans' Statesman, whom Judy Bradwell had put champion at the Royal Highland over Mr Hunnable's Glenstawl and Manifesto, ridden by Allister Hood. This decision fairly put the cat among the pigeons, for it was a Waterford Crystal Championship which qualified for the title at the Horse of the Year show, and at none of the English shows are small hunters eligible for the championships.

But the Royal Highland always was a law unto itself, which is why it does not affiliate to the Hunters' Improvement Society or invite its judges from their approved panel. Presumably its championship is therefore null and void in the eyes of the sponsors, the Horse of the Year show and the HIS itself.

The working hunter classes were once again monopolised by Gill Oliver and Mrs Peter White's Dual Gold, who won the working championship at Windsor, the Royal and Wembley. Another successful contender was the former Toulson show hunter, Mastermind, produced from Cumbria by Mrs Reta Wicks, who in 1969, as Reta Burch, won this title with a horse called Goodwill, later to be bought by the Queen and ridden in numerous British teams, including that for the 1976 Olympic Games, by Princess Anne.

The surprise of the year was the Waterford Crystal Hunter Championship at the Horse of the Year show, which was won by Mr and Mrs Robert Healey-Fenton's The Brigadier (by Halsafari), who had won his class in Dublin as a four-year-old and again this year, but had few pretensions to championship status.

But with The Consort, Flashman and Assurance all missing from the heavyweight class, The Brigadier duly won it from Vin Toulson on Spring Close and Allister Hood on Thomas Hunnable's Super Coin, another Irish five-year-old by Prince Riza. The Brigadier's owners had bought him as a youngster and brought him with them when they moved back to Exmoor after several years in Co. Wexford.

The championship was judged in the evening, and Mrs Richard

Hawkins stood valiantly by her guns and defended the winning lightweight, Whaddon Way, who seemed the most worthy champion. But Mr Vivian Bishop, who rides heavyweights himself and may not have liked the length of the lightweight's hind pasterns, went for the weight-carrier and slowly but surely broke down the opposition, and The Brigadier was duly deemed to be the Hunter of the Year. What a homecoming for his owners!

Led Hunters

This was an unusual year in the breeding classes, in that time after time the brood mares won the breeding, or indeed the overall championship at the expense of the three-year-old geldings who usually rule the roost at this level. Four of them — an unusually high proportion — qualified for the Horse section of the Lloyds Bank in-hand championship.

It is axiomatic that the led youngstock champions have only rarely gone on to success in other spheres. Indeed, the chances are that they may be ruined for life: developing one-sided mouths through being led invariably from the same side, round of their joints through being trotted endlessly on sunbaked going with no give in it, and even more so by being driven literally thousands of miles on non-slip matting, which prevents accidents but at the same time plays havoc with unformed fetlocks, which take all the strain.

Only those who are sufficiently strong-minded to limit their showing to from four to six shows a year should do it at all — say, at their own county show for experience and to assess the form, then at the Hunter Show, the Royal and perhaps the Royal Bath and West or Three Counties or East of England. This will not only suffice, but a carefully planned programme will preclude the temptation to follow the circus around all summer. Just as young children are better in their nurseries, so are young horses better in their fields, thus not being exposed to the sophistications of adult life while their gums are still studded with milk teeth.

Perhaps, then, it is a logical progression — if, hopefully, the lesson has been learned — to the dominance of the brood mares, many of whom were better than their own progeny, with a few remarkable exceptions.

The most successful mare was the Hon. Mrs R.N. Crossley's

homebred grey mare, Cuillin Hills, by Count Albany (who stood near Malton in North Yorkshire), out of Loch Ness, who was by that renowned Irish sire of showjumpers such as The Rock and Rockette, Water Serpent, out of an Irish Draught mare. Mrs Crossley hunted her for five seasons and then started to breed from her while she herself was having her last child. Her first foal, Spy Hill, by Archie Thomlinson's Ancient Monro, was champion at the Great Yorkshire and was sold for a lot of money as a show horse but sadly was discovered to have a soft palate, so Colonel and Mrs Crossley took him back and have leased him to Domini Lawrence for dressage work. Cuillin Hills is so hard to get in foal — 'only Archie Thomlinson has succeeded' — that she has been given a year off and carried Mrs Crossley at the Opening Meet of the Middleton, of which Colonel Crossley has resumed the joint-mastership.

Cuillin Hills — named after the place where Bonnie Prince Charlie lay in the heather awaiting Flora MacDonald — was supreme at Staffordshire, reserve at the Royal Highland, reserve at the Hunter show, champion at the Royal, champion and Lloyds Bank qualifier at the Great Yorkshire, overall breeding champion at Peterborough, and second in the Horse section of the Lloyds Bank in-hand championship at the Horse of the Year show: not a bad record for a part-time matron who still goes fox-catching.

Ian Thomas, too, had a very successful season with Lucky Strike, who won Devon County, was overall breeding champion at the Three Counties and qualified for the Lloyds Bank championship, and was overall champion at the City of Leicester. Better still, her son Lucky Dip, a yearling by Don't Look, won his class at the Hunter show and was reserve youngstock champion at the Royal.

Sam Luxton, whose farm in North Devon has produced so many good horses over the years, qualified his brood mare Cheal Rose for Wembley after she had won the HIS brood mare championship at the Hunter show. At the Devon County he also qualified his three-year-old Cannabis gelding, The Doper, who won the Horse section at Wembley.

But three-year-olds — apart from The Doper, who won championships at the Devon County, Royal Cornwall and Royal Bath and West — failed, in the main, to cover themselves with

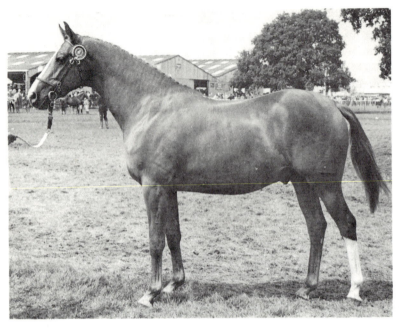

Mr R. Mason's and Miss S.A. Jeanes's Royal Fiddler — '. . . one of the most outstanding youngsters to be shown for many a long year.' (*Kit Houghton*)

glory. Exceptions to this were Mr and Mrs F. Allin's Ladywell Grenadier, whom Mrs Hugh Gingell made champion at the Shropshire and West Midland show and subsequently bought (Ladywell Grenadier is a well-grown son of the premium stallion Major Sol); and Mr Miles Stimpson's Red Ensign by Red Canute from the opposite side of the country, Norfolk.

But the one who finished third to The Doper and Cuillin Hills at Wembley was the chestnut son of The Dame and a show-jumping mare, namely Mr R.R. Mason's and Miss S.A. Jeanes's Royal Fiddler. He was and is one of the most outstanding youngsters to be shown for many a long year.

Fillies competing with colts seldom have enough presence to make much of a mark in hand, but one filly who must be mentioned is the Royal champion, Mermaid, owned and bred by Colonel Neil Foster, president of the HIS and chairman of its stallion committee.

The most successful of them all, however (even if his triumph was a one-off, which it was), was Creative Television Workshops' Keyston Kelly who won the Edward Prince of Wales Cup at the National Hunter show from The Doper and then sank without trace thereafter but, nevertheless, with the top award for youngstock under his girth.

Hacks

It is impossible, notwithstanding the excellent entries in the hack classes at shows such as Royal Windsor, South of England, Three Counties, Royal International and Horse of the Year shows, not to feel that the show hack has gone into decline. Just after the war there was an abundance of hacks, each of them ridden with considerable artistry and erudition by people of the calibre of Count Robert Orssich (son of a cavalry officer in the Austro-Hungarian empire, and himself a former pupil of the Spanish Riding School in Vienna); his pupil, Miss Ann Davy (now Mrs Ross); Captain Tony Collings, who trained the first British three-day event team after winning the second Badminton three-day event in 1950; Mrs Christopher Mackintosh; Mrs Lisa Shedden; George Brine; Jane Kent (now Mrs McHugh); Shirley Gilbert (now Mrs Harry Hindle); and numerous others. These people selected their horses with care, trained them assiduously to a high standard, and produced them skilfully to give an impression of ease and elegance as they tittuped around the ring at a very slow canter (scratching, some called it, but it was elegant) or trotted, putting their toes out almost 'into the next parish'.

There are still some capable of producing a top-class hack today, such as Robert and Gillian Oliver, Mrs Loriston-Clarke and Mrs Holderness-Roddam, Mrs Dorian Williams, Allister Hood, Carole Gilbert-Scott, Mrs John Keen and Stella and Christine Harries to name only a handful, while David Tatlow is a loss to the hack world now that he has decided that he prefers hunters; but only Robert and Gillian Oliver consistently produce horses to win the major championships, most notably Mrs D.M. Goodall's homebred Tenterk (by Tenterhook), Black Gold and Chanceley Voo Doo, who was supreme at the Royal and the Royal International in 1980 before sadly being measured-out after an objection had been lodged concerning his height.

Mrs McHugh, I think, put her finger on the reason for the decline after judging at the Royal this year when she told me:

Carole Gilbert-Scott with Dr and Mrs Gilbert-Scott's winning hack,
Chanceley Voo Doo. (*Kit Houghton*)

'We seem to have lost the type.' How, I wonder, has this happened
— perhaps because there are now so infinitely many more things
to do with horses than there were between the wars? And, more

important still, are we ever going to be able to get it back, and does it matter if we don't?

The photograph of the late Mrs Christopher Mackintosh on Blithe Spirit, winning at the Royal Show at Windsor in 1954, exemplifies, to my mind, the show hack at its best: full of quality and presence, with excellent limbs and bone, a lovely front, light in hand with a kind and generous expression and natural balance. He was also a glorious mover. Archie Thomlinson found him and sold him to Sheila Willcox, who produced him successfully and sold him on, deciding to devote her full attention to the three-day event, which she did with great ability.

If Blithe Spirit's double could be found today, I am sure that he would still be the lost type for which all the most experienced judges are seeking.

Mrs Christopher Mackintosh with Blithe Spirit, a superb show hack, winning at the Royal Show, Windsor, 1954. (*Sport & General*)

Cobs

The same thing that is happening now to hacks had almost over-taken the cob until very recently, when the redoubtable Irish journalist Muriel Bowen, who has always had a penchant for the horse, decided that the renaissance of the cob was a *cause célèbre* worthy of her attention.

She campaigned as energetically for Cromwell, an Irish-bred grey gentleman whom she had leased, and in whom she subsequently acquired a half share, as ever she had when standing for Parliament some years ago. She persuaded sponsors to put up more money for the cob classes and found a number of new sponsors. She lobbied those who could provide the publicity to please those who had contributed, and slowly but surely the entries increased until, in 1979, there were sufficient to comprise two classes, for lightweights and heavyweights — a state of affairs that had not obtained since the early 1950s. As the cob is an all-round family animal, suitable both for the youth just grown out of the pony stage to hunt, and for the elderly and over-weight, and costs but little to keep, there is every reason to suppose that the new-found popularity of the show cob will continue in the foreseeable future.

They are, however, difficult to breed and to find, and thus will always be in short supply. Some good ones have been bred in England, usually with strong Welsh connections. There was for instance, Kempley, who won the Show Cob of the Year title in 1977, 1978 and 1979. He might have won it for a fourth time too, had he not got a little too 'sharp' after all those years of London applause; thus he was beaten by the less volatile Brock, shown by Bill Bryan for Mr E.E. David, Master of the Llangeinor in Glamorgan.

But since the war, the best cobs have come traditionally from Ireland: Mrs Z.S. Clark's Sport reigned supreme for five years after winning Dublin for Marshall Parkhill; and Cromwell, by the Thoroughbred Autumn Gold by Nearco; Huggy Bear by Golden Gordon, one of many good ones shown by Roy Trigg over the years; Grandstand by The Commett, sold by Mrs Jack Gittins and now owned by Keith Luxford the saddler; and Mr Roger Biss's The Royalist, who won Dublin two years ago and was then owned by Captain Michael Hall, Managing Director of Goffs, the bloodstock auctioneers of Kill, Co. Kildare.

The Royalist is by the Connemara pony stallion, Clonkeehan Nimbus, out of Lougher Lass, by the Thoroughbred sire Audience out of Lady Luck, by the Irish Draught stallion Laughton.

Championship results at the major shows

March to October (Newmarket to Wembley)

HIS Stallion Show Newmarket (6 March 1980)

King George V Challenge Cup: L.S. Ivens's Osiris
    Reserve: J. Snell's Saunter

Macdonald-Buchanan Cup: L.S. Ivens's Lord of Arabia
    Reserve: E. Smith's Evening All

Henry Tudor Cup: T.M. Abram's Ascertain
    Reserve: T.M. Abram's Better by Far

Newark and Nottinghamshire (2–3 May 1980)

Ridden Hunters: South Essex Insurance Group's Fleet Street
    Reserve: N. Sykes's Master Kempley

Led Hunters: M. Wilson's Evaluate
    Reserve: Mrs Gray's Heddings Courage

Hacks: Mrs J.B. Wyman's Keston Refund
    Reserve: Dr and Mrs M. Gilbert-Scott's Fair Change

Cobs: P. Rackham's Red Robin
    Reserve: R. Biss's The Royalist

Ridden Ponies: Dr and Mrs Gilbert-Scott's Cusop Heiress
    Reserve: Mr Jago's Nantcol Anwyl

Lloyds Bank In-Hand Qualifier: Miss S.P. Sage's Daldorn Charmaine (pony brood mare)
    Reserve: Mrs Trimingham's Riaz (Arab stallion)

Royal Windsor (7–11 May 1980)

Hunters: Mrs A.P. Bamford's Silversmith (R. Oliver)
    Reserve: Lady Zinnia Pollock's Whaddon Way (D. Barker)

Working: Mrs P. White's Dual Gold (Mrs R. Oliver)
  Reserve: Mrs E. Littlejohn's Sedlescombe Sultan

Cobs: Miss M. Bowen's Cromwell

Hacks: Mrs D.M. Goodall's Tenterk (R. Oliver)
  Reserve: Mrs B.M. Morgan's Chanceley Voo Doo

Ponies: Cusop Heiress
  Reserve: Mrs N.A. Rogers's Chirk Caviar

Devon County (15–17 May 1980)

Ridden Hunters: F. Rodford's Zatopek (D. Tatlow)
  Reserve: South Essex Insurance Group's Assurance (V. Toulson)

Led Hunters: S. Luxton's The Doper
  Reserve: S. Luxton's Moonlight Saunter

Brood Mares: I. Thomas's Lucky Strike
  Reserve: Mr and Mrs R. Burrington's Bally Autrey

Small Hunter Brood Mares: Mrs A.G. Loriston-Clarke's
Catherston Lonely Breeze

Lloyds Bank Qualifier: The Doper
  Reserve: Mrs M.E. Mansfield's Keston Royal Occasion (Welsh
  Section B)

Shropshire and West Midlands (21–22 May 1980)

Ridden Hunters: Miss R. Dudley's Freckles
  Reserve: Mrs A.P. Bamford's Silversmith

Led Hunters: Mr and Mrs F. Allin's Ladywell Grenadier
  Reserve: Mrs Graham's That's Best

Hacks: Mrs and Miss C. Rogers's Black Gold
  Reserve: E. Crow's Serendignette

Royal Bath and West (4–7 June 1980)

Ridden Hunters: Mobility Ltd's The Consort
  Reserve: South Essex Insurance Group's Assurance

Led Hunters: S. Luxton's The Doper
  Reserve: Mr and Mrs R. Burrington's Bally Autrey

Small Hunters: Mrs D.M. Hurndall-Waldron's Kestor

Hacks: Mrs D.M. Goodall's Tenterk
   Reserve: E. Crow's Serendignette

Cobs: Miss M. Bowen's Cromwell

Pony Breeding: Mrs Dorian Williams's Wingrove Stormaway
   Reserve: Mrs D.E.M. Alexander's Forge Celtic Air

Ridden Ponies: Cusop Heiress
   Reserve: Dr and Mrs Gilbert-Scott's Arden Vol-au-Vent of
   Creden

Lloyds Bank Qualifier: Wingrove Stormaway
   Reserve: Bally Autrey

South of England (5–7 June 1980)

Ridden Hunters: South-Essex Insurance Group's Assurance
   Reserve: F. Rodford's Zatopek

Horse and Hound Working Hunters: Mrs P. White's Dual Gold

Led Hunters: Mr and Mrs C. Cope's Bramlands Sunrise
   Reserve: J.L. Burgess's Sarah's Birthday

Hacks: Mrs D.M. Goodall's Tenterk
   Reserve: Wilson Caterers's Ashwell High Society

Cobs: R. Biss's The Royalist
   Reserve: K. Luxford's Grandstand

Lloyds Bank Qualifier: Llanarth Stud's Llanarth Flying Comet
   Reserve: Mrs C. Caffyn Parsons's Richmond Gay Fantasy

Royal Cornwall (5–7 June 1980)

Ridden Hunters: Mobility Ltd's The Consort (N. Oliver)
   Reserve: Mrs M. Priest's Brewster

Led Hunter: S. Luxton's The Doper
   Reserve: D. Kellow's Lillie Langtry

Lloyds Bank Qualifier: Lillie Langtry
   Reserve: Mr and Mrs A.L. Masters's Twylands Fiesta (pony
   brood mare)

Three Counties (10—12 June 1980)

Ridden Hunters: Mrs P. White's Flashman
  Reserve: Mobility Ltd's The Consort

Hacks: Mrs D.M. Goodall's Tenterk
  Reserve: Mrs N. Rogers's Black Gold

Cobs: Mrs P. White's Kempley
  Reserve: E.L. David's Brock

Ridden Ponies: Dr and Mrs Gilbert-Scott's Cusop Heiress
  Reserve: Mr and Mrs C. Cooper's Piran John Halifax

Led Hunters: I. Thomas's Lucky Strike
  Reserve: Mrs M. Priest's Abbey Mill

Led Ponies: Mrs D.E.M. Alexander's Forge Celtic Air
  Reserve: Mrs B.M. Morgan's Beverley Jocelyn

Lloyds Bank Qualifier: Lucky Strike
  Reserve: Llanarth Stud's Llanarth Meredith ap Braint

Essex County (13—14 June 1980)

Ridden Hunters: T. Hunnable's Foggy Wood
  Reserve: Lady Zinnia Pollock's Sun Sovereign

Led Hunters: Miss A. Vos's Adventurous Acorn
  Reserve: Mrs V. Ward's Cilerna Rock

Hacks: Wilson Caterers's Ashwell Hi-Society
  Reserve: T. Hunnable's Brown Buzzard

Ridden Ponies: Mr and Mrs W. McAlpine's Oakhalls Halloween
  Reserve: Mrs N.A. Rogers's Chirk Caviar

Lloyds Bank Qualifier: Forge Celtic Air
  Reserve: J. Gardiner's and Miss D. Golding's Happy Rhapsody
  (Small hunter/hack breeding)

Royal Highland (16—19 June 1980)

Led Hunters: Mr and Mrs A. McCowan's Free and Easy
  Reserve: Hon. Mrs R.N. Crossley's Cuillin Hills

Ridden Hunters: Mr and Mrs A. McCowan's Statesman
    Reserve: T. Hunnable's Glenstawl

Ridden Ponies: Mrs H. Parkinson's Cusop Harmony
    Reserve: Messrs Hollings' Gay Sovereign

Lloyds Bank Qualifier: Lennel Stud's Lennel Top Cat (yearling riding pony)
    Reserve: Free and Easy

Lincolnshire (18–19 June 1980)

Led Hunters: M. Stimpson's Flagship
    Reserve: M. Stimpson's Red Ensign

Ridden Hunters: T. Hunnable's Foggy Wood
    Reserve: R. Appleyard's Matches

Ridden Ponies: Mr and Mrs W. McAlpine's Oakhalls Halloween
    Reserve: Mrs N. Rogers's Ocean So Fair

HIS National Hunter (25 June 1980)

Prince of Wales Cup: Creative Television Workshops' Keyston Kelly
    Reserve: S. Luxton's The Doper

Walker-Okeover Cup (fillies): Mr and Mrs C. Trembath's Daisy Hill
    Reserve: Miss H. Day's Miss Tallulah

Longcross Cup (by premium stallion): W.D. Lewis's Henry II
    Reserve: Miss S.A. Jeanes's Royal Fiddler

Jarrett Cup (best non-TB): S. Luxton's The Doper
    Reserve: Henry II

HIS Cup (brood mares): S. Luxton's Cheal Rose
    Reserve: Hon. Mrs R.N. Crossley's Cuillin Hills

Cahal Trophy (heavyweight): Cuillin Hills

Kadir Cup Trophy (foals): Mr and Mrs F.E. Wigley's Meltem

Lloyds Bank Qualifier (best in show): Cheal Rose
    Reserve: Keyston Kelly

Royal Norfolk (25—26 June 1980)

Led Hunters: M. Stimpson's Red Ensign

Ridden Hunters: T. Hunnable's Grenadier
    Reserve: South Essex Insurance Group's Assurance

Hacks: Wilson Caterers's Ashwell Hi-Society
    Reserve: Mr and Mrs J. Keen's Royal Appointment

Lloyds Bank In-Hand Qualifier: Mrs M.E. Mansfield's Trellech
Giselle (in-hand pony)
    Reserve: Mrs C. Trimingham's Riaz (Arab)

Ridden Ponies: Hon. Mrs T. Ponsonby's Jackets Celeste
    Reserve: Mrs N. Rogers's Chirk Caviar

Royal Show (30 June—3 July 1980)

Hunter Brood Mares: Hon. Mrs R.N. Crossley's Cuillin Hills
    Reserve: Mr and Mrs R. Burrington's Helwell Melody

Foals: Miss J. Vardon's colt

Fillies: Col. N.P. Foster's Mermaid

Young Hunters: R. Mason's and Miss Jeanes's Royal Fiddler
    Reserve: I. Thomas's Lucky Dip

Overall: Royal Fiddler
    Reserve: Cuillin Hills

Riding Pony Breeding: Mrs D.E.M. Alexander's Forge Celtic
Ballad
    Reserve: A.G. Loriston-Clarke's Catherston Lonely Breeze

Lloyds Bank Qualifier: Royal Fiddler
    Reserve: Mrs B.N. Morgan's Beverley Jocelyn (pony brood
    mare).

Ridden Hunters (*Horse and Hound* Cup): Mrs A.F. Bamford's
Silversmith
    Reserve: F.Rodford's Zatopek

Working Hunters: Mrs P. White's Dual Gold
    Reserve: T. Hunnable's Manifesto

Ridden Ponies: Dr and Mrs Gilbert-Scott's Arden Vol-au-Vent of Creden
  Reserve: Dr and Mrs Gilbert-Scott's Cusop Heiress

Hacks: Mrs B. Morgan's Chanceley Voo Doo
  Reserve: Mr and Mrs J. Keen's Royal Return

Cobs: Misses M. Bowen's and A.M. Griffin's Cromwell

Great Yorkshire (8–10 July 1980)

Hunter Breeding: Hon. Mrs R.N. Crossley's Cuillin Hills

Ridden Hunters: F. Rodford's Zatopek
  Reserve: B.B. Fuels's Bunowen

Hacks: Wilson Caterers's Ashwell Hi-Society
  Reserve: Mrs M. Wright's Mark Anthony

Lloyds Bank Qualifier: Cuillin Hills
  Reserve: Mr and Mrs C. Furness's Crimchard Firefly

Pony Youngstock: Mrs Stilwell's Lennel Topcat

Pony Brood Mares: Miss S. Sage's Daldorn Charmaine
  Reserve: Mrs B. Morgan's Beverley Jocelyn

Ridden Ponies: Messrs Hollings's Gay Sovereign
  Reserve: Derby House Saddlery's Leighon Isaac

Kent County (10–12 July 1980)

Ridden Hunters: Daks Simpson Ltd's Daks Harvest Light (R. Trigg)
  Reserve: Lady Zinnia Pollock's Sun Sovereign

Led Hunters: M. Stimpson's Red Ensign
  Reserve: R. Bothway's Knot Him

Hacks: Mr and Mrs J. Keen's Royal Return
  Reserve: Miss J. Watts's Bonny Hill

Cobs: Mrs Hurst's Duckyls Huggy Bear (R. Trigg)

Ponies: Mr and Mrs W. McAlpine's Oakhalls Halloween

Lloyds Bank Qualifier: Red Ensign
   Reserve: Mr and Mrs T. Armstrong's Glenfield Chocolate
   Soldier

Royal International (14—19 July 1980)

Hunters: Mobility Ltd's The Consort
   Reserve: Lady Zinnia Pollock's Whaddon Way

Hacks: Mrs B. Morgan's Chanceley Voo Doo
   Reserve: Mr and Mrs N. Rolfe's Sunny Wonder

Ponies: Mr and Mrs W. McAlpine's Oakhalls Halloween
   Reserve: Dr and Mrs Gilbert-Scott's Cusop Heiress

Cobs: Mrs P. White's Kempley

East of England (15—17 July 1980)

Led Hunters (Overall): The Hon. Mrs R.N. Crossley's Cuillin Hills
   Reserve: Mr and Mrs D.A. Shirley's Silver Jubilee March

Ridden Hunters: F. Rodford's Zatopek
   Reserve: Miss P. Mansergh's Game Prince

Hacks: Mr and Mrs J. Keen's Royal Return
   Reserve: Mrs R. Winch's The Duke of Perth

Cobs: Misses Bowen and Griffin's Cromwell
   Reserve: Mrs Hurst's Duckyls Huggy Bear

Pony Youngstock: Miss J. Morgan's Costock Choir Boy

Pony Brood Mares: Mrs M.E. Mansfield's Trellech Giselle

Lloyds Bank Qualifier: Costock Choir Boy
   Reserve: Silver Jubilee March

Ridden Ponies: Dr and Mrs Gilbert-Scott's Cusop Heiress
   Reserve: Dr and Mrs Gilbert-Scott's Arden Vol-au-Vent of
   Creden

Royal Welsh (22—24 July 1980)

Ridden Hunters: P. Hobbs's Hilly Leys
   Reserve: W.F. Caudwell's March Entanglement

Lloyds Bank Qualifier: R.A. Swain's Crossways Merle (Welsh Section A)
  Reserve: Mrs P. Johns-Powell's Weston Glimpse

Rutland (3 August 1980)

Ridden Hunters: T. Hunnable's Glenstawl
  Reserve: Lady Zinnia Pollock's Sun Sovereign

Led Hunters: I. Thomas's Lucky Strike
  Reserve: M. Stimpson's Red Ensign

National Pony Show (6–7 August 1980)

Riding Pony Youngstock: Miss J. Morgan's Costock Choir Boy
  Reserve: Mrs D. Alexander's Forge Celtic Air

Brood Mares: Mrs Dorian Williams's Wingrove Stormaway
  Reserve: J.S. Hurst Ltd's Rosevean Springsong

Stallions or Colts: Miss S.E. Ferguson's Rosevean Eagle's Hill
  Reserve: Mrs B. Morgan's Barnaby

Overall: Rosevean Eagle's Hill
  Reserve: Wingrove Stormaway

14.2 – 15.2 hh Youngstock: Mrs D. Alexander's Celtic Ballad
  Reserve: Miss J. Leedham's Starlyte Christina

Ridden Ponies (Children's): Dr and Mrs Gilbert-Scott's Cusop Heiress
  Reserve: Mrs C. Caffyn Parsons's Keston Fayleen

Lloyds Bank In-Hand Champion: Mrs E. House's Bincombe Venture (Shetland Stallion)
  Reserve: Lord Kenyon's Gredington Judith (Welsh Section A)

Horse of the Year Show (6–11 October 1980)

Addison Small Hunter of the Year: Mrs N. and Miss G. Rogers's Royal Gossip
  Reserve: L.S. Cronin's Sea Lord

Hunnable Riding Pony of the Year: Mrs J. Hussey's Kateslea Zindle
  Reserve: Dr and Mrs Gilbert-Scott's Cusop Heiress

Waterford Crystal Show Hunter of the Year: Mrs R.
Healey-Fenton's The Brigadier
   Reserve: Lady Zinnia Pollock's Whaddon Way

Waterford Crystal Hunter Points Championship: South Essex
Insurance Group's Assurance

Bing and Grondahl Hack of the Year: Mr and Mrs J. Keen's
Royal Return
   Reserve: Mrs D.M. Goodall's Tenterk

Lloyds Bank In-Hand Champion of the Year: Llanarth Stud's
Llanarth Flying Comet (Welsh Cob Stallion)
   Reserve: S. Luxton's The Doper

Lombard Working Hunter of the Year: Mrs P. White's Dual Gold
   Reserve: Miss J. Bradwell's Castlewellan

Cob of the Year: E.L. David MFH's Brock
   Reserve: Mrs P. White's Kempley

16

The Use and Abuse of Medications

Edited from a number of sources by HRH The Prince Philip, Duke of Edinburgh, President of the International Equestrian Federation (FEI)

Equestrian competition under the FEI Rules is a human endeavour in which the horse shares his role with the rider. It is a test of man and beast – a test of their ability, experience and conditioning and of the rapport established between them to form a winning partnership. Horses of all shapes, sizes, and descriptions participate – the highly pedigreed against those of unknown origin.

The important point is that the FEI is only concerned with the control of its four disciplines. These sports bear no comparison with flat-racing and its associated Thoroughbred racehorse breeding industry. Although there are a number of professionals in the equestrian sports, the majority are amateurs and much of the administration is by volunteers. Racing and breeding, on the other hand, are almost entirely professional and commercial and in addition the public spends a good deal of money on betting.

Furthermore, the demands on racehorses and their racing and stud career structure is completely different to the life of the average competition horse. It is therefore quite unrealistic to suggest that the rules governing the use of drugs and medications in racing are relevant and directly applicable to the sports controlled by the FEI.

By the time a horse reaches a level of experience and ability which makes him a suitable mount for FEI competition at the higher national levels or the international level, he has accumulated considerable wear and tear from repeated maximum effort in training and in competition on good going and bad. The damage is for the most part of a nature which does not respond to attempts at complete cure but can be managed with good husbandry, training and ethical veterinary treatment, thus permitting the horse to compete comfortably and safely up to his innate ability.

The veterinary responsibility of the FEI is threefold — it must:

1. Ensure the health and welfare of every horse entered in competitions under its jurisdiction.
2. Ensure that the competition is equitable for all contestants.
3. Ensure that abuses are prevented.

Injury, fatigue and even exhaustion are inherent in athletic competition. When the horse serves as an integral member of the team it too sometimes suffers related injury and varying levels of fatigue. Man, as the rational partner of the man—horse team, has a moral responsibility to protect the horse, to preserve his useful life, and to ensure his health, comfort and safety so far as it is possible within the requirements of the sport.

So far so good. Difficulties, however, soon begin to arise because the dividing line between the treatment of injury and disease, on the one hand, and the preparation of horses for competition, on the other, is not easily defined. It is obviously right in principle to use medications to cure injuries and disease, but it is obviously wrong to use drugs or surgery to influence the performance of a horse.

The problem is to decide which purely therapeutic medications, and in what quantity, and which types of surgery, are reasonably certain to have no significant influence on the normal performance of a horse. There are those who say categorically, and hold it almost as an article of faith, that any exogenous substance whatever may have some influence on a horse's performance. On the other hand, there are those who maintain that a genuine therapeutic substance, in reasonable quantity, used for a genuine curative purpose and for which there is no evidence that it has, or will have, any significant influence on performance should not be categorically forbidden. This would allow, for example, a horse with a wasp sting on the end of its nose to be treated with an anti-histamine or a corticosteroid cream rather than ice-packs, or a horse with a small skin wound to be stitched under a local anaesthetic.

In the case of athletics, for example, a substance given to alleviate toothache or a mild sleeping pill in cases of what is known as jet-lag, and substances to control tummy trouble are not categorically forbidden.

The most notorious of these borderline therapeutic substances used on horses come under the heading of non-steroidal anti-inflammatory drugs. While there is quite a lot of evidence that the over-use of these drugs can produce harmful, and consequently disadvantageous side-effects, there is little, if any, evidence to show that, given in properly prescribed doses and at the appropriate time, they have any significant influence on the normal performance of a horse. Neither is there any evidence that they prevent the consequences of bumps and strains if they are given before the competition. But the point is, that treating a wasp sting or a cut is not intended to, and in practice does not, give a horse an unnatural advantage and as far as any evidence available suggests, neither does the treatment of inflammatory conditions by NSAIDs.

The Veterinary Regulations cover a multitude of administrative details, but the most important sections are those concerned with the definition and detection of what are known as Prohibited Substances. These are intended to include all those classes of drugs which are known to be capable of influencing the normal performance of a horse.

However, the FEI recognises that in practice it is simply not possible to enforce any regulations about the use of such substances anywhere except at the international events. It is not that it condones the use of substances that are not directly therapeutic at other times, there is simply no practical way of controlling it. The only way of enforcing the Regulations is to follow the practice of the Racing Authorities by testing a horse either before or after a competition to see whether it is acting under the influence of a Prohibited Substance.

This, of course, implies that all Prohibited Substances can be detected and, in addition, that there is a reasonable likelihood that those horses which have been treated with such substances will be detected. The improvement in analytical techniques is such that the chances of getting away with an undetectable drug are a great deal slimmer than they were only a few years ago. As for catching treated horses, it would be possible to make absolutely certain by sampling every single horse in every competition, but this would be extremely expensive. So for the moment it is specified that 10 per cent of the horses at an event should be sampled at random. So far this regime has only produced about half a dozen positive results in a year.

In an effort to determine the level of Phenylbutazone use (and abuse) in American competition, official testing laboratories have been analysing routine samples collected at shows and events. The figures accumulated since the survey was initiated almost two years ago indicate that the national average of horses in competition which show detectable levels of Phenylbutazone or its metabolites is 10 per cent, somewhat lower early in the year when the going is soft and correspondingly higher in late summer and autumn when the going is hard.

Of the 10 per cent treated (100 horses in every 1000 sampled) only 1.5 per cent (1—2 horses in every 1000) demonstrated excessively high levels which might be interpreted as abusive treatment with Phenylbutazone.

One or two out of a thousand is not convincing evidence of abuse. There are many reasons why the odd horse might suffer impaired metabolism, excretion and/or detoxification which would account for the retention and accumulation of Phenyl-butazone residues in the body.

A comparable pilot study was conducted at the 1980 World Cup in Baltimore. Of the samples taken all but one showed detectable levels of Phenylbutazone and only one showed a level which could be interpreted as the result of abusive treatment.

Similar projects were conducted at the international shows at Washington and New York in 1979. All horses sampled showed detectable levels of Phenylbutazone. None showed abuse.

In summary the findings of a continuing comprehensive survey of routine samples indicated that:

1. There appears to be little or no abuse of Phenylbutazone in competitions regulated by the American Horse Shows Association.
2. The use of Phenylbutazone in the international horse is commonplace — *but*
3. The abuse of Phenylbutazone is minimal — low enough to be of no practical regulatory concern.

Critical studies are convincing that Phenylbutazone toxicity is very real if dosage exceeds 4 gms per day for the 500 kilo horse (approx 10 mgm per kg) or dosage at that level exceeds four consecutive days.

Studies conducted at Cornell University by Drs Dewey, Maylin and co-workers support for the most part the work done in Switzerland by Professor Gerber and in the United Kingdom by David Snow. The work done at Cornell, which is soon to be published, utilised Thoroughbred and standardbred horses in work.

A 4 gm daily dose at the end of five days resulted in a decrease in total white blood cells. A 6 gm daily dose at the end of five days resulted in addition in colic and the 'Colitis-X' syndrome.

The most obvious clinical change at all levels of administration upwards of 4 gms per day was a marked decrease in appetite on the fourth and fifth day — a symptom frequently observed in practice, but for some obscure reason rarely regarded as a symptom of toxicity.

In America in the competing horse of 500 kilos the typical regimen for the management of lameness which does not lend itself to definitive treatment would start with the administration of 4 gms orally on the first day. If the desired response is achieved, the dosage is dropped to 3 gms orally. If the desired result persists at the 3 gm level dosage is again lowered, to 2 gms. If the desired response can be maintained at 2 gms per day the client is instructed to discontinue dosage except when needed and then only at the lowest possible dose at which satisfactory results can be obtained. Some clients learn that they can eliminate the 'loading dose' on the first and second day and obtain satisfactory results at the lower levels of administration.

Some few professionals will administer a 2 gm dose intravenously shortly before a competition even though the horse is being managed on oral administration. It is doubtful that this practice is of value, it may in fact lower its competitive efficiency, and probably only helps to heighten the rider's courage coefficient. The practice is not widespread.

Many people maintain, on moral grounds, that no horse should be allowed to compete under the influence of any exogenous substance whatever. This looks to be a simple and straightforward solution, but unfortunately it causes some very awkward anomalies. Apart from preventing any medication for injuries other than soap and water and various electrical treatments even under qualified and official supervision, it creates uncertainty in the minds of grooms and competitors about the use of such things as anti-insect and fly sprays, the treatment of skin conditions, homoeopathic substances and various 'tonics' and feed supplements. There have been a number of cases in racing where a Prohibited Substance has been detected in a horse which had been given, or taken, a piece of chocolate or a sweet.

This raises a whole new set of problems in the subject of medications control. The fact is that the dramatic improvement in the techniques of chemical analysis in the last few years has not only made it possible to detect drugs which were for a time undetectable, but also to detect much smaller quantities of drugs.

This means, of course, that detectable traces of a Prohibited Substance may now be found after a much longer interval after the medication has been given and in a quantity far below anything which could conceivably influence the performance of a horse. Furthermore, the risk of disqualification because a trace of a compound may remain in the body fluids days after it was administered has increased very considerably.

A possible solution to this problem is to specify the maximum residue levels permitted to be present in a sample. This may be a rather daunting prospect but at least it would allow genuine therapy to be used, and in addition it might well provide a satisfactory solution to the NSAID neurectomy dilemma.

Research in Britain involved the administration of single and multiple doses of Phenylbutazone to thirty-six horses over varying periods and the taking of a series of blood samples from two hours to twenty-four hours after dosing.

The experiments showed a wide variation of residue levels in the blood in the first twelve hours after administration that did not necessarily match the size of the dose given. However, after twenty-four hours there was a more consistent relationship between the size of the dose administered and the residue levels that could be measured.

It was felt that, with further work, it may be possible to arrive at an arbitrary level of Phenylbutazone circulating in the blood that should not be exceeded in a horse during competition. Together with the establishment of such an arbitrary level a warning would then have to be given that any administration of

Phenylbutazone to a horse within at least twenty-four hours before sampling could result in the permitted level being exceeded because of the big individual variation in absorption during the twenty-four hours after administration of the substance.

The additional research work that needs to be done is:

a) A comparison of levels reached at various time intervals after administration
   (i) by mouth
   (ii) by intravenous injections
   (iii) by intramuscular injections

   (All the work done at the Royal Veterinary College was based on an oral administration as currently used in the United Kingdom. In France, intramuscular injection is routinely used.)

b) The standardisation of testing techniques between laboratories. This is essential if disciplinary proceedings on an international level are to follow.

Research in Germany suggests that by using Gas Chromatography (GS) and High Pressure Liquid Chromatography (HPLC) the concentration of Phenylbutazone can be determined up to seventy-two hours after application of 10 mg per kg of body weight. There is no doubt that with more sophisticated analytical methods and modifications of the current routine procedures the time interval between administration and detection could be extended and the accuracy of the determination increased.

The basic alternatives before the FEI are whether to try to follow the line of absolute purity with the consequent increase in the difficulty of effective control and the added uncertainty and anxiety for veterinarians, owners and riders, or on the other hand, whether to attempt to concentrate on the control of the abuse of drugs and medications with the consequent difficulties of establishing permissible residue levels of therapeutic medications dependent on adequate analytical techniques.

17

Review of the Pony Classes

Dr and Mrs Gilbert-Scott's lovely little bay pony, Cusop Heiress, did not win the Royal International championship nor the Show Pony of the Year title at the Horse of the Year show, but she was runner-up for each title and had so many triumphs again this season — as champion at Newark, Royal Windsor, the Royal Bath and West (where her stable companion, Arden Vol-au-Vent, was reserve), the Three Counties, the National Pony Society show (again with Vol-au-Vent in reserve), Greater London and several more including the British Show Pony Society championships — that she was really the moral victor of the Show Pony title.

Having said that, it must be added that at the Royal, under Mrs Betty Gingell, the diminutive Vol-au-Vent actually succeeded in beating Cusop Heiress for the championship. This was indeed a feather in the cap of this mighty *multum in parvo,* by Creden Valhalla (by Bwlch Valentino) out of Mrs Glenda Spooner's Arden Bronze. Mrs Spooner is the progenitor of the Ponies of Britain Club and show, and Bronze is one of the many lovely and successful ponies that she bred by her small Thoroughbred stallion, Ardencaple, who has been a prolific winner of 12.2 hands classes. Vol-au-vent's dam was another extremely successful pony mare, Criban Biddy Bronze, owned by Lady Reiss. Pure Welsh, she derived from those wonderful Criban ponies bred on the Brecon Beacons by Llewellyn and Dick Richards at Talybont-on-Usk, where their forebears had bred ponies for two hundred years before them.

Although Biddy Bronze (by Criban Gay Snip out of Criban Belle) could out-gallop most of her larger rivals, she had a wonderful temperament which she passed on to her progeny. In fact her owner's smallest daughter, aged three and a half, rode her at home and brought her into the nursery for tea!

Cusop Heiress, foaled in 1972, was bred by Mr Vivian Eckley at Hay-on-Wye, where for so many years at his Cusop stud he stood the immortal riding pony stallion Bwlch Valentino, whom he bought as a four-year-old from the late Mrs Nell Pennell who bred him, his son, Bwlch Zephyr, and his grandson, Bwlch Hill Wind. Heiress is by Cusop Dignity out of Cusop Hostess.

Dignity is a son of Valentino out of Norwood Delilah, who was by the Arab sire Samson out of Edward Crow's old pony Angela, by the Thoroughbred Perion. Caroline Akrill bought Cusop Heiress as a two-year-old from Vivian Eckley and the following year sent her to the Gilbert-Scotts to break. Later they had the opportunity to buy her, and did so.

As a four-year-old (she is now eight) she had only three outings and without any kindergarten preliminaries she made her debut at the South of England, which she won, then went to the Royal International where she stood third to Christmas Carol of Bennochy (another illustrious stable companion) and her final show was the Horse of the Year, where she was second.

The following year she had a few more shows and by the

Dr and Mrs Gilbert-Scott's lovely little bay pony, Cusop Heiress.
(*Kit Houghton*)

time she was six she started her triple Royal Windsor crown and went from strength to strength.

All of the Gilbert-Scott ponies live 'in the garden' — or at least in their stable yard in what used to be the orchard, where they have eleven boxes. 'One has ferrets in it!' says Carole Gilbert-Scott, who does the horses and ponies with her sister Simone.

'Mum was the original enthusiast. Now we're all involved. Dad (who practices in Windsor) used to sail, then he came to a few shows and liked them so he sold his boat and bought a horse-box. As well as transporting ponies and horses to the shows, last summer it also took twenty-two-year-old Andrew (Gilbert-Scott) to Formula Ford race meetings. After exercising a couple of ponies, I go and help him grind the valves. It's all great fun and a real change. We have no grooms here, and no mechanics either!'

The family regard their animals as ponies, and not as 'rosette machines'. They still have their first show pony, Cusop Pirouette, as they could not bring themselves to sell her. They also have her four children, some still unbroken, who are simply pets. 'It's not really economic!'

For the same sort of reason, they did not take Sarah Williams off Heiress for the Horse of the Year show, even though she had shot up during the summer and was vastly too big for a 13.2 hands pony. 'You couldn't deprive her of one last show with her.' How refreshing it is, in this highly commercial sphere, to hear such sentiments expressed!

Equally, the Gilbert-Scotts are delighted that Lucinda McAlpine has done so well with the pony they produced for her in 1979, Oakhalls Halloween, who was champion at the Royal International in 1980 and at the Essex, Kent County and Lincolnshire meetings. He has now been sold to Gerald Harper, the Scottish criminal lawyer.

Another family who treat their ponies as pets are Mr and Mrs Rogers of Bedford. Their sons and daughter are no longer in the pony category, but the family still own their first ridden pony who is thirty-four years old, and have three daughters of the immortal Pretty Polly, Polly Pollyanna, Pollyanthus and Polly Perkins, now brood mares. They live on the 200-acre farm, from which Mrs Rogers has drafted all the chickens and cattle to make room for more horses.

Oakhalls Halloween, owned by Mr and Mrs W. McAlpine, became the 1980 Champion Ridden Pony at the Royal International.
(*Kit Houghton*)

Their daughter Jinny, who is now twenty-one, started showing when she was nine and was 'made' by Davina Whiteman (née
Lee-Smith), who gave her the invaluable opportunity to ride a
great many different animals from 11 hands 2 ins to 15 hands
2ins. Her enthusiasm for ponies has never ceased but now the
animals are shown by local children — notably Chirk Caviar,
who won at Royal Windsor and the National Pony Society show;
Twylands Fidelio, who was third to Cusop Heiress at the
Championship show and has been sold to Mr Harper; and the
outstanding 12.2 hands chestnut mare Ocean So Fair, who, to
her owners' delighted disbelief, won the Show Pony of the Year
title at Wembley as a five-year-old in 1979 and a year later won
the height class despite having brewed up during the final judging
after being exposed to the clanking chains of some heavy horses
in the inside collecting ring.

Ocean was bred by Mrs Leahy near Harrogate, by the Welsh
Section B pony, Brockwell Chipmunk, who consistently breeds
excellent progeny to little ponies, out of Set Fair of Oakleigh
from Mrs Colledge's successful stud, bred up from her part-bred
Arab mare, Bubbles. She won at Stoneleigh as a four-year-old,
where Mrs Rogers saw her and was very impressed with her
potential — so much so that she not only bought her by telephone
but rang Australia to do it.

Jack Edwards of the Weston stud was then visiting there, and
having heard that he intended to settle, she telephoned and said
what a waste it would be to send such a pony out there, where
they only have classes for 12, 13 and 14 hands ponies. She must
have been very persuasive, for Ocean is now on the farm and will
join the brood mare band when her ridden-pony career has ended.

As if all this were not enough, Jinny also has the top hack
Black Gold, the small hunters Footpath and Why Worry (who
do indoor jumping all winter), and Royal Gossip, who won the
1980 title, and the top hunters Swanbourne and Whaddon Way,
the latest arrival from Lady Zinnia Pollock and a blissful ride.

In the 14.2 hands class at the Horse of the Year show it was
gratifying to find two judges as level-headed and as knowledgable
as Mrs Hugh Gingell and Mrs Dorian Williams putting an amateur-
produced little-known ten-year-old with bone and substance,
who could actually go hunting, at the top of the assembly, and
eventually awarding him the championship. Jane Hussey and

Mrs J. Hussey's Kateslea Zindle, Pony of the Year at Wembley's Horse of the Year show. (*Kit Houghton*)

Kateslea Zindle, an old-fashioned sort of bay pony, were worthy of their title, and one's first reaction when the rider brushed away a tear on realising that she had won, was revised as soon as it became known that this was no child professional overcome with joy at having defeated another of its ilk. Sadly, over-exposure to all but the *crème de la crème* of the pony-showing scenario can lead only to the depths of cynicism — which is sad because people like the late Mrs Nell Pennell, who bred the ancestors of most of the champions of today (Bwlch Valentino, Bwlch Zephyr and Bwlch Hill Wind — three generations of as near perfection as it is possible to get in this far from perfect world) were so very uncynical concerning animals at all events.

Kateslea Zindle was bred by Miss Margaret Singleton from Nottinghamshire, and is by the premium stallion The Zipper out of the family's outgrown pony, April Showers, whose sole progeny he was. She produced him at the age of twenty-one in 1968. He was called Jonathan Joe, and as he was somewhat full of himself he was sent to Mrs Denzil Oxby, who sold him to

Vin Toulson, and he then went to Colin Rose. He was sent as a
four-year-old to Davina Whiteman, who produced him and
renamed him before selling him into Wales, where he was found
by Mr Vivian Eckley and sold to the Husseys.

In the breeding classes, Miss Elspeth Ferguson's Rosevean
Eagles' Hill, who had already won two Lloyds Bank In-Hand
Championship titles, continued to hold his own, winning the
stallion and overall championship at the National Pony Society
show at Malvern in August, when his covering season was over.

Reserve to him was Mrs Dorian Williams' new brood mare,
Wingrove Stormaway, who won the Lloyds Bank qualifier on
her first outing as a matron at the Bath and West and emerged
as champion National Pony Society mare. Wingrove Stormaway
is a grey 14.0 hands mare by Croft Mantino out of Cusop
Sailaway.

Mrs Daphne Alexander, who came to fame with the small
Thoroughbred stallion McGredy which she owned in partnership
with Mrs Nell Pennell, won the reserve to the youngstock
champion, Joanne Morgan's Costock Choir Boy, at the National
Pony Society show, with Forge Celtic Air. She also won the
14.2−15.2 championship with Forge Celtic Ballad. Forge Celtic
Air was reserve youngstock champion at the Royal and supreme
in-hand champion at the Ponies of Britain show, where he wound
up supreme overall champion. A three-year-old dark bay gelding,
he is by Celtic Ballad out of Forge Mistral and was bred by his
owner on her stud near Marlborough.

Of the native breeds, the most successful was the Llanarth
Stud's Welsh cob stallion, Llanarth Flying Comet, who actually
retained the Lloyds Bank In-Hand Championship at the Horse
of the Year show under Mrs Yeomans and Colonel Dick Spencer.
But he was run close in the class by the runner-up, Mrs Edward
House's diminutive black Shetland stallion from the Quantocks,
Bincombe Venture − a seven-year-old who became supreme
champion at the National Pony Society's show at Malvern, winning the Lloyds Bank qualifier to gain his ticket to Wembley.

At the Royal the top matron was Mrs B.M. Morgan's Beverley
Jocelyn, who was runner-up to the young hunter Royal Fiddler
for the Lloyds Bank qualifier. Mrs Morgan's daughter had the
youngstock champion at the Royal show, Costock Choir Boy,
by Twylands Troubadour.

18

Martin Whiteley Takes Horse Trials Chair

Martin Whiteley was elected unanimously as Chairman of the Horse Trials Committee of the British Horse Society in October, 1980. He has been involved with horses all his life and rode with the British team during its golden age, helping to win the European Championship at Punchestown in 1967 and finishing second individually on The Poacher.

His father, J.P. Whiteley, had gone from the Army into politics and was MP for North Buckinghamshire. Martin and his two brothers were born and brought up at Bletchley, riding from the age of two and hunting from the age of six, originally with the Whaddon Chase. His father (known as 'William' to his friends 'after the shop, which unfortunately we did not own') was killed in 1943, as a Brigadier, and five years later the family moved to Mixbury in the Bicester country, whose hounds his brother Peter took on for a couple of seasons after coming down from Cambridge.

After Eton, he joined the Army, not originally intending to remain. He did his National Service in Germany, with the Green Jackets, and started to ride racing. There were superb opportunities to ride out there in those days, and he rode on the flat, over hurdles and over fences for five seasons from 1949 to 1953. English meetings were held at Hannover and Dortmund every fortnight, on Sundays, with six races. Horses were commandeered initially and then leased or imported, and racing soon became his first love.

In 1953, when he was leading amateur rider in the BAOR, he had the misfortune to break his back in a racing fall at Hannover. Two years later, as the Army did not believe in the operation, he had a spine graft at his own expense in London. He left the Army in 1959.

His godfather, Michael Beaumont, was MP for mid-Buckinghamshire in the 1930s, and as the pipe of port that he had laid down

for Martin's twenty-first birthday present had gone up in the
Blitz, he said: 'I want to give you a really good present — what
about a horse?'

Martin allowed that he would love to win the Grand Military.
But Major Beaumont, who was Master of the Kildare Hounds
and who bought the 1954 Dublin champion, What a Walk, had
been to Badminton that spring and gave him instead a potential
three-day event horse, St Nicholas, who went clear over the
European Championship course at Windsor in 1955.

That gift horse was destined to change the course of Martin's
riding life, for though he never found dressage easy he thoroughly
enjoyed cross-country. He went to Mrs Lisa Shedden at Kingham,
and from then on for eight or nine years until 1961 he always
had horses with her. During his career he had, in fact, eighteen
event horses, of which he rode eight at Badminton.

'I always hunted them, and did not get them up for the
autumn three-day events at Harewood but just aimed for Badminton. Maybe one big three-day event a year is what more
people should aim for now.'

Certainly, in the years when Britain was invariably at the top,
from 1967 until 1972, the team had the very great advantage of
being able to call on the services of four completely sound horses
in Major Derek Allhusen's Lochinvar, Mary Gordon-Watson's
Cornishman V, Richard Meade's Barberry and Martin Whiteley's
The Poacher.

In the first few of the fourteen years during which he competed in horse trials, as well as the Great Badminton Championship there was always a competition called Little Badminton,
over exactly the same cross-country course, for up-and-coming
horses, and in 1960 he won it on a horse called Peggoty. Two
years later he was sixth in Badminton proper. Then in 1965 he
won Little Badminton on The Poacher, a wonderful horse, bred
in Ireland, full of courage but always a man-eater in his box.
The following year, competing in the World Championships at
Burghley, he finished fifth individually.

A highly predictable selection for the European Championships at Punchestown, Co. Kildare, where he won a team gold
medal and an individual silver, he seemed certain to be picked
for the Olympic confrontation in Mexico. His mother, Mrs Trixie
Whiteley, also had an Olympic candidate called Foxdor, who

had been loaned to Sergeant Ben Jones of the King's Troop RHA. Both horses were being got ready by Michael Herbert, who now trains the Canadian team. Just before Burghley they were given a gallop, and Foxdor suddenly went slower and slower and then dropped down dead, with an unsuspected heart condition. This was not only bad luck for Ben Jones but also for Mrs Whiteley, who had hunted all her life — side-saddle before the war, and afterwards, when she became a victim of arthritis, on a pony.

Martin then showed just what sort of person he is. His great ambition was to ride for his country in the Olympic Games, but he realised that his back was not reliable and that Ben Jones was without a horse, so he gave up the ride on The Poacher. Five days later, Ben Jones and the horse established an immediate rapport, so they went off to Mexico and helped to win the team gold medals.

In 1969 there was another European Championship, this time at Haras du Pin in Normandy. Here, The Poacher and Staff-Sergeant Ben Jones helped to win the team title again for Britain.

Martin Whiteley and that unique horse, The Poacher, competing at Eridge, 1965. (*Pony/Light Horse*)

Nor was this great horse done yet, for in 1970, ridden this time by Richard Meade, he won the Whitbread Championship at Badminton and was runner-up to Cornishman in the World Championships in Punchestown; in 1971 he was in his third European-Championship-winning team at Burghley. The Poacher competed in six CCIOs running (one Olympic Games, two World Championships, three European Championships), and only once finished outside the first five individually — a unique record. When he eventually retired it was to the hunting field, where Mrs Dick Hawkins, wife of one of the joint-Masters of the Grafton Hounds, hunted him regularly.

One of the great strengths of horse trials in England is that the vast majority of those in the top echelon are foxhunters and understand and appreciate horses. Martin Whiteley told me, 'They argue things out rationally and democratically, and quietly find the general consensus of opinion, because basically they are all on the same side.'

He should — and does — know, having served the sport on all sides. Some twenty years ago, with the owner of Everdon, Captain Dick Hawkins, he started the Everdon novice horse trials, and he has been a committee member of the Horse Trials Group since 1961, and Vice Chairman since 1972. He joined the selection committee in 1963, and was chairman from 1969–1972. He has been a steward of the BHS at horse trials such as Windsor, and Technical Delegate at Bramham, Burghley and in Canada. He was also responsible for forming the Horse Trials Support Group, which as a sub-committee of the British Equestrian Olympic Fund is responsible for fund-raising and the purchase and training of International, Olympic and potential competition horses.

A housemaster at Eton College, where he was educated, he and his wife, formerly the Lady Anne Nevill, daughter of Lord Abergavenny, have three daughters.

19

National Showjumping

The national scene was considerably enlivened early in 1980 with the announcement by Lister Welch, David Broome's agent, that he intended to stage a £10,000 winner-take-all challenge at Mr Thomas Hunnable's new Towerlands Equestrian Centre near Braintree. The competition was to be known as the Rimas Challenge because the money was put up by Mr Samir Mahmoud (no prize for working out that his christian name, backwards, is Rimas) and would be fought out between David Broome, Harvey Smith and Eddie Macken.

The British Show Jumping Association did their best to prevent it from taking place at all, for the existing rules do not cater for such a contingency. However, as it was only a one-off affair it was eventually allowed to go ahead. Despite the fact that the officials of the governing body, in their wisdom, decided to boycott the event and were conspicuous by their absence, an enjoyable evening ensued – particularly for Eddie Macken, whose journey from Ireland was rewarded when he landed the spoils of victory. This may have provided some compensation for his loss, some months later, of the services of the quadruple British Jumping Derby winner, Boomerang, who fractured his pedal bone and brought his career to a halt. Still, he had been a wonderfully consistent horse despite being denerved twice (some say three times).

The only one who failed to derive much enjoyment from the evening was, ironically, David Broome. Queensway Sportsman elected to stop in the last round, sending his rider over the fence without him as luggage in advance, thus losing him £10,000 – a very expensive refusal indeed.

Three weeks earlier, at Robert Old's Park Farm Equestrian Centre at Northwood, Middlesex, David Broome had won his fifth Lancia motor car at the Lancia Championships, where Derek Ricketts took the Lancia Trophy on Col. and Mrs Rodney Ward's Hydrophane Coldstream.

The *Birmingham International* show in March at the National
Exhibition Centre was Britain's first big show of the new season,
and though Paul Schockemöhle on El Paso and Hugo Simon on
Gladstone shared the Grand Prix, Broome was prominent among
the winners, as was Derek Ricketts (puissance winner on Coral's
Denham, equally with four others). The latter's horses were
then leased to Coral Racing.

At *Bicton* (Devon), Malcolm Pyrah was an early qualifier for
the Radio Rentals Championship on Towerlands Chelsea Girl.
Before long, he was to acquire Anglezarke and Chainbridge;
Trevor Banks decided to sell them on when Mick Saywell left
him to ride again for Lincolnshire farmer John Taylor. Later still,
shortly before the Horse of the Year show, Trevor Banks declared
that he was about to acquire a new string and that they would
be ridden for him by Ann Moore, the 1971 Women's European
Champion and 1972 Olympic Silver medallist on Psalm. She
retired from the sport to marry a Birmingham butcher but is
now making a comeback.

The first major outdoor meeting for 1980 was the Everest
Double Glazing International at *Hickstead* from 1st–5th May,
where Robert Smith won the Everest Trophy on Team Sanyo's
Video, Jeff McVean took the Everest Speed Stakes on Persian
Shah for Australia and sold the horse on to Michael Mac, Derek
Ricketts won the International Open on Coral's Wonder, Caroline
Bradley claimed the Grand Prix on Tigre, James Kernan annexed
the Fault-and-Out for Ireland on Debbie Johnsey's former horse,
Speculator, and Douglas Bunn was the proud owner of the
Everest champion, The Rascal IV, ridden by Raymond Howe.

Newark, traditionally, heralded the start of the agricultural
shows, and the Everest Double Glazing Championship was a
triumph for Vicky Gascoigne on Trevarrion, while Michael
Whitaker had a good win on Samir Mahmoud's Disney Way and
Paul Platten won the TSB Championship on Eastern Playboy.

The *Royal Windsor* drew Ferdi Tyteca from Belgium, and on
Ransome he was the only foreign winner. Chris Parker won the
Calor Gas Stakes with a rejuvenated Brackenhill, fully restored
to soundness after a year off the road. Another winner was Nick
Skelton on FMS Barbarella, as was Ray Howe on Douglas Bunn's
The Rascal and Michael Whitaker on Samir Mahmoud's Disney
Way. Jeff McVean won two classes for Australia on his King

George V Cup winner, the little chesnut mare Claret and Persian Shah, and Michael Whitaker brought off a double with Brackley Way.

Maureen Holden brought off the BSJA National Women's Championship on Mister Vee, homebred by her husband, and the men's equivalent went to Harvey Smith on Sanyo Mangon. Paddy McMahon on Capercaille and Nick Skelton on Everest Stud's Wallaby divided the St George of England Championship, but they were all beaten for the Modern Alarms Supreme Championship by veteran Fred Welch on True Grit.

Derek Ricketts made a good start to the *Devon County* show by winning both competitions on Coral's Nice 'n' Easy and Coral's Classic, and on the second day the last-named won again, with Chris Parker and Brackenhill. But on the last day David Broome had things all his own way, winning the Area International Trial (AIT) on Tabac Original and the Grand Prix on Harris Homecare (Sunny Side Up).

The *Shropshire and West Midlands* meeting at Shrewsbury belonged to the young entry, with Robert Smith scoring a good victory in the Radio Rentals AIT on Alabama while John Brown took the proceeds of the Agaheat Scurry back to Scotland, thanks to Campbell Graham's Paddy Connelly, his tried and tested partner since they won two young riders' titles at Hickstead.

The final season of Wills' sponsorship at *Hickstead* — the twentieth — started over the last weekend in May with the Lambert and Butler International, when Britain and France dominated the Prince of Wales (Nations) Cup. Victory finally went to the home side (see International chapter). Individual winners were Rowland Fernyhough and Bouncer, Harvey Smith with Team Sanyo's Music Centre (formerly Graffiti), Robert Smith and Video, Eddie Macken and Carroll's Spotlight, and Liz Edgar with Everest Double Glazing's Forever, who won the Grand Prix.

At the *Hertfordshire* show, Chris Parker and Brackenhill scored again in the Everest AIT and Michael Mac won the Marconi Topscore on Tauna Dora, a consistent winner previously for Graham Fletcher.

The *Surrey County* at Guildford, a regular Whit-Monday engagement for those in the South-of-London catchment area, brought Paddy McMahon's new sponsors, Husky, into the spotlight with Husky Streamline, who won the Radio Rentals AIT jointly with David Broome on Eyelure Ltd's Tabac Original (formerly Heatwave). John Brown won the Topscore (accumulator) on Campbell Graham's Dutch-bred Pinxter.

The *Staffordshire* show brought Sue Pountain into the limelight with Ned Kelly IV, owned by the JCB Jumping Team and later to do so well at the Royal International. He has a great jump, and what a hunter he would make with his bone and substance, though sadly he may not have sufficient turn of foot for that job. He seems genuine and keen on jumping, however, and he won both the Jenkinson's Stakes and the Bass-Worthington's AIT, his passport to Wembley.

Douglas Bunn's The Rascal, with Ray Howe, was the hero of the *Suffolk County* fixture, where he won the Championship and the Everest AIT, while his stable companion, More Candy, won the Ransome Plough Stakes.

Malcolm Pyrah and Pam Dunning were the leading riders at the *Royal Bath and West*, but the spoils were well spread with the Cockburn's Special Reserve Stakes going to Malcolm on P.J. Conway's Charles Fox, that night's speed event to Robert Smith on Sunningdale, the Babycham Gold Cup to Robert again on Video, and the Eterna Stakes to Derek Ricketts on Coral's Classic.

Tony Newbury won the Topscore with Tudor Doublet; Caroline Bradley and Landmine took the coveted Lancia qualifier; Lionel Dunning and Jungle Bunny won the Radio Rentals Stakes; and Nick Skelton won the A & B with Barbarella.

Nick then embarked upon a phenomenal round of success at the *South of England* meeting at Ardingly, winning the Everest Double Glazing Stakes on Maybe, the Corona Topscore on Wallaby, the Aga Cooker Jubilee Stakes on Barbarella, who also won the Radio Rentals AIT, and the Elizabeth Ann Prizewinners' on Wallaby. John Brown with Paddy Connelly (Continental Grain Stakes), Michael Mac with Persian Shah (Calor Gas Stakes) and Fred Welch with Rosslea (Maxicrop Triple Strength Stakes) were about the only others to get a look-in.

Equally, the *Royal Cornwall*, which runs concurrently at Wadebridge, was David Broome's benefit meeting. He won the Aga Cooker Stakes on Tabac Original and the Everest Double Glazing competition on Harris Homecare.

David continued his run of success at his neighbouring *Three*

Counties show at Malvern, where Tabac Original got off to a
good start by winning the Continental London Stakes, and
Harris Carpets' Red A won the Elizabeth Ann Power and Speed.
Still Nick Skelton ground on inexorably, to win the Radio
Rentals AIT on Barbarella. Caroline Bradley won the Everest
Double Glazing Stakes on Fieldmaster and finally Harvey Smith
and Sanyo Music Centre won the Lancia Stakes.

So to the *Benson and Hedges* show at Cardiff Castle, where
en route for the amateur and professional titles (won respectively
by Peter Robeson and David Broome) John Brown and Paddy
Connelly won the first competition, Harvey Smith and Sanyo
Music Centre the second, and the same two riders came up again
when Pinxter took the Accumulator and Music Centre the
Topscore. Finally, Peter Robeson took the amateur title from
Chris Smith of Australia and Belgium's Ferdi Tyteca. The
professional title fell to David Broome, with Steve Hadley and
Derek Ricketts disputing the runner-up position. The Match-
Play Championship went to Caroline Bradley on Landmine.

The *Royal Highland* at Ingliston, Edinburgh, had a more
parochial flavour than usual as not so many International riders
made the trip north. Geoff Billington and the big roan cob
Snowdonia, who is such a trier, won the Bank of Scotland Quaich
Puissance, James Aird and Castle Pollard the Topscore, Mark
Fuller and Channel Five the Calor Gas Stakes, John Greenwood
and Magee the House of Fraser Championship and Peter
Richardson on Folly Hill the Everest Double Glazing class.

Harvey Smith, though he used the meeting as a recla-
mation site for another rogue horse that he is rehabilitating, also
won the Radio Rentals class on Sanyo Music Centre. But the
young Scots triumphed outstandingly, with James Aird winning
the Points Trophy, while Gary Gillespie (whose father, a miner's
son, made a fortune when he bought a farm in Lanarkshire on
which to turn out the horses, and discovered a rich seam of coal
beneath it) came to the attention of the media when he rode
Chico to win the Crawfords Scotch Whisky Championship
Knock-Out.

Nick Skelton swept the board once more at the *Lincolnshire*
show, winning the Radio Rentals Stakes and the Everest AIT on
Everest Double Glazing's Maybe. At *Charlton Park*, a Cotswolds
event which goes from strength to strength thanks to the inspi-

ration and hard work of Mrs Hamish Munro and her family, Nick Skelton went on to win the Radio Rentals Power and Speed on Wallaby and the Wilts AIT on Maybe, adding the Colt Car Speed on Wallaby to his tally for good measure. Caroline Bradley and Landmine scored in the Olympus Camera Stakes and Sally Mapleson won the Grand Prix on Con Brio.

At the *Royal Norfolk*, the predictable local winners of the Everest Double Glazing class were Malcolm Pyrah on Mr Hunnable's Towerlands Chelsea Girl, while Paul Platten's Eastern Playboy won the Holden Motors' Accumulator. The other classes went to Yorkshiremen: the AIT to Mark Fuller's Channel Five and the Holden Motors' Open to Graham Fletcher's veteran, Buttevant Boy.

Nick Skelton was still in dangerous form at the *Wales and West* meeting, held in the fields behind the Broome family homestead at Crick, near Chepstow. Everest Double Glazing's Hardly Ever won the Sparkford Ballywillwill Stakes and their Jet Lag won the AIT. On the last day, David Broome won the Sanyo Olympic Talent Spotters' Stakes with his new German horse, Pikant, and the Radio Rentals went to Helen Dickinson, fresh out of the junior classes, on Old Smuggler.

So to *The Royal*, where John Whitaker started well by winning the Calor Gas Stakes on Rush Green, Harvey Smith and Sanyo Music Centre brought off the double of the Hunting and Topscore competitions, Sue Pountain and Ned Kelly IV won the Elizabeth Ann Stakes, Malcolm Pyrah won the Lancia Championship qualifier on Thomas Hunnable's Towerlands Chain Bridge, and Derek Ricketts took the Radio Rentals Stakes, which incorporated the BSJA National Championship, on Hydrophane Coldstream.

But the heroine of the leading agricultural show in England was Liz Edgar, who won the Everest Double Glazing competition on Forever and the £3,000 caravan offered to the leading rider of the show.

Liz and Forever also won the Bass Grand National at the *Great Northern* show at Charnock Richard the following week, where her brother, David Broome, took the Stones Bitter Stakes on Tabac Original and the Berger Paints International Championship on Harris Homecare. On Philco, he went on to win the Midland Bank Great Yorkshire Championship at the *Great*

David Broome and Philco on their way to winning the
Midland Bank Great Yorkshire Championship. (*Leslie Lane*)

Yorkshire show, where his brother-in-law, Graham Fletcher,
pulled off the coveted Cock o' the North Championship on
Preachan, in his first English season. John Whitaker on Ryan's
Son and Rowland Fernyhough on Autocrat scooped the other
big prizes.

Meanwhile, at the *Kent County*, Nick Skelton won the Lancia
Stakes on Wallaby and the Championship on Maybe, while
Wallaby also won the Aga Cooker Stakes, Westbourne Top Score
and Radio Rentals AIT.

The *Lambert and Butler* Hickstead meeting was dominated
by the Americans on the first day, when Norman Dello Joio on
Johnny's Pocket won the first class, to be followed by his team-
mate, Melanie Smith, with Vivaldi. Then Graham Fletcher arrived
from his county show to redress the balance. On Sowerby Parks
he won the International Stakes and on Double Brandy he
brought off the Grand Prix in a magnificent double.

Often the behind-the-scenes side of showjumping is far more

interesting than what goes on in the ring, and the prevailing situation at the *Royal International* at Wembley was a case in point. It became known on the grapevine that David Broome had made a large bid for Tigre, the grey German-bred horse which was co-owned by Caroline Bradley (and which riders such as Paul Schockemöhle and Johan Heins have tried in vain to ride). His joint owner, Donald Bannock, who owns a masonry group near Birmingham, advertised for sealed tenders for the horse from interested parties.

Thanks to Bob Dean of British Equestrian Promotions, who met with the joint owners for five hours, it all ended happily and Tigre won the Queen Elizabeth II Cup as well. But it was touch and go whether this horse, who goes so well for Caroline, would join the Harris Carpets team — and though he is difficult, Caroline admitted: 'David can get the best out of any horse.'

David won the opening Wembley Stakes on Harris Homecare, and Nick Skelton asserted himself shortly afterwards to win the Philips Industries Championship on Barbarella, but the first night's major competition, the *Horse and Hound* Cup, went to America's Melanie Smith on the Dutch-bred Calypso. Tuesday brought a double victory for John Whitaker with Rush Green and Miss Tina, and found another Yorkshire winner in Mark Fuller on Channel Five. That night's puissance was divided between Johannsmann of West Germany on Excellenz and Armand Leone on Wallenstein for the USA. Wednesday saw Harvey Smith and Sanyo Music Centre winning one of the lesser events, and Eddie Macken on Carrolls' Onward Bound another. The big guns were trained on the Queen Elizabeth and King George V Cups, won by Caroline Bradley with Tigre and David Bowen with Scorton respectively.

Nick Skelton and Maybe won the Jean Machine Stakes on Thursday, and John Brown took the Norwich Union Stakes on Paddy Connelly. The *Daily Mail* Cup, one of the oldest trophies on offer, went to Jean Germany with Whistling Song.

On Friday, Harvey Smith and Music Centre brought off their double in the Lancia Stakes, and John Whitaker had his third win of the week and second on Rushgreen in the Lancome International. The Whitbread Pair Relay went to Everest's Jet Lag and Wallaby, but the John Player Grand Prix went to Terry Rudd of the United States on Semi Tough.

Vicky Gascoigne won the Two-Horse Calor Gas stakes on the last day with McGinty and Upstream, David Broome achieved his double on Homecare in the Topscore and Jean Germany won the Radio Rentals Champion Horseman, before Chris Smith of Australia beat all comers to win the Everest Supreme Championship on Sanskrit.

During the third week in August, Michael Whitaker became, at twenty, the youngest-ever winner of the W.D. & H.O Wills's British Jumping Derby at *Hickstead*. He was riding Owen Gregory, whose owner is Mrs Raymond Fenwick, mother of Ann Wilson, who used to ride him but is now in New Zealand with her husband, Harvey. Owen Gregory jumped the only clear round (and only the twentieth since the competition was first held in 1961).

John Whitaker and Ryan's Son made all the running with 4 faults at the last rustic parallel and finished up sharing second place with Derek Ricketts, whose objection against a technical refusal coming off the 10ft 6 ins Derby Bank was upheld.

Rowland Fernyhough and Bouncer won the Derby Trial.

Eddie Macken's Boomerang, four times winner of this classic, made a farewell appearance and was enthusiastically applauded when the saddle was removed in the ring and replaced by a pad of flowers. In 1979 Eddie Macken and Boomerang were the only horse and rider ever to win the Derby Trial and the Derby in the same year.

At the *Greater London* show on Clapham Common, Fred Welch brought off a double on Norstar and True Grit and David Broome a treble with Harris Homecare and Queensway Sportsman (Everest Double Glazing, Johnson Power and Speed, and Radio Rentals AIT). The following week, at the *Wales and West* show, Jabeena Maslin won the Welsh Jumping Derby on No Obligations.

Nick Skelton distinguished himself yet again at the *Everest Double Glazing Championships* at Park Farm, Northwood, the week before Wembley. FMS Barbarella won the North Face Stakes, Maybe the Soloramic Stakes and Jet Lag the Accumulator. But the Championship went to Derek Ricketts with Hydrophane Coldstream.

Nick's winning streak continued for the *Horse of the Year* show at Wembley, where on Maybe he won the Butlin Championship on the first night. On Tuesday it was the turn of Michael Whitaker and Disney Way to win the Philips Industries Stakes, but the Championship went to Johan Heins riding Laramy for Holland. Then the coveted Foxhunter Champion-ship was won by Derek Ricketts on Roy Trigg's Morning Glory, a former show hunter, bred in the Scottish Border country by the late Mr 'Roly' Harker, Master and huntsman of the Jed Forest. Morning Glory is by the premium stallion Barbin out of a mare called Dunkery III, also by a premium stallion who was the top heavyweight at the National Hunter Show in 1969 and 1970. Roy bought Morning Glory as a two-year-old from the late Jack Gittins.

On Wednesday Nick Skelton won again, this time on Everest Double Glazing's Wallaby. Eddie Macken won the Topscore on the young Carrolls Royal Lion, and Malcolm Pyrah well merited his victory in the Leading Showjumper competition on Tower-lands Anglezarke, owned by Tom Hunnable. Finally, Ferdi

Nick Skelton and Everest Double Glazing's Maybe, a combination which enjoyed a very successful season in 1980. (*Leslie Lane*)

Tyteca took the *Daily Telegraph* Cup back to Belgium, thanks to the good offices of his Irish horse, Ransome.

The next day he won again with his brilliant young T'Soulaiky. Team Sanyo's Music Centre and Harvey Smith won the Lancia Stakes and young Gary Gillespie from Scotland triumphed in the Norwich Union Puissance on the Hannoverian Goldfink which Ted Edgar (Gary is one of Ted's pupils) bought from Paul Schockemöhle in July.

Robert Smith had a winner on Friday when Alabama took the Jean Machine Stakes. Steve Hadley and Sunorra took the William Hanson Trophy, while Ferdi Tyteca and the Belgian-bred T'Soulaiky won one of the biggest prizes of the week, the Continental Grain Stakes for the *Sunday Times* Cup. It is interesting to note that Ferdi Tyteca has fallen foul of the Belgian federation for refusing to push this youngster by taking him to the alternative Olympics in Rotterdam, for which he did not consider the horse to be ready.

Jayne Tickle, Ted Edgar's niece, won the Calor Gas Championship on Condico; John Brown and Paddy Connelly won the *Country Life & Riding* Cup; Lionel Dunning and Jungle Bunny took the *Horse and Hound* Cup; and finally, young Nick Skelton, a credit to Ted and Liz Edgar whose pupil he has been since he was sixteen, scooped the richest prize of the week, the £3,000 Radio Rentals Championship, with Everest Double Glazing's Maybe.

20

Junior European Championship

Junior European Horse Trials Championships
(26–28 September 1980)
It may be a sign of the times that goes a considerable way towards justifying the 'youth cult' that has been gaining increasing momentum over the last ten years all over the Western world but, whatever the reason, there is no gainsaying the fact that the British junior teams have done far better than their seniors.

The horse trials team of Virginia Strawson (on Greek Herb), Claire Needham (Solo), Nicola May (Commodore IV) and Susanna Brooke (Super Star IV) won the team championship from eight other nations at Achselschwang in Bavaria, Southern Germany. Denmark and Switzerland were represented by individuals only.

Britain also had two additional individuals in Tim Dudgeon on Tom Faggus and Maija Söderholm on Sica Dream, and all six were within twelve marks of the best dressage score, while Britain finished 50 points better overall with a total of 161.2 penalty points, than the Swedes, who were second with 211.8 points, and the French, third on 212.05.

Major Lawrence Rook, who has just retired as chairman of the Combined Training Committee, judged the dressage with Frau Erike Andersen and Herr Ruprecht von Butler for the host nation, and was considerably stricter than either of his colleagues, but the British tests, thanks to Gill Watson, who was appointed trainer by Colonel Hubert Allfrey, made a good impression all round. The team finished 10 points behind the hosts but 18 ahead of France.

By happy chance, the cross-country course had been built by Otto Pohlmann. He was also the designer of that marvellous course for the Munich Olympics in 1972, which produced all the right results without causing injury to horse or rider. This year's course had been shortened to somewhat less than 5 km with twenty fences, and British riders emerged with just a few time penalties and one refusal, when Maija Söderholm and Sica Dream had a difference of opinion concerning the recommended two strides at the road crossing: the horse considered one stride more suitable. The steeplechase course of 2.25 km with two changes of rein was likewise trouble-free.

Claire Needham and Solo were fast and clear, which put the rest of the team in good heart. Tom Faggus had a good clear round within the time and Sica Dream was only penalised by his involuntary refusal. Greek Herb pulled like a train but made nothing of the fences, so when Super Star was clear in the best time of the day, Britain appeared to be in a commanding position, with Super Star in the lead individually.

The last to go was the defending individual champion, Nicola May with Commodore IV. They finished just 10 seconds outside the time and the team title seemed certain to go to Britain. Three of the French and Swedish teams were round safely but their fourth men had been eliminated after two falls, but of the fifty-six starters, twenty-five got round without jumping penalties. Six were eliminated for two refusals, two for two falls (a new condition introduced at the request of the FEI), and three were spun by the vets during the ten-minute halt.

Though the British team were home and dry, so to speak, the individual scores were so close that one showjumping mistake could alter the whole picture — and did. All but seven of the forty-three survivors went clear over a straightforward course with a few turns to test suppleness and a double.

Three entries, among them Greek Herb, had negligible time faults. Susie Brooke, in the lead but with no margin for error, must have been under immense pressure as she awaited her turn, hardly unmindful of the fact that three elder brothers had ridden for the team in former years on that marvellous dun Connemara pony, Olive Oyl. Sadly, a pole rolled from the fifth fence and dropped her back to fourth place. Individual victory went to Carmen Berger of West Germany with Bacardi 9, on 48.2 penalties. Claire Needham won the silver medal for Britain on 50.6 and Richard Funder the bronze for Austria on Dac with 51.2.

The spoils were well spread at this happy and well-organised event, and it is to be hoped that those who took part in it are never made to feel cynical as some of their seniors inevitably do about what can be a thoroughly estimable sport.

Junior European Showjumping at Millstreet
(21—24 August 1980)
Though the all-conquering French took the junior European showjumping team championship from the Netherlands, with the British team in fifth place behind West Germany and Belgium, for the second year in succession Britain won the gold and silver individual medals. Last year Vicky Gascoigne and Gillian Milner took the honours, this time the winner was Michael Mac, riding the grey Australian-bred Persian Shah which he bought from Jeff McVean; and in second place was Jane Sargeant, who hunts with the Grafton, on Ladiesman.

Ten nations — Belgium, Finland, France, West Germany, Italy, the Netherlands, Spain, Switzerland, Ireland and Great Britain — sent teams to Millstreet, Co. Cork, the home of Mr and Mrs Noel C. Duggan. There were also two riders from Austria.

The British team comprised Michael Mac with Persian Shah, Jane Sargeant with Ladiesman, Zoe Bates with Craven V, Mark Heffer with Marco VIII and Alan Fazackerley with Learner. The *chef d'équipe* was Robin Leyland, who farms at Oakham and has wide experience as a competitor and is so good with the young.

As in Rome, the opening day's competitions were comprised of one for newcomers to the Championships and one for previous competitors. Michael Mac, who was a 1979 'veteran', qualified for the barrage in the second class, and was well up on time but failed to achieve a second clear, finishing second to Philippe Rozier of France who had the only double clear round on Fetiche d'Armor.

The competition for the first-timers was held over a small course and nine went clear, with Jane Sargeant and Ladiesman eventually finishing fourth.

The first leg of the individual championship took place on the following day, still on faults and time over a small course, but one with more problems for riders to solve. Of forty-eight starters fifteen went clear, and they, together with one who incurred a time fault and a further eleven with 4 faults, went on to the second round on the final day. Jane Sargeant and Michael Mac were both clear, the former finishing second to Guido Flass of West Germany on Minus, the latter finishing fifth.

On the third day, the British team of Michael Mac, Jane

Sargeant, Zoe Bates and Mark Heffer was drawn first over a longer course. Michael went well clear, Mark picked up 8¼ faults, Zoe had a fence down, and Ladiesman had 8½, so Britain's first-round score was 12¼; Belgium, France, West Germany, Ireland and the Netherlands had 4 and Italy was on 8.

In the second round the British team was assisted by the fact that some of the fences were raised and widened and the horses felt that they had at last something to jump. Michael achieved his second clear, Zoe and Jane were clear as well and Mark had just 4, which gave Britain a second-round total of zero and a final score of 12¼. But France too had three second-round clears to capture the title beyond all doubt. The Netherlands won the silver medal on 8 and West Germany and Belgium each finished on 12. The Germans won the bronze medal after a jump-off.

On the final day, the second leg of the individual championship took place over the biggest track of the meeting, and from a field of twenty-seven, only four who had gone clear the first time were able to retain their status — among them, Jane and Michael.

Caterina Vachelli from Italy on Edelweiss jumped-off first and was clear again in 47.07 secs. Then Danny van der Bossche of Belgium on Asco had two down in trying to match the time. Michael and Persian Shah were splendidly clear again in 36.45 secs to win. Jane's clear round was in 39.61 secs for second place, and Caterina Vachelli was third. With their previous placings, Michael and Jane were also leading boy and girl riders respectively.

Junior European Dressage Championships
(12–14 September 1980)
Britain did not this year send a team to the Junior European Championships in Germany, but seventeen-year-old Karen Ruggles from Hampshire competed as an individual on her horse, Kanzler, and finished very creditably in eighteenth place.

She had qualified at all the national championships and won the final of the Spillers novice dressage with jumping championship at the Horse of the Year show riding Lord Richard.

Dressage *per se* has never been a British enthusiasm and, as long as foxhunting continues (and long may it) to delight and thrill all ages of horsemen and women from eight to eighty, I doubt that it ever will.

21

Encouraging the Young

In 1977 Pat Bowman, head of public relations for Lloyds Bank, discussed with Anne, Duchess of Rutland, the then chairman of the National Pony Society, and Raymond Brooks-Ward of British Equestrian Promotions the possibility of promoting some form of educational activity for young people in the horse world. They came up with the Lloyds Bank Young Judge of the Year competition.

The first stage was arranged in conjunction with *Pony* magazine. In January, 1978, they published a selection of eight photographs of native ponies, and competitors were invited to identify them and to write, in not more than forty words, which was their favourite breed, and why. Those who identified the breeds correctly would have their entries judged by Anne, Duchess of Rutland, chairman of the National Pony Society Council, and Richard Meade.

From an entry of over five hundred, only three correct ones were received — from thirteen-year-old Nicola Furness from Berwick-on-Tweed and from two boys, thirteen-year-old James Carter from Newbury and Nigel Hollings, seventeen, from Blackburn. The judges then examined the written statements of a number who had correctly identified seven ponies, and selected a further seven to go forward to the second stage. The identification of the ponies was deliberately hampered by the inclusion of two Dartmoors and the exclusion of any Welsh ponies. Nicola, however, was able to take advantage of the fact that she has always lived among Dartmoors, which her parents breed.

The second stage of the competition took place at the Royal Windsor show, where the owners of nine native ponies kindly made their animals available for judging by the competitors. Mrs Miles Staveley, whose husband was president of the National Pony Society, and whose mother, Mrs Molly Cail, bred so many outstanding young hunters while she herself bred

Welsh and riding ponies, judged on the same lines as the Young Farmers' Club stock judging competitions, and interviewed each entrant.

Competitors were asked to write down the order in which they would place the nine ponies in a mixed mountain and moorland class and to give their reasons for doing so. The main essential was to look at each pony individually, decide whether or not it was a first-class representative of its breed, then judge the class and place the ponies accordingly. Although Nicola had placed them in reverse order to that which the judge would have done, her reasons were so good that without hesitation she was deemed the winner and presented with the Bank's trophy and other prizes by Richard Meade.

As Lloyds Bank Young Judge of the Year she was then invited with her parents to attend the National Pony Society show at Malvern three months later, where she acted as a probationer judge and joined Mrs David Bourne in judging the qualifying round of the Lloyds Bank In-Hand Championship. Their selection, Miss Elspeth Ferguson's Rosevean Eagle's Hill, then three years old, went on to win the supreme title at the Horse of the Year show.

The object of the competition was to encourage new probationer judges, to promote interest in ponies and a greater understanding of the points of a pony. The sponsors were delighted by the interest shown and the high standard of knowledge of the prizewinners – a standard of knowledge concerning conformation that is uniquely British, one might add.

The success of the first competition led to its establishment as a regular annual event in the NPS calendar. Following the same general pattern, but with a more difficult photographic test in *Pony* in which entrants had to identify common faults and malformations, the 1979 competition was judged by Jane Holderness-Roddam and Anne, Duchess of Rutland. The ten finalists were assessed at the Royal Windsor show by Mrs David Bourne who chose as winner Susan Esau, fourteen, of Bideford.

Susan, whose achievement was all the greater because she does not come from a family background of horses, is a member of the Stevenstone and Torrington Farmers Hunt branch of the

Pony Club. She, too, went on to stand as a probationer judge for the qualifying round of the Lloyds Bank In-Hand Championship at the National Pony Show.

In 1980 the competition was judged by Mrs Joanna McInnes, of the NPS, and Susan King, presenter of the television programme *Horses Galore*. This time the young entrants were faced with the problem of identifying the breeds of mountain and moorland ponies from photographs of their heads only, and then matching the correct head to one photograph of hindquarters.

The final was held at the National Pony Show and the ten young experts were examined by Mrs Frank Furness, who selected Alison Blake, sixteen, of Bournemouth as the third Lloyds Bank Young Judge of the Year. Alison, who is a member of West Hants Pony Club and Bournemouth and West Hants Horse Society, also stood in on the judging of the In-Hand Championship qualifier at the show and was the Bank's guest at the final at the Horse of the Year show.

In 1979, Lloyds Bank and the NPS started another project along the same lines: the Pony-Judging Study Day, held at the British Equestrian Centre at Stoneleigh in September. It was an extension of the Young Judges' theme, which it took a step further, with lectures by a panel of experts and a selection of top-class animals on hand to illustrate various points.

A lecture was first given on conformation and movement by Mrs Nigel Pease, one of the few judges who has ridden champion hunters and hacks and bred and exhibited countless pony champions. Daughter of Colonel John Smith-Maxwell, late hunting correspondent to *The Field*, her Lemington Stud has been at the top for a great many years, breeding riding and working hunter ponies who could do a job of work. She illustrated her talk with the help of a brown mare who she wished to remain anonymous but was a good sort, if not a top show animal.

Mr P.R. Hastie, the Buckinghamshire veterinary surgeon, came next, illustrating his lecture on blemishes and unsoundness with diagrams drawn on a blackboard and with another live exhibit. Both speakers emphasised the prime importance of good conformation to the ability to remain sound.

Then followed talks on mountain and moorland breeds,

working hunter ponies and riding ponies, all with live exhibits drawn from top studs, thanks to the generosity of their owners. Robin Gosling talked about Shetlands, Mr T.W. Gwyn-Price about Welsh breeds, Mrs R.M. Taylor about Highlands, New Forests and Dartmoors, Peter Dean on Exmoors, Pat Lyne on Connemaras, Mrs E. Ball on Fell ponies and Mrs Miles Staveley on ponies from the Dales.

Mrs Pease returned to discuss working ponies, illustrated by Mr Tom Hunnable's highly successful Toyd Bewildered, and riding ponies, with Miss Elspeth Ferguson's Rosevean Eagle's Hill as the paramount example. During question time, all the ponies came back into the ring together. The point was made that these are our breeding stock, a priceless heritage left to us by generations who knew a great deal more than most of those who are striving to follow in their footsteps today. Ponies were put on earth to be ridden, driven and enjoyed, and if they cannot stay sound and perform these duties they are of little use, however beautiful, for 'handsome is as handsome does'.

A second Lloyds Bank Pony Judging Study Day took place at the British Equestrian Centre at Stoneleigh in September 1980.

It began with a lecture/demonstration by Mrs Nigel Pease on the schooling and preparation of a pony for ridden mountain and moorland classes.

Next, Mrs Frank Furness, wife of the past president of the NPS, illustrated, with a commentary, the judging of a mixed mountain and moorland ridden class. She is strongly involved with the educational work of the NPS and with the Stud Assistants' Diploma examinations.

Finally, after the luncheon interval, Mrs I.M. Yeomans presented a lecture/demonstration on showing in hand. She has, of course, a worldwide reputation as a breeder and judge of thoroughbreds and ponies, both riding and native, and is well-known for being the first show commentator just after the war.

These are the people, with their rich fund of experience, who can pass on to the young the knowledge that they have acquired over the years. How lucky we are that they are willing, indeed anxious, to do so, so that it is not lost to succeeding generations.

Lloyds Bank is helping to ensure that the standard of the best ponies in the world does not decline because future generations of judges are not possessed of sufficient knowledge to put up only the best as a criterion for breeders. It seems likely that the study day will be an annual NPS fixture.

In 1980 another pioneering departure undertaken by the Bank was the sponsorship of the Young Instructor of the Year awards, whose aim is the encouragement of young professional instructors to advance their standards of training, to help plan their careers and to provide them with some financial assistance towards continuation training.

Four promising young British Horse Society Assistant Instructors and four Intermediate Instructors from all over the country benefited from the seven-day course held at the British Equestrian Centre from 17th–23rd May. At the end of the course, each student was awarded a training bursary varying from £250 for the top student, £150 for the second, £100 for the third and £50 apiece for the next five.

Lloyds Bank already sponsor the BHS *Training for a Career* leaflet, of which 10,000 copies are issued from the training and examinations office each year.

The Young Instructor of the Year award in 1980 went to Susan Nevill-Parker, aged twenty-three, of Weston House, Pembridge, Leominster, Herefordshire. Susan achieved her Intermediate Instructor's exam in 1978 and became a List VI dressage judge at the same time. Since July 1977 she has worked from home, teaching riders of all ages and ability. Chief instructor for the Radnor and West Hereford branch of the Pony Club, she coaches the team for inter-branch competitions, teaches at camps and rallies of other branches, and schools horses for other people. She also competes in dressage, show-jumping and eventing and has three horses: one just broken; one a novice event horse; and a third which has attained the Advanced category.

In second place came Duncan S. Smith, aged twenty, from Mount Pleasant Farm, Yardley Gobion, Towcester, Northamptonshire. Formerly an active member of both Pony Club and Riding Club, after taking the two-year BHSAI course at Newark Technical College he passed the AI exam in 1977 and afterwards worked in a number of yards to gain practical experience with the emphasis on teaching. As a result of his dedication he

Sue Nevill-Parker, the 1980 Young Instructor of the Year, receiving her Lloyds Bank trophy from Sir Daniel Pettit, chairman of the Bank's Birmingham and West Midlands regional board. (*Findlay Davidson*)

saved sufficient money to go the The Wirral, where he gained his BHS Intermediate examination. He is now at the Newark Equestrian Centre where he schools young horses and is aiming for the BHSI exam.

The third-placed student, twenty-one-year-old Greer Hendry of Peters Muir House, Haddington, East Lothian, passed all her Pony Club exams as well as those for Grade IV and the BHSAI and BHS Intermediate certificates. She runs her own small yard of approximately fourteen horses, all of them top eventers and showjumpers. She instructs in dressage, showjumping and cross-country and in the summer spends from four to six weeks instructing at Pony Club camps. A keen follower to hounds and a regular competitor in hunter trials, BHS events and show-jumping competitions, she has ridden all her life.

Just how good an instructor she is was demonstrated shortly after when the East Lothian Pony Club teams came second in the showjumping and equal seventh in the horse trials in the championships at Stoneleigh. Greer trained both teams and at twenty-one is little older than the members she guided so well.

The latest sponsorship for young people is the Lloyds Bank Equestrian Year Scholarship, devised by Alan Smith, editor of *Equestrian Year*. The scholarship takes the form of a £500 training grant to help a promising rider under twenty-one who has shown special ability in dressage, horse trials or show jumping to gain further experience.

The first winner was Karen Ruggles, seventeen, of Ringwood, Hants, who was selected on the basis of her outstanding dressage work. She qualified for five classes of the national championships and was chosen by the BHS as the only rider of high enough standard to go to the European Junior Championships with her horse Kanzler.

Karen, who is trained by her mother, decided to use her prize to buy video equipment so that she can analyse her own performance.

22

The Lloyds Bank In-Hand Championship

During the 1960s there used to be held an in-hand championship for horses and ponies which was sponsored by Fredericks Limited and based on the lines of the best-in-show award for breed champions at Crufts. It always evoked a good deal of controversy and criticism, on the grounds of the near-impossibility of comparing a Shetland pony stallion, for instance, with a Thoroughbred brood mare, and it foundered and eventually died.

Among those who regretted its demise was Lord Kenyon, a director of Lloyds Bank and chairman of their North-Western Regional Board, as well as chairman since 1963 of the Welsh Pony and Cob Society.

Formerly a foxhunter with Sir Watkin Williams-Wynn (The Wynnstay) Hounds, when his eyesight became too bad to continue, he decided, rather than let grass grow in the stable yard, to breed Welsh ponies, in which he had an inherited interest from his mother. Starting in 1946 he developed the Gredington stud at his family home near Whitchurch, which is now being demolished three hundred years after it was built.

One of his first stallions was the red roan Criban Victor, bought as a three-year-old in 1946, little dreaming how great a champion he would become. A pony of true Welsh type, he was one of the best-natured horses imaginable and so kind, both in the stable and out of it, that even a child could manage him. He was always handled by Gordon Jones, whose father, John Jones, was Miss 'Daisy' Brodrick's stud groom when she started the Coed Coch Stud in 1926.

Criban Victor sired many good ponies and was himself a consistent champion in the show ring: at the Royal Welsh in 1947, 1958-60 and in 1964; at the Ponies of Britain Show 1959-62 and 1965-66; and at the National Pony Society Show

Lord Kenyon's superb Welsh section A stallion, Coed Coch Planed.

in 1956, 1959 and 1960. At the ripe old age of twenty-five he was section B champion and reserve supreme champion at the North Wales Association show at Caernarvon.

Five years later he developed an arthritic shoulder and was put down for humane reasons. He was followed by two section A stallions, Coed Coch Planed (foaled in 1952, by Coed Coch Madog out of Coed Coch Pelen by Tregoyd Starlight) and the homebred Gredington Simwnt, who qualified at the Royal and was third in the Wembley final in 1978. A top mare, Coed Coch Symwl, was bought at Miss Brodrick's reduction sale in 1936 for the then record price of 1100 guineas.

Lord Kenyon thought that the idea of an in-hand championship should be revived, and conceived a new approach. He says: 'I decided that, to succeed, it should have a far wider franchise.

Welsh section A stallion, Gredington Simwnt, homebred by Lord Kenyon at his Gredington stud.

It was widened in scope to take in nine shows and include horses and ponies of every category, except heavy horses.'

Lloyds Bank was persuaded to take over the sponsorship and the championship, which has grown over the years to cover seventeen shows, leading to the final at the Horse of the Year show, is not only now recognised as the premier event of its kind in the country, but formed the basis of the Bank's current programme of horse sponsorships.

The aim of the championship is defined clearly: to find the supreme in-hand pony or light horse in any one year, based on rounds at shows where winners of in-hand classes are eligible to go forward to the qualifier.

From the start, it has always presented even the most experienced judge with a challenge: comparing unlikes is never easy and to decide between quality animals which is the best representative of its breed or type can be a daunting task.

Nowadays not only have many of our top judges found their

own ways to tackle this problem, but there is great enthusiasm among breeders to get through to the Wembley final. A side benefit that was not envisaged by the sponsor is that breeders, who were often segregated into esoteric little groups, have now got to know one another in a thoroughly friendly, although keenly contested competition.

It brings together those who breed hunters, Arabs, Cleveland Bays and others, riding ponies and all nine native breeds of ponies with their ramifications. The Welsh, for example, have sections A (Welsh mountain), B (riding pony, a hand bigger), C (ponies of cob type), and D (cobs). Arabs, too, are subdivided — into pure-bred, part-bred and Anglo-Arabs (Thoroughbred crosses).

The breeders, whether they go in for hardy native ponies or Thoroughbreds, are themselves a special type of person. They are content to bide their time, philosophical in the face of disappointment, resigned to occasional bad luck, happy to work hard, quick to note and to remedy failing condition, good husbandmen and horsemasters, and indeed much more.

Whether one meets them on the showgrounds of the British Isles or at the party which Lloyds Bank gives to the finalists at the Horse of the Year show, the breeders of our horses and ponies are as much a source for pride as are the animals they produce — usually for little reward. Breeding is a way of life rather than a means of livelihood, but there are few occupations so satisfying.

At the 1980 Horse of the Year show at Wembley, Mrs I. M. Yeomans and Colonel C. R. (Dick) Spencer, representing the pony world and the hunter world respectively, dealt first with the nine ponies. There were four brood mares present, the highest-placed of whom was Miss Sage's sixteen-year-old Daldorn Charmaine, who finished third. Mrs Edward House's Shetland stallion, the seven-year-old Bincombe Venture, was given reserve place, and the winning animal in this section was Llanarth Flying Comet, a twelve-year-old black Welsh cob stallion, owned by the Llanarth Stud, University College of Wales.

There were eight finalists in the horse section, three of which were brood mares, including Sam Luxton's thoroughbred mare Cheal Rose, who qualified at the National Hunter Show where

Llanarth Flying Comet, Supreme Champion in the 1980 Lloyds Bank
In-Hand Championship. (*Leslie Lane*)

she was champion mare. Colonel and Mrs R. N. Crossley's
Cuillin Hills was placed reserve, with Sam Luxton's other
finalist, The Doper, in first place.

Then came the most difficult part of this championship for
the judges — when the first two animals in each section are
judged against each other to determine the Supreme Champion.
Victory went to the defending champion, Llanarth Flying
Comet, whose action pulverises the opposition in the very best
tradition. Comet is the only animal ever to have carried off the
title of Supreme Champion in two successive years. The Doper
was awarded Reserve.

LLOYDS BANK IN-HAND CHAMPIONSHIP: QUALIFYING ROUNDS 1980

Show	Winning Owner	Qualifier	Reserve Owner	Reserve
Newark & Notts (May 2)	Miss S. P. Sage Trelawn Stud Samsons Lodge Farm Aldham Hadleigh, Suffolk	Daldorn Charmaine chesnut riding pony brood mare	Mrs G. S. Trimingham The Grange Arabian Stud Carrington Boston Lincs	Riaz 6-year-old pure-bred liver Arab stallion
Devon County (May 17)	S Luxton, Hele Barton Petrockstowe Okehampton Devon	The Doper 3-year-old chesnut hunter gelding	Mrs M. E. Mansfield Rotherwood Stud Nook Farm Ashby de la Zouch Leicestershire	Keston Royal Occasion 7-year-old chesnut Welsh stallion (section B)
Bath & West (May 30)	Mrs Dorian Williams Foscote Manor Buckingham Bucks	Wingrove Stormaway 10-year-old grey riding pony brood mare	Mr & Mrs R. J. Burrington Helwell Barton Kenton Devon	Bally Autrey 12-year-old bay hunter brood mare
Royal Cornwall (June 6)	Douglas Kellow Woodlands Farm Sweetshouse Bodmin Cornwall	Lillie Langtry 2-year-old bay thoroughbred filly	Mr & Mrs A. L. Masters St Lawrence Stud Farm Bodmin Cornwall	Twylands Fiesta pony brood mare (brown)
South of England (June 6)	Llanarth Stud University College of Wales Llanarth, Dyfed	Llanarth Flying Comet 12-year-old black Welsh cob stallion	Mrs C. Caffyn-Parsons Waverey Court Farm Monks Walk Farnham Surrey	Richmond Gay Fantasy 6-year-old bay brood mare

LLOYDS BANK IN-HAND CHAMPIONSHIP: QUALIFYING ROUNDS 1980 *continued*

Show	*Winning Owner*	*Qualifier*	*Reserve Owner*	*Reserve*
Three Counties (June 12)	Ian Thomas MVO Springfield Lodge Billerton Priors Warwickshire	**Lucky Strike II** 9-year-old brown hunter brood mare	Llanarth Stud University College of Wales Llanarth Dyfed	**Llanarth Meredith ap Braint** 11-year-old Welsh cob stallion
Essex Show (June 14)	Mrs D. E. M. Alexander Forge Farm Stud Ramsbury Marlborough Wilts	**Forge Celtic Air** 3-year-old bay pony gelding	J. Gardiner & Miss D. Golding 'Holmfield' Pilgrim's Way Trottiscliffe Maidstone, Kent	**Happy Rhapsody** 12-year-old bay pony brood mare
Royal Highland (June 18)	Mrs C. Sitwell Lennel Stud Coldstream Berwickshire	**Lennel Top Cat** brown yearling riding pony colt	Mr & Mrs Andrew McCowan Horncliffe Mains Berwick-upon-Tweed	**Free and Easy** 3-year-old chesnut hunter gelding
National Hunter Show (June 25)	Mr S. Luxton Hele Barton Petrockstowe Okehampton Devon	**Cheal Rose** 6-year-old brown thoroughbred brood mare	Creative Television Workshops c/o Far Poden Honeybourne Evesham, Worcs	**Keyston Kelly** 3-year-old thoroughbred gelding
Royal Norfolk (June 26)	Mrs M. E. Mansfield Rotherwood Stud Nook Farm Ashby-de-la-Zouch Leicestershire	**Trellech Giselle** bay pony brood mare	Mrs G. S. Trimingham The Grange Arabian Stud Carrington Boston, Lincs	**Riaz** 6-year-old pure-bred liver Arab stallion

LLOYDS BANK IN-HAND CHAMPIONSHIP: QUALIFYING ROUNDS 1980 *continued*

Show	Winning Owner	Qualifier	Reserve Owner	Reserve
Royal Show (July 3)	Miss S. A. Jeanes & Mr R. R. Mason East Lodge Farm Bromsgrove Worcestershire	**Royal Fiddler** 2-year-old chesnut hunter gelding	Mrs B. M. Morgan c/o Chancley Stud Glebe Farm Michaelchurch Escley, Hereford	**Beverley Jocelyn** 10-year-old bay pony brood mare
Great Yorkshire Show (July 10)	The Hon. Mrs R. N. Crossley Westfield Farm Malton N. Yorkshire	**Cuillin Hills** 13-year-old grey hunter brood mare	Mr & Mrs C. G. Furness Mordington House Berwick-upon-Tweed	**Crimchard Firefly** 7-year-old brown Dartmoor stallion
Kent County (July 11)	Mr M. Stimpson c/o The Poplars Wreningham Norfolk	**Red Ensign** 3-year-old chesnut hunter gelding	Mr & Mrs T. Armstrong The Glenfield Stud Great Oaks Farm Chiddingfold Godalming, Surrey	**Glenfield Chocolate Soldier** 9-year-old grey Welsh mountain pony stallion
East of England (July 17)	Miss J. B. Morgan 45 Slade Road Rugby Warwickshire	**Costock Choir Boy** 3-year-old bay riding pony gelding	Mr & Mrs D. A. Shirley c/o Hallemead House Shiplake Henley-on-Thames Oxon	**Jubilee March** 3-year-old brown hunter gelding
Royal Welsh (July 24)	Mr R. A. Swain Oakfields Church Stretton Salop	**Crossways Merle** 8-year-old grey Welsh mountain pony brood mare	Mrs T. Johns-Powell Sheepcourt Bonvilston Nr Cardiff, S.Glam	**Weston Glimpse** 9-year-old grey Welsh pony brood mare

LLOYDS BANK IN-HAND CHAMPIONSHIP: QUALIFYING ROUNDS 1980 *continued*

Show	Winning Owner	Qualifier	Reserve Owner	Reserve
Arab Horse Society Show (August 2)	Miss V. E. Bates Gunsite Stud Theobalds Park Waltham Cross Herts	**Theobalds Flying Colours** 5-year-old Anglo-Arab stallion	Mr G. Plaister Diana Lodge Collins Lane Purton Swindon, Wilts	**Zarafah** 2-year-old pure bred Arabian filly
National Pony Society Show (August 7)	Mrs E. W. House Bincombe Bridgwater Somerset	**Bincombe Venture** black Shetland stallion	The Rt Hon. Lord Kenyon CBE, LLD, DL Gredington Whitchurch Shropshire	**Gredington Judith** Welsh Mountain pony brood mare

LLOYDS BANK IN-HAND CHAMPIONSHIP: HORSE OF THE YEAR SHOW SUPREME CHAMPIONS

Year	Name	Age and breed	Qualifying Show	Owner	Breeder
1972	Fresco	3-year-old hunter gelding	Newark & Notts	Norman Crow Ercall Park High Ercall Telford, Salop	
1973	Whalton Ragtime	11-year-old pony brood mare	Royal Highland	Mr & Mrs J. C. Alton Manor Farm Hunsingore Wetherby, Yorks	
1974	Sammy Dasher	2-year-old hunter gelding	East of England	L. S. Ivens & Mrs P. Jackson Cuckoo Hill Farm Hanslope, Wolverton Milton Keynes	Mrs P. Jackson Laurels Farm Wappenham Towcester
1975	Clipston	3-year-old hunter gelding	Royal Cornwall	Mrs A. V. Ferguson 'Roscrea' Village du Putron St Peter Port Guernsey, CI	S. K. Spokes 'Nobold Stud' Clipston Northants
1976	Rosevean Eagle's Hill	Yearling pony colt	Royal Highland	Miss S. E. Ferguson Rose Vean Stud Bishampton Pershore, Worcs	Owner

LLOYDS BANK IN-HAND CHAMPIONSHIP: HORSE OF THE YEAR SHOW SUPREME CHAMPIONS *continued*

Year	Name	Age and breed	Qualifying Show	Owner	Breeder
1977	Three Wishes	3-year-old bay hunter filly	Royal Highland	Mr & Mrs A. McCowan Horncliffe Mains Berwick on Tweed Northumberland	Mr & Mrs Skinner Hillgrounds Stockland Honiton, Devon
1978	Rosevean Eagle's Hill	3-year-old riding pony colt	National Pony Society	Miss S. E. Ferguson Rose Vean Stud Bishampton Pershore, Worcs	Owner
1979	Llanarth Flying Comet	11-year-old black Welsh cob stallion	South of England	Llanarth Stud University College of Wales Llanarth Dyfed	Owner
1980	Llanarth Flying Comet	12-year-old black Welsh cob stallion	South of England	Llanarth Stud (address above)	Owner

23

Who's Who

Aly Adsetts (Great Britain)
Aly Pattinson came up through the show pony classes to ride in one-day events and the British junior team, as a dressage pupil of Mrs Marjorie Hance. In 1973 she won several trials on Olivia and Bleak Hills, and in 1974 she came right to the front when she rode Alex Colquhoun's Carawich to win the Midland Bank open championship at Cirencester. In 1975, also on Carawich, she achieved her biggest success to date, winning the Raleigh Trophy at the Burghley three-day event on Carawich from Captain Mark Phillips on Gretna Green and Richard Meade on Tommy Buck. Is now married and rides as Mrs Adsetts.

Major D. S. Allhusen (Great Britain)
Educated at Eton and Cambridge, he joined his father's regiment, the 9th Lancers. After the war he brought back from Germany two mares which cost £48 and £50. On the more expensive Laura he competed in the pentathlon at the 1948 Olympics in Switzerland, and on her daughter Laurien by Davy Jones, he joined the British team for the European three-day event championships of 1957 and helped win the title.

Riding Lochinvar, by Battleburn, bought in Ireland as a three-year-old, he was in the winning British team for the European championships of 1967 and 1969 and captained the team that won the Olympic gold medals in Mexico in 1968, in addition to winning the individual silver medal. Laurien, mated to the HIS premium stallion Happy Monarch, bred Laurieston, on whom Richard Meade was a member of the winning Olympic team in Munich in 1972, in addition to winning the individual gold medal.

Otto Ammermann (West Germany)
Born 1932 in Kleinensiel, Otto Ammermann has ridden since the age of ten. He was the West German three-day event

champion in 1969, bronze medallist in the German Championship 1971, and won the Champions' competition at Aachen in 1963 and the Grand Prix in 1964. He rode in the European three-day event championship at Luhmühlen in 1975, in the Montreal Olympic Games in 1976, where he was a member of the silver medal team. In 1977 he was also in the silver medal team in the European championships at Burghley, and in 1978 he helped to win another team silver medal in the world championships at Lexington, Kentucky. His usual mount is Volturno, an Oldenburger.

Colonel Sir Michael Picton Ansell (Great Britain)

Mike Ansell, whose determination to beat the foreigners at all costs sent the first British team into Europe in 1947, has many other claims to fame. Like his father before him, he commanded the 5th Royal Inniskilling Dragoon Guards. Before World War II, he hunted, played polo, rode racehorses, and was a member of the British showjumping team in the late 1930s, in addition to putting on a famous trick and activity ride at the same time.

Wounded early in the war, he was captured at St Valery and lost his sight as a result of war wounds and a prolonged period in a prisoner-of-war camp in Germany.

Repatriated, he became chairman of the British Show Jumping Association, in 1944, and held the chair for twenty-four years. He also served as chairman of the British Horse Society and of the British Equestrian Federation, which brought the two together in 1972, and is an honorary member of the Bureau of the FEI (International Equestrian Federation). From their post-war years until 1975, he directed both the Royal International and the Horse of the Year shows.

It is due to his inspired leadership that the sport of showjumping in Britain has flourished since 1946. He was responsible for the establishment of the National Equestrian Centre (now the British Equestrian Centre) at Stoneleigh, now the headquarters of both the BSJA and the BHS. A former High Sheriff of Devonshire, he was knighted in 1968 for his services to showjumping. In 1977 he was awarded the silver medal of the IOC (International Olympic Committee).

David Barker (Great Britain)
Born in 1935, the son of a hunting farmer from Yorkshire, David came on from the junior classes and in 1960 was a member of the British Olympic team in Rome riding Franco, a Thoroughbred former racehorse by Como, but was eliminated at the last fence. In 1962 he won the men's European championship in London on Andrew Massarella's Mister Softee, from Hans Gunter Winkler and Piero d'Inzeo, in a photo-finish for second place. David Barker now runs a stud and shows hunters successfully. He is joint Master of the Whaddon Chase and hunts to hounds.

Donald Beard (Great Britain)
Younger brother of highly successful professional showjumping rider, 'Curly' Beard, Don set up the first British high jump record at Olympia in 1937. Riding Swank for the late Fred Foster, he cleared 7ft 6¼ins, but it is worthy of note that after establishing the record, Swank was never much use again. Donald is married to the former Sylvia Massarella, of the famous Yorkshire showjumping family, and is a very successful farmer in the West Riding of Yorkshire.

Gilles Bertran de Balanda (France)
This well-known showjumper was born in 1950 and lives in the area famous for the French Thoroughbred, Chantilly. Horses are in his blood — his uncle was a leading rider and his grandfather, Capt. M. L. Bertran de Balanda, won the individual silver medal at the Amsterdam Olympics and later became a director of the French team. Gilles' best horse is the eight-year-old stallion, Galoubet A, one of fifteen he keeps at Meaux, 10km from Chantilly.

Harry Boldt (West Germany)
Born in 1930 in Insterburg, he is married with one child and has ridden from the age of twelve, instructed by his father, Heinrich Boldt. He won a gold medal for dressage in the 1966 German championships, a silver in 1967, another gold in 1973, a silver in 1974 and a bronze in 1975. In European championships he has won four team gold medals and four individual silver medals, in world championships two individual silver and two

team gold medals, and in the Olympic Games two individual silver and two team gold medals, in Tokyo and Montreal. At Goodwood in 1978 on Woycek he was one of the gold medallist team but only fifth individually.

Caroline Bradley MBE (Great Britain)
The world's leading, most distinguished and hard-working lady rider, Caroline first joined the British team in Dublin in 1966, aged twenty, winning on the Russian-bred Ivanovitch and on David Barker's former horse, Franco, on whom she was runner-up for the Grand Prix in New York the following year. In 1973 she rode True Lass, brought out as a novice by Harvey Smith, to be runner-up for the European title, in Vienna, and won the puissance in Nice on Archie Thomlinson's New Yorker. In 1974 he won her the puissance at the Horse of the Year show at Wembley – the first-ever lady rider to win this class.

In 1974 Caroline finished third in the last-ever women's world championship in La Baule, but because she took out a professional licence in 1973, following pressure from the Establishment, she has lost her chance of riding in the Olympic Games. In 1975 she became the second woman to win the Hamburg Jumping Derby, on New Yorker in 1977 she was second in six competitions at the Royal International and won the Leading Showjumper title at the Horse of the Year show on Marius. In 1978 she rode this Dutch horse to win the Queen Elizabeth II Cup and on the Grey Hannoverian, Tigre, won the Nice Grand Prix, and helped to win the World team championship in Aachen, besides winning the Rothmans Grand Prix of Canada in Calgary, Alberta. In 1979 she helped to win the European team championship on Tigre and clinched the Presidents Cup for Britain in the winning team at Calgary as well as being the leading rider at Wembley's Royal International, and the Tissot Grand Prix winner on Tigre in Paris, where she also, as at Hickstead, helped to win the Nations Cup. She won the Volvo World Cup Qualifier in Dublin in November, and the Queen Elizabeth Cup (again on Tigre) in 1980.

Hans Heinrich Brinckmann (West Germany)
A pre-war German cavalry officer who followed in his father's footsteps and was a successful international rider, 'Mickey'

Brinckmann is now one of the most outstanding course-builders in the world. The architect at Aachen, the West German CSIO, where the courses are renowned as the toughest, though fairest, in the world, he enhanced his reputation at the 1972 Olympic Games in Munich and at the 1978 World Championships.

David Broome OBE (Great Britain)

Born in Cardiff in 1940, David Broome won Olympic bronze medals in 1960 on Sunsalve, and in 1968 on Mister Softee; the European championships of 1961 in Aachen, on Sunsalve, and of 1967 and 1969 on Mister Softee; and the men's world championship in La Baule, in 1970, on Douglas Bunn's Beethoven. He has also won the King George V Cup on no less than four occasions.

His first good horse was Wildfire, a King's Troop reject bought by his father, Fred Broome, for £75. He rode him to be leading money-winner of the year in 1959, when he was nineteen, and he topped the list again two years later with the Argentinian Olympic horse, Discutido. In addition, he won a great many competitions with Ballan Silver Knight and Bess, but he had to borrow Jacopo from his brother-in-law, Ted Edgar, to ride in the 1964 Olympics in Tokyo.

At the end of 1965 he took over John Massarella's Mister Softee and his fortunes changed dramatically. In 1966 they won the King George V Cup, and, in addition to two more European titles and an Olympic bronze medal, this great horse won him the British Jumping Derby at Hickstead.

In La Baule, in 1970, he won a hard-fought contest for the men's world title, the most difficult part of which was riding Mancinelli's headstrong German-bred Fidux. Having ridden in his fourth Olympic Games in Munich in 1972, when Manhattan proved an unworthy partner, he turned professional in 1973, riding four horses leased to the Esso Petroleum Company. The contract was not renewed in 1974, due to the oil crisis in the Middle East, but David still did well enough soldiering on without a sponsor. He was second to Rodney Jenkins in the American Grand Prix in San Diego, and won the Benson and Hedges professional championship in Cardiff and the individual championships in New York and Toronto.

In 1975, sponsored by Phil Harris of Harris Carpets, he had a brilliant season and won no fewer than seven competitions at the Horse of the Year show at Wembley with the American-bred Philco, Sportsman and Heatwave. And on Heatwave, who had never before competed in a Nations Cup, he jumped the crucial round to give Britain victory in the Prince of Wales Cup at Hickstead, and again in the Aga Khan Trophy in Dublin. In 1976 he won many good competitions abroad and was the star of the Royal International at Wembley, taking the Saddle of Honour as leading rider, having won the Philip Cornes Champion Horseman and the *Daily Mail* Cup, on Sportsman. In 1977 he was the leading rider at the Royal International and Britain's top rider once again. In 1978 he was in the team to win the world championship in Aachen and was again the leading rider at the Royal International, while Heatwave (Tabac Original) won the Irish Horse Board's special award as the leading Irish-bred international horse. In 1979 he helped to win the European team championship in Rotterdam on Queensway Big Q and won the Irish Grand Prix at Dublin on Sportsman, as well as assisting British team victories at Paris, Hickstead and Dublin. He also won the Netherlands Grand Prix, on Big Q, and the Amsterdam Grand Prix, on Sportsman. In 1980 he won the Professional Championship in Cardiff.

William Brown (USA)
From South Salem, New York, William 'Buddy' Brown joined the US team at eighteen, in 1974. A year later he won an individual silver medal in the Pan-American Games.

His best horse, the grey A Little Bit, was loaned to the team by his parents, Mr and Mrs William Brown. A former racehorse, who won a race on the West Coast only seven months before coming to Europe, as a six-year-old, in 1974, he won in England and in Dublin. Buddy also did well on his parents' chesnut seven-year-old, Sandsablaze, who had three seasons campaigning at home before joining the team. In the 1978 world championships in Aachen, he had the misfortune of his horse Viscount breaking down, but he was in the team which won the bronze medals.

Douglas Bunn (Great Britain)
Douglas Bunn's contribution to showjumping has been, and is,

inestimable. After Cambridge he was called to the Bar, but in his spare time he joined the British team, having started his sporting career before the war as a child rider, and rode in many international shows. It was then that he realised how great a disadvantage British horses and riders laboured under without the benefit of an international arena, with permanent obstacles, at their disposal.

In 1960 he opened, at his home at Hickstead in Sussex, the All England Jumping Course, enlisting in 1961 the support of W. D. & H. O. Wills, which has continued so generously ever since, and the beginnings of Hickstead marked a renaissance in the fortunes of the British showjumping team. Also in 1961, and again with the help of Wills, he put on the most richly endowed showjumping championship in the world, the British Jumping Derby. It carried stakes of £6,000 and was contested over 16 fences, including the Derby Bank with its 10ft 6in drop, and it set the seal on Hickstead's success. This was underlined when it was the setting for two junior European championships, one ladies' European, a ladies' world, and, in 1974, the men's world championship.

Douglas Bunn's best horse was the brown Irish gelding, Beethoven, bred in Ireland, by Roi d'Egypte out of a draught mare, bought from Jack Bamber of Ballymena in 1961. Narrowly beaten for the King George V Cup four years later, he won the Grand Prix in Toronto and carried David Broome to victory in the men's world championship of 1970 in La Baule. Douglas Bunn was chairman of the BSJA in 1969.

Commandant Ned Campion (Ireland)

Born in 1937, Ned Campion hails from Co. Tipperary but now lives with his wife and family in Co. Dublin. He joined the Irish Army equitation team at McKee Barracks, Phoenix Park, in 1958, and rode in his first international show three years later. He has won in London, New York, Vienna, Nice, Rome, and Ostend and was leading rider in Nice in 1967. His most successful horse was the chesnut mare Garrai Eoin, by Candelabra, bought from her breeder, the late Lady Daresbury, in 1962. Garrai Eoin died in the winter of 1975–6 and was replaced by the promising Sliabh Na mBan. He is now *chef d'équipe* of the Irish team.

Frank and Mary Chapot (USA)

Born in New Jersey in 1934, Frank Chapot joined the United States equestrian team in 1956 and became its captain when Bill Steinkraus retired in 1973. In Rome, during the 1960 Olympic Games, he rode Trail Guide helped to win the team silver medal. From 1961 until the horse was retired, he rode the giant 17.3 chestnut Thoroughbred, San Lucas, winning grand prix and puissance competitions at the leading shows, in addition to being a cornerstone of the team itself. He was equal third in the men's world championship in 1974 at Hickstead on Main Spring, and rode him to win the King George V Cup in the same year, having won an Olympic team silver medal, on White Lightning, two years earlier in Munich. He captained the USA Olympic showjumping team in Montreal, and is now concerned with its administration.

In 1965 he married Mary Mairs, from California, already a successful international rider in her own right. On her chestnut mare Tomboy, she rode in the 1963 Olympics and in London that same year won the John Player Trophy for the Grand Prix, the Saddle of Honour, and the Loriners Cup, for points gained on two horses. In 1968, on White Lightning, she won the Queen Elizabeth II Cup, the first American to do so. She was only eighteen when she joined the team in 1962, and the following year she was the first American rider ever to win a gold medal at the Pan American Games in São Paulo.

Lorna Clarke (Great Britain)

Winner of the mini-Olympics at Munich in the autumn of 1971 on Peer Gynt, Lorna Sutherland, as she then was, first rode to fame when she won the Burghley three-day event on her skewbald cob, Popadom, in 1967. Since then she has been a consistent trials winner on horses such as Nicholas Nickleby and Peer Gynt, foaled in 1962, by The Admiral out of Foggy Morn. Lorna competed in the world championships at Punchestown as an individual on Popadom in 1970. At Badminton that year she rode three horses, rivalling the record of the Australian captain, Bill Roycroft. With Peer Gynt, she was shortlisted for the 1972 Olympics and went as a reserve, and in 1973 won at Boekelo in the Netherlands. After taking a sabbatical after her marriage, she staged a comeback and won Burghley again in 1978 on Greco.

Tad Coffin (USA)

Winner of the Olympic three-day event gold medal, riding the twelve-year-old Thoroughbred mare, Ballycor, Tad (Edmund) Coffin is a twenty-five-year-old rider who lives in Vermont, just south of the Canadian border — thus Bromont, where he gained his great victory, was almost a local show for him. He also won the gold medal at the Pan American Games the previous year, 1975, when he joined the US three-day event team. In 1977 he finished fifth at Ledyard, and in 1978 he was in the US world championship team which finished second in Lexington.

Chris Collins (Great Britain)

Chris Collins, who started his equestrian life riding steeplechasers and won the famous Pardubice 'Chase in Czechoslovakia, first joined the British team in 1974 for the world championships at Burghley, riding his Irish-bred brown gelding Smokey VI. In 1977 they were in the team which won the European championship at Burghley, and in 1978 they competed in the world championships at Lexington, Kentucky, as members of the British team. In 1979 he rode Gamble for the British team in the European championships in Luhmühlen, West Germany, when the team won the silver medal. In 1980 he was appointed chairman of the Horse Trials Selection Committee.

Captain The Hon. Patrick Conolly-Carew (Ireland)

Patrick Conolly-Carew rode in many three-day events while serving in the Royal Horse Guards, and is now a very successful *chef d'équipe* to the Irish three-day event team.

Colonel Dan Corry (Ireland)

Dan Corry rode with the Irish Army jumping team for over thirty years and became its captain. Won many big prizes all over Europe and the United States. Is a frequent visitor to English shows where he is in great demand as a judge of the show classes and an international jumping judge.

Frédéric Cottier (France)

Born in 1954. He has an outstanding horse in Flambeau C and helped to win five Nations Cups in 1980 to give France the Presidents Cup for the first time.

Paul Darragh (Ireland)

The son of a doctor from Co. Kildare, Paul Darragh has always wanted to ride showjumpers as a career, and he spent a season in England with Trevor Banks to learn all he could about the game, returning to Ireland to join Iris Kellett, for whom he rode Pele to win the British Jumping Derby at Hickstead in 1975. Now he rides Carrolls Heather Honey, who was his mount in the world championships in Aachen in 1978, and changed hands for a mere £60 when bought by her owner, due to her disconcerting habit of going into reverse gear when asked to go forward. In 1979 they were members of the winning Aga Khan Cup team in Dublin for the third successive year.

Bruce Davidson (USA)

Bruce Davidson, a member of the United States team that won the team silver at the 1972 Olympics, became the world three-day event champion at Burghley in 1974, riding Irish Cap. Born in 1950 in New England, of Scottish and Irish stock, he started riding when he was six. At his public school in Baltimore, Maryland, he was captain of riding for three years, and he has hunted since he was nine or ten.

He and his wife Carol — they married early in January 1974 — met at the United States equestrian team training centre at Gladstone, New Jersey. The daughter of Mrs John D. Hannum, Master of Mr Stewart's Cheshire Foxhounds in Pennyslvania, she was shortlisted for the Olympic team in 1968 and rode Paddy to be the top horse in the United States in 1972. On their return from a season in England in 1974, they moved to their own farm in Pennsylvania to breed and produce event horses.

Bruce rode the veteran Plain Sailing in the 1972 Olympics, but his individual successes have been gained on Irish Cap, an Irish horse he bought in Ohio. On him he competed at Badminton, finishing third, and won at Ermington; he also won at Bramham Park, riding Paddy. In 1975 he rode Roger Haller's English-bred Golden Griffin to win the Ledyard Farm trials in

Massachusetts, and the Pan American team and individual gold medals in Mexico. In 1976 he helped his team to win the Olympic gold medals. In Lexington, Kentucky, he retained his world title in 1978 riding the big grey Thoroughbred, Might Tango.

James Day (Canada)

Jim Day, who won the individual gold medal at the 1967 Pan-American Games when he was only twenty-one, did even better the following year in Mexico. Riding his big chesnut Canadian Club, who was then only eight years old and is one of the best horses that Canada has ever produced, he was one of the team which won the Olympic gold medal. Jim is son of a famous horseman, Dick Day of Aurora, who has trained and produced many good hunters and jumpers, and his mother is also a well-known judge. Is married to the former Janet Burns, whose father, Charles Burns, owns the winner of the 1969 Grand National, Highland Wedding.

Jim won the North American Junior Championship in 1964 and joined the Canadian team in the same year, winning the international championship in Harrisburg. In 1975, he was runner-up to Virginia Holgate in the Montreal mini-Olympics three-day event, and in the 1976 Olympics he made history by riding for both the Canadian three-day and showjumping Olympic teams.

Norman dello Joio (USA)

Born in 1957, showjumper Norman dello Joio comes from South Salem, New York. He was third in the first World Cup in Gothenburg in 1979, on Allegro. He won at Hickstead and Wembley in 1980, on Johnny's Pocket.

Bertalan de Nemethy (USA)

Hungarian-born Bertalan de Nemethy, a former cavalry instructor, is a naturalised American who was appointed coach to the United States Equestrian Team's Prix des Nations squad in 1955 and has officiated in that capacity ever since. Was a member of the Hungarian Olympic team for the 1940 Games, which were cancelled due to the war, but he has coached five American Olympic contingents, and his team has won the Presidents Cup on two occasions. His products won the silver medal in Rome in 1960 and one of his riders, Bill Steinkraus, won the individual gold medal in Mexico City. 'Bert' operates from the team centre at Gladstone, New Jersey, where he spends a lot of time training young horses and young riders. In 1980 he built the World Cup courses in Baltimore and his team won the Aga Khan trophy in Dublin.

Colonel Piero d'Inzeo (Italy)

Born in 1923. The elder of the two brilliant Italian brothers, sons of a rough-riding sergeant in the Italian cavalry, Constante d'Inzeo. Piero rode from boyhood and joined the army as an officer cadet. He passed out in 1946 and has spent most of his life in finding, training, and riding showjumpers. First came to the fore in the early 1950s and in 1956 helped to win a team silver with an individual bronze medal in the Olympic Games in Stockholm on Uruguay. Won the men's European championship on Uruguay in 1959. In the Rome Olympics in 1960 he rode The Rock to a team bronze and individual silver. By 1964 he was a major, and on Sunbeam he helped Italy to win another bronze in Tokyo. Has won the King George V Gold Cup in London on three occasions. His best horses have been Irish with the exception of Uruguay, who was bred in France. The Rock, Sunbeam, and Ballyblack all came from Ireland, as did Red Fox, a former hunter winner in Dublin.

Piero d'Inzeo staged a great comeback in Rome in 1973, where he won four of the major competitions, including the Grand Prix, on his Olympic horse Easter Light. He rode in the 1976 Olympic Games. In 1977 he won on Pioneer in Tehran.

Lt-Colonel Raimondo d'Inzeo (Italy)

Born in 1925, Raimondo's life followed a different course from his brother's. Initially less keen on riding and less concerned with the classically correct style, he went to Rome University before he, too, joined the cavalry, transferring in 1950 to the mounted police, the famous Carabinieri.

Over the years his record has been better than his brother's, perhaps because he is endowed with a more competitive spirit, maybe because he establishes a real rapport with his horses and they all have complete confidence in his judgement. He has a fine Olympic record — a team and individual silver on Merano in 1956, a team bronze and an individual gold on Posillipo in 1960, and a team bronze on the same horse four years later. He won the world championship in 1956 on Merano and retained it four years later on Gowran Girl. The Quiet Man, Merano, Posillipo and Bellevue (all but Merano bred in Ireland) have been his best horses. For the future his hopes were pinned on the Italian-bred Fiorello and the Irish Gone Away, who like Piero's Red Fox is a former winning hunter in Dublin for Mrs Tom Morgan, Master of the West Waterford. But Fiorello, his Olympic horse in Munich, was still comparatively inexperienced, and having started favourite for the individual gold, did not come up to expectations. Afterwards he was sold to Dr Vittorio Orlandi, who rode him in the men's European championship at Hickstead in 1973. In 1974 Raimondo was leading rider in Rome and Dublin on Bellevue, then aged seventeen, but still going strong as he showed in 1975 in winning the rich Grand Prix at Dublin, where Raimondo was only narrowly beaten by Harvey Smith as the leading rider. In 1976 he went straight from the Montreal Olympics to Dublin where he won again on Bellevue. In 1977 he was second in the Shell Puissance at Dublin behind Eddie Macken on Kerrygold and in 1979 he was the joint winner on Stranger.

The Marquis Jean d'Orgeix (France)
Jean d'Orgeix, better known to his fellow competitors as 'Paqui', won the Olympic individual bronze medal on Sucre de Pomme at the 1948 Games at Wembley. Jean was a frequent visitor to London in the 1940s, both with Sucre de Pomme and another active little French-bred Anglo-Arab, Kama, but he then went to live in Cambodia and so left the sport. However, he later returned to his native land, and in 1973 was appointed coach to the French showjumping team, which won the Olympic gold medals in 1976.

Pierre d'Oriola (France)
Born in 1920, Pierre Jonquéres d'Oriola is the only double Olympic individual showjumping gold medallist. He won on Ali Baba in 1952 and on Lutteur B in 1964, when France also won the team silver medal. Has also won the men's world champion-

ship, on Pomone in Buenos Aires in 1966, besides finishing second and third in 1953 and 1954, and has won major competitions all over the world. D'Oriola runs a farm in the French Pyrenees and he and d'Orgeix were the first civilians to break into the hitherto entirely military French team after the war. On the mare L'Historiette he won the Grand Prix in Zurich in 1946, and he won the first post-war King George V Cup in London on Marquis III in 1947. He has achieved success with a truly remarkable number of horses — Marquis, Ali Baba, Virtuoso, Voulette, Arlequin, Lutteur, Gingembre, Nagir, Pomone, and many more.

Anneli Drummond-Hay (South Africa)
Born in 1937, a grand-daughter of the Duke of Hamilton, Anneli started her competitive riding life in horse trials — following in the footsteps of her sister Jane, now Mrs Timothy Whiteley, who was once second at Badminton. Anneli's first victory came at Burghley in 1961, a year after she had finished second at Badminton on Perhaps. She won Burghley on Merely-a-Monarch, a brown gelding by Happy Monarch out of a mare by Merely-a-Minor, and the following spring consolidated her position by winning well at Badminton on the same horse. A wish to ride in the Olympic Games, from which at this time women were debarred in the three-day event, led her then to switch her allegiance to showjumping, at which Merely-a-Monarch proved to be equally adept. He won the Imperial Cup at the Royal International Horse show during his first season over artificial fences and was later short-listed for the 1964 Olympic team. His owner then sold Monarch to Mr Robert Hanson on the understanding that Anneli should continue to ride him. But when the horse lost his form — due to physical causes — and was given for a brief period to David Broome, Anneli repurchased him and nursed him back to health and fitness. When he returned to the fray, Monarch was owned in partnership with Colonel Tom Greenhalgh. In 1967 he won the Grand Prix in Geneva and the following year Anneli won the ladies' European championship with him and Xanthos. In 1970 he won the Queen Elizabeth Cup. Xanthos, a little liver-chesnut horse who started life with Captain Brian Fanshawe in the Warwickshire Hunt stables, won both the Rome and the British

Jumping Derbies in 1969 and repeated his Rome triumph at Olgiata the following year. Married during the 1971–72 winter to Errol Wucherpfennig of South Africa, Anneli has pursued her highly successful riding career there.

Anton Ebben (Holland)
A businessman from Hilversum, Toni Ebben was a most success-ful rider in his mid-thirties, when he was a pupil of the late Colonel Jack Talbot-Ponsonby. His best horse was Kairouan, an Anglo-Normand by that famous sire of jumpers in France, Furioso. Having won his rider the Harringay Spurs at the Horse of the Year show for his consistency with his stable companion, the puissance horse Prins Ayax, Kairouan went on to win Grand Prix in many European shows and Toni Ebben was fortunate to replace him with Jumbo Design, who in 1977 was in the winning European championship team in Vienna.

Ted and Elizabeth Edgar (Great Britain)
Born in 1933, the son of Warwickshire farmer Tom Edgar, who was for many years the BSJA area representative, Ted started riding jumping ponies as a boy. He first joined the British team in Rotterdam in 1957 on Jane Summers, who was rescued from the knacker's in her youth for the sum of £5. She jumped two clear rounds in her first Nations Cup to give Britain victory by one quarter-fault. Ted won a lot of point-to-points in the West Midlands before he bought an ex-American rodeo horse, Uncle Max, from Neal Shapiro in 1968. Together these bombastic characters, eminently suited to one another, won the puissance at the Horse of the Year show shortly afterwards and in 1969 won the King George V Cup and the Leading Showjumper title event.

Elizabeth Edgar (née Broome) won the W. D. & H. O. Wills Young Riders' Championship at Hickstead during the first two years it was held, 1960 and 1961, on Ballan Excelsior and Bess. Then she took Bess into other international competitions until the mare (now retired to stud) was annexed by her brother, David.

Ted and Elizabeth are now riding a string of horses, nearly all of them German-bred, for the Everest Double Glazing company, and Ted joined the ranks of the new professionals in

1973. In partnership with Mr and Mrs David Kingsley of Everest, they have also founded the Everest Stud to breed and lease showjumping horses. In 1975, Elizabeth was very successful on Everest Maybe, including among her successes the ladies' national championship at Royal Windsor, and she won some good competitions in 1976, both at home and abroad. In 1977, a record year for both, Elizabeth won the Queen Elizabeth II Cup and was leading amateur in the Benson and Hedges Championships at Cardiff Castle, where Ted was leading professional. On the British team's North American tour of 1977 Liz won the Grand Prix in New York on Wallaby. In 1979 she won the Queen Elizabeth II Cup on Forever, a brilliant seven-year-old by a Thoroughbred son of the distinguished sire of jumpers Furioso (by Precipitation) out of a Hannoverian mare. In 1980 she declined to ride in the alternative Olympics and turned professional after being leading rider at the Royal Show.

James Elder (Canada)

Born in 1934, Jim Elder was the deciding factor in the Canadian showjumping team's Olympic victory in Mexico in 1968. His father, Robert Elder, was for very many years Master of the Toronto and North York Hunt, and brother Norman was in the Canadian Olympic three-day team in 1960 and 1968. Jim, president of a refrigeration company, won a team bronze medal in the Olympic three-day event in 1956 and was tenth individually in 1960. Eight years later he was riding showjumpers. He rode O'Malley, after two years' training, to win the international puissance as a six-year-old in Toronto, after which he was sold to the Yorkshire businessman, Robert Hanson. O'Malley was one of his four best horses, the others being Johnny Canuck, Pieces of Eight, and The Immigrant, who jumped the vital round to assure the Canadian Olympic victory in Mexico. In 1976 he was again in the Canadian team. In 1978 he rode the roan Wow to several high placings in European Grand Prix and in 1980 was a member of the gold medal team in the alternative Olympics in Rotterdam.

Alexander Evdokimov (USSR)

Winner of the European individual three-day event championship in 1973, riding the seven-year-old Thoroughbred stallion

Jeger in Kiev. Evdokimov was born in 1949 and brought up in the village of Khrenovskoye, the home of the famous state stud, as well as an equestrian sport centre. In 1964, when he was still at high school, he beat all the contenders for a place on the Soviet Union's Olympic team by winning the national championship. Though he was still a year too young to go to Tokyo, he did ride for his country in the Mexico Olympic Games in 1968.

John Fahey (Australia)
Born in 1943, John lost the individual Olympic bronze medal to Peter Robeson and Firecrest only after a final jump-off at the Tokyo Olympic Games in 1964. He was then riding Bonvale, who also took him to Mexico four years later and had the best score of all the Australian team. A year later Bonvale broke down and Fahey brought two new horses, Warwick III and The Red Baron, to tour British shows in 1972. Before leaving for home early in 1973, John Fahey sold Warwick to a nineteen-year-old rider from Exeter, Tony Newbery, who made him a top international horse.

Rowland Fernyhough (Great Britain)
A young rider who comes from Montgomeryshire (now Powys) in mid-Wales, Rowland's first major assignment when leaving the young rider category was to ride Mrs Brian Crago's grey Irish horse, Bouncer, in the British team at the 1976 Olympic Games in Montreal. He has also been very successful with Autumatic and Autocrat. He joined the senior team in 1973, having graduated from the junior. A farmer's son, he was born in 1955.

Graham Fletcher (Great Britain)
Born in 1951. Son of Yorkshire farmer Ken Fletcher from Thirsk, Graham was the brightest hope to come out of the county since Harvey Smith. He started on ponies and graduated to young riders, first coming to prominence on his own four-year-old, Buttevant Boy, and Joe Pullen's Talk of the North.

Had a meteoric rise to fame at the Horse of the Year show in 1970, winning the Cortina Crown for points gained throughout the show. Joined the British team in Rome, Fontainebleau, and

Aachen in 1971 and won the Dublin Grand Prix on Buttevant
Boy. Also won the Olympic trial at the British Timken Show
and was shortlisted for the British team at the end of the
season. He won the Aachen Grand Prix in 1975 on Buttevant
Boy, and rode Hideaway with the Olympic team in Montreal.
One of Britain's top Internationals, he won the Queensway
Masters in 1978. He is the brother-in-law of David Broome, who
married Elizabeth Fletcher, and the only rider of that vintage
and ability who is still amateur. He and his wife Karen have
twin daughters, born in 1979.

Thomas Gayford (Canada)

Major Gordon Gayford, who rode for Canada, blazed the trail
now followed by his son Tom, who was born in 1929 and
joined the team twenty years later. Like so many of his com-
patriots, Tom started in three-day events, riding in his first
Olympic trials at Helsinki in 1952 in the team managed by his
father. Both work for the same firm of stockbrokers in Toronto
and share a farm north of the city. A consistent winner in both
New York and Toronto on Blue Beau, who joined the team in
1955 and created a record by jumping with it for ten seasons.
Tom Gayford's finest hour came at the Mexico Olympic Games
in 1968, when he rode Big Dee to a team gold medal. In 1976
he built the Olympic courses in Bromont and Montreal and in
1980 was *chef d'équipe* to the victorious alternative Olympic
team.

Mary Gordon-Watson MBE (Great Britain)

Whose great horse Cornishman V was ridden by Richard Meade
in the winning British team for the Olympic three-day event in
Mexico in 1968, rode him herself at Haras du Pin in Normandy
a year later to win the European championship at the age of
eighteen. Then, in 1970, she rode him at Punchestown to take
the world title. Cornishman, who is by Golden Surprise, was
bred in Cornwall by David Moore out of a point-to-point mare.
Mary's father Brig. Mark Gordon-Watson bought him as a
newly-broken four-year-old, undaunted by the fact that the
horse bucked him off when he went to try him. In 1972,
Cornishman and Mary helped win the team gold medal in
Munich, the second of his great career. After his win at Liphook

in 1973, Cornishman was short-listed for the British team at the European championships in Kiev, but he developed a cough shortly before the final team trial at Osberton, keeping him out of the team. In October he competed as an individual in the Ledyard Farm three-day event in Massachusetts, USA, and finished fourth. He has now been retired to the hunting field, and Mary is bringing on some younger horses.

Francisco Goyoaga (Spain)

'Paco' Goyoaga, born in 1921, is the best civilian rider his country has produced since the war. A nephew of the former captain of the Spanish Army team, the late Col Jaime Garcia-Cruz, he owns a chain of dry-cleaning shops in Madrid. On the army horse, Quorum, he won the very first world showjumping championship, in 1953 in Paris, beating d'Oriola on his gold medal horse Ali Baba, Fritz Thiedemann with Diamant for Germany, and Piero d'Inzeo with Uruguay. In 1956 in Aachen he was runner-up, riding Fahnenkonig, to Raimondo d'Inzeo with Merano. He favoured the heavier breeds of German horse and his best were Baden, Fahnenkonig, Toscanella, and the French Kif-Kif, which he sold to the government when he retired after leading his team to victory at Geneva in 1965. He is now *chef* to the Spanish team.

Michele Grubb (USA)

Michele McEvoy was twenty-one years old when, in the spring of 1974, she won the invitation championship on the Sunshine Circuit in Florida from Rodney Jenkins, the holder. Soon afterwards she came to Europe with Sundancer, Mister Muskie, the quarter horse (now dead), and the young Vesuvius to compete at the Hickstead Easter meeting before going on to Rome, where she won three competitions. Selected to represent the United States in the women's world championship in La Baule, she finished second on Mister Muskie behind the defending champion, Janou Tissot on Rocket.

In 1979 she married Tim Grubb, the Leicestershire rider who helped to win the Presidents Cup at Calgary, Alberta, where he was in the winning British team for the Nations Cup, a feat he also achieved in 1980.

Jean-Jacques Guyon (France)

Riding Pitou, Jean-Jacques Guyon won the individual three-day event gold medal in the 1968 Olympic Games in Mexico. He jumped magnificently in the speed and endurance test during the second day, scoring a bonus of 27.2 on the steeplechase and of 17.2 on the cross-country to take up the running with a score of 28.61 penalty points. Major Derek Allhusen and Lochinvar, for Britain, had an even better score — 35.2 for the steeplechase and 29.2 for the cross-country but his round was marred by a refusal at the fourth fence, a feeding trough leading out of an enclosed pen. Both were fortunate to go before the deluge, a storm of tropical violence.

Nils Haagensen (Denmark)

The twenty-four-year-old winner of the individual championship in the European three-day title fight at Luhmühlen in 1979 on Monaco, having led through all three phases. Nils was taught by his father, Ejner Haagensen, who owns a men's clothing shop at Naestved, forty miles from Copenhagen. Nils was a member of the Danish dressage team at the 1976 Olympic Games. He first tried his hand at eventing only thirteen months before his title victory. He proved his success to be no fluke when he won the alternative Olympic event at Fontainebleau on Monaco.

Frank and Cynthia Haydon (Great Britain)

Frank and Cynthia Haydon are the leading breeders and exhibitors of the hackney horse and pony. Mrs Haydon is the daughter of the late Bob Black, who with his brother James came south from York between the wars and set up the two most successful hackney establishments in the country. Cynthia Haydon was taught to drive a team by the late Bertram Mills, and drove his team at Olympia before World War II. She was the first woman ever to compete in the international driving three-day event, both in the European and world championships, and the first to bring a team of hackneys into this highly competitive scene. She is as well known in the USA and Canada as she is in this country, for she competes regularly in New York and at the Royal Winter Fair in Toronto.

Seamus Hayes (Ireland)

Seamus Hayes, whose father, Maj.-Gen. Liam Hayes, bought so many world-beating showjumpers for the Irish Army team in the 1930s, came to England in 1946 to ride for Tommy Makin, then for the Massarellas, and finally for Phil Oliver. He was leading rider here in 1949, 1950 and 1952, and then returned to Dublin to take up an appointment as civilian instructor to the Irish Army team, before setting up on his own on the Curragh. He will always be associated with his own Snowstorm, Tommy Makin's Sheila and Planet, and Lord Harrington's Goodbye, the liver-chesnut son of Renwood, Goodbye, who cleared 7ft 2in on six occasions before he retired in 1967, won the inaugural British Jumping Derby at Hickstead in 1961 and took the title for the second time three years later. Seamus is married to the former Mary Rose Robinson, sister of Mill House's jockey, Willie Robinson.

Johan Heins (Holland)

Born in 1947, Johan Heins lives in Maastricht and is married with two children. Riding Severn Valley (for the Zangersheide Stable) bred in England by the former premium stallion Iron Ore, Johan Heins, a pupil of Alwin Schockemöhle, won the European championship in Vienna in 1977 and was also a member of the winning team. One of his first major wins was the Grand Prix in Dublin and three years afterwards he won his title at the age of twenty-nine, having been selected by Leon Melchior to ride the horse he had bought, with its brother Severn Hills, from Lincolnshire farmer John Taylor.

Bertie Hill (Great Britain)

Son of a North Devon farmer, Bertie was enormously successful as a point-to-point rider just after the war, when he was still in his teens, and established a quite remarkable partnership in pony races over banks with a memorable blood horse called Brownie III. An outstanding natural horseman, he was taken in hand by the late Tony Collings, who reasoned that, with a good knowledge of dressage, Bertie would make a world-class three-day event rider. He rode in the 1952 Olympic Games and helped to win the gold medals in 1956 on Countryman. He also won the European championship on Crispin in 1954. Hill trained the team which won the gold medals in Mexico and Munich, and now operates a successful training establishment for both horses and riders from his farm at South Molton. His son Tony followed in his footsteps as a member of the British junior team and was runner-up for the European title in 1972; and his daughter Sarah was in the junior team in 1974.

George Hobbs (Great Britain)

Born in 1924, Sussex farmer George Hobbs took out a professional steeplechase jockey's licence which kept him out of the Olympic showjumping team. But he rode in many winning British international teams on Royal Lord, with whom he won the National Foxhunter Championship in 1955, and during an international career which stretched over fifteen seasons he was successful with Attila, Brandy Soda, Battling Pedulas, and War Lord. Hobbs is a very active and valuable member of the BSJA selection committee and is also chairman of the BSJA's rules sub-committee. In 1974, he was competing again only fifteen weeks after sustaining a heart attack.

Jane Holderness-Roddam (Great Britain)

Jane Holderness-Roddam is the second daughter of the late Colonel and Mrs J.F.S. Bullen of Catherston Manor, Charmouth, Dorset, who after the war started the Catherston pony stud. Like her sister Jennie before her, she started her equestrian career riding show ponies, and then hacks, before graduating to combined training. She won Badminton on Our Nobby in 1968 and on the strength of this victory on a small but gallant horse was selected for the British Olympic team in Mexico, where she helped to win a team gold medal six months later. She was known then as 'the galloping nurse', for she was a full-time nurse at the Middlesex Hospital in London. After her marriage to Tim Holderness-Roddam, who works for Tate and Lyle, now her sponsors, she rode Warrior for Mrs Suzy Howard of the United States to win Burghley in 1976. She won Badminton on Warrior two years later, after which she was in the British team for the world championships in Lexington, Kentucky. Warrior was third at Burghley in 1980 and has now retired from three-day eventing.

Kurt Jarasinski (West Germany)
Born 1938. A pupil of that great horseman, Fritz Thiedemann, Kurt Jarasinski followed the maestro as stable jockey to the Holstein stud at Elmshorn and rode Torro in the winning German Olympic team in Tokyo in 1964.

Rodney Jenkins (USA)
The top professional showjumping rider in the United States, Rodney Jenkins, the son of a professional huntsman in Virginia, began his riding career in the hunting field at the age of eight in 1948, and inevitably graduated to the hunter classes in the show ring and thence to showjumping. He joined the US team for the first time in 1973, on the North American Fall Circuit, with the brown gelding Idle Dice — the most successful horse in the annals of American showjumping, with more than $100,000 in stake money to his credit. Selected to represent the United States, with Frank Chapot, in the men's world championship at Hickstead in 1974, he was not among the qualifiers for the final. But on his second-string horse, Number One Spy, he won the Grand Prix in London and later took the valuable San Diego Grand Prix in California from David Broome, who had beaten him in the professional championship in Cardiff, where he won the Pro-Am match.

Heinrich-Wilhelm ('Der Kaiser') Johannsman (West Germany)
Born in 1951, Johannsman is a saddler by profession and is married with one child. He made his international showjumping debut in the 1978 World Championships in Aachen. Thereafter he has been a regular team member with Sarto.

Debbie Johnsey (Great Britain)
Junior European champion in 1973, Debbie Johnsey is more than just another talented young showjumping rider. Even in 1972, competing against adults in the top class, she was runner-up on Speculator both for the Wills British (National) Championship at Hickstead, and for the Leading Showjumper of the Year title at Wembley. She started her career on ponies in Wales and the Borders — she lives near Chepstow, not far from the Broome family — and was selected for the British junior team with her pony stallion, Champ, at the age of eleven.

But the rules laid down that she was too young to compete internationally, even in a junior team. On Speculator, who is by the premium stallion Specific, sire of the Grand National winner Specify, she also won the Whitbread Young Riders title at Wembley in 1973. In 1975, she was also successful on the American-bred Croupier and on Moxy, whom she took to the 1976 Olympics, where she was the only girl and the youngest rider in the field. She did exceptionally well to finish fourth in the individual Grand Prix, narrowly missing a bronze medal. She was in the British European championship team in 1977. Moxy had to be put down in March, 1978. Debbie Johnsey is now married to Peter Gotz of South Africa.

Lieutenant Reuben Jones (Great Britain)
Ben Jones, as an NCO in the King's Troop, RHA, rode Master Bernard in the Olympic three-day event team in Tokyo, 1964. When Foxdor died a few months before the 1968 Olympic Games, he took the ride on Capt. Martin Whiteley's The Poacher and helped to win the team gold medal in Mexico. Rode regularly with the team until the end of 1969. He is now stationed with the RAVC, and his daughter Joanna is a promising event rider on Col Sir John Miller's Sapphire Star.

Iris Kellett (Ireland)
Iris Kellett, who won the Queen Elizabeth II Cup on Rusty when it was first presented, in 1949, and recaptured it two years later, is the daughter of a Dublin veterinary surgeon and has run a successful riding school (which has now moved to Co. Meath) since the 1940s. In 1969, after a career spanning more than two decades, she finally won the ladies' European championship at Dublin riding Morning Light, who was then sold to the French for £30,000 and his name changed to Moet et Chandon. Miss Kellett has now given up riding internationally but she has a number of promising pupils coming on to the international scene. Former pupils include Eddie Macken and Paul Darragh, both successful showjumpers.

James Kernan (Ireland)
The son of the well-known Northern Ireland dealer, Frank Kernan of Crossmaglen who has sold so many top international

horses all over the world, James won the junior European showjumping championship individual title in 1974. In 1977 he helped to win the Aga Khan Trophy for Ireland and again in 1978 and 1979, on the brilliant young horse, Condy.

Larry Kiely (Ireland)
Born in 1941, Captain Larry Kiely is a former All Ireland hurler from Tipperary. He joined the Irish Equestrian School in 1962 and rode in his first international show four years later, winning his first class, the puissance, in 1969 at Ludwigsburg. After breaking his leg in early 1971, he won the Grand Prix in Wulfrath and was in the winning Nations Cup team in Ostend.
  His best horse, the bay mare Inis Cara, foaled in 1961, by Golden Years, was bought in 1965 from Jerry Rohan in Midleton, Co. Cork. She won the puissance in Ludwigsburg and Ostend, clearing 7ft 2in. In Rome in 1972 she was runner-up to Raimondo d'Inzeo and Bellevue in the puissance, and in 1974 tied with Bellevue in the Shell puissance in Dublin.

Kathy Kusner (USA)
Born in 1940. The daughter of a Maryland school teacher. Kathy Kusner joined the US team in 1962, having set up the American women's high jump record of 7ft 3in. at the age of eighteen. She won the Irish Grand Prix in 1964 on Untouchable, and retained it in 1965. Rode in both the Tokyo and Munich Olympic Games. Was second to Stroller and Marion Mould for the 1965 ladies' world title at Hickstead, and won the European championship in 1967. After a court case, Kathy became the first woman to hold a jockey's licence in the United States.

Mark Laskin (Canada)
Showjumper Mark Laskin, aged twenty-three, comes from Edmonton, Alberta. In 1980 he was the youngest member of the winning gold medal team at the alternative Olympics in Rotterdam. A Rothmans Equestrian of the Year in 1978 and 1979, he also won two World Cup events in Vancouver and Toronto.

Captain Guy Lefrant (France)
Born in 1923. Guy Lefrant's sojourn on the active list, which

extends from 1948, must be a record in any nation. Rides in both showjumping and three-day events with equal virtuosity. Won the individual three-day event silver medal on Verdun in the 1952 Olympics and a team bronze on Nicias in Rome. First rode with the Olympic showjumping team in Tokyo, and on M de Littry, by Furioso, helped to win the silver medal with Janou Lefebvre and d'Oriola.

Jack Le Goff (France)

Born in 1932, the son of a French cavalry officer. Trainer to the United States three-day eventers for Munich 1972, where they won the team silver medal. Was champion of France in 1956 and 1963; he competed in the 1960 and 1964 Olympic Games and led the French team to the bronze medals in Rome, finishing in sixth place individually. At the end of his riding career, Le Goff coached the French team which finished fourth in Mexico in 1968, in addition to producing the individual gold medallist, Pitou, ridden by Jean-Jacques Guyon. Formerly a successful race-rider, under both codes, and an Army instructor, he coached the French junior and senior teams from 1965 and joined the American three-day event team as their trainer in 1970, enjoying considerable success with them since then. In 1972 they were Olympic silver medallists, then in 1974, at Burghley, they won both the team and individual titles at the world championships. They then achieved the logical progression of the Olympic gold medals (and an individual gold and silver) in 1976. In 1978 they won the team silver medals in the world championships in Kentucky, where Bruce Davidson retained the individual title.

Armand Leone (USA)

Showjumper Armand Leone was born in 1958 and comes from Franklin Lakes, New Jersey. He is a second-year student at New York Medical School. On Encore he won the final selection for the United States equestrian team in 1978.

Fritz Ligges (West Germany)

A member of the winning German Olympic team at Munich, in 1972, the highly talented Ligges had previously won the individual bronze medal in the Olympic three-day event at

Tokyo in 1964, riding Donkosak, before he took up showjumping. He rode Robin in the Munich Olympics to a team gold. At Wembley, in 1975, he won the Norwich Union puissance with Ramiro and Genius. Three years later he broke his collar bone there.

Alan Lillingston (Ireland)

Owner of the Mount Coote Stud at Killmallock, Co. Limerick, Alan Lillingston is a most versatile rider. He is the last of the only two amateurs ever to win the Champion Hurdle at Cheltenham, a well-known hunter judge, and in 1968 won the supreme hunter championship at Dublin on his own horse, Josh. In 1979 he helped Ireland to win the European Three-Day Event championships in Luhmühlen, on Seven Up.

Colonel Sir Harry Llewellyn KBE (Great Britain)

Born in 1911, second son of Sir David Llewellyn. Educated at Oundle and Trinity College, Harry Llewellyn, who rode Ego into a place in the Grand National while he was still at Cambridge, forged an unforgettable alliance with the immortal Foxhunter. Probably the most famous partnership in the world, they joined the British team in 1947 and gained a team bronze medal in the 1948 Olympic Games at Wembley — in a team mounted wholly by Llewellyn. He captained the team to victory in Helsinki in 1952 — and these were the only gold medals to come back to Britain from the 1952 Games. Has made an inestimable contribution to showjumping, first as a rider in the team for nine seasons, and more recently as an administrator. As chairman of the BSJA he was instrumental in the engaging of an ex-mounted policeman as stipendiary steward with a roving commission, and as chairman of the international affairs committee he still makes a valuable contribution to the running of the sport at this level. He is also chairman of the Sports Council for Wales. He was Master of the Monmouthshire Hounds, 1952—57 and 1963—65, and was chairman of the British Equestrian Federation until 1980. He was knighted in 1977 and succeeded to a baronetcy in 1978.

Jennie Loriston-Clarke MBE (Great Britain)
As Jennie Bullen she went through all the pony and hack stages
of her younger sister, equally successfully, and then started to
do dressage on her former champion hack, Desert Storm. She
soon discovered just what sort of world she had happened upon,
her father told me, when at the Royal Windsor Horse Show she
had her first success and no one spoke to her at all, let alone
congratulated her. This may well have strengthened her
ambition to make good, and she soldiered on to such effect that
at Goodwood in 1978 she won the bronze medal in the World
Championship Grand Prix on Dutch Courage, a horse she
bought and trained herself. They were sixth in the alternative
Olympics at Goodwood in 1980.

Eddie Macken (Ireland)
Born in 1950 in Granard, Co. Longford, Eddie Macken was the
most successful pupil of Iris Kellett's riding establishment.
Eddie first joined the Irish team with Morning Light. Then he
took over the brilliant Pele, on whom, in 1974, he was runner-
up for the men's world championship at Hickstead, having led
the field for the first two days. He also won the Wills Hickstead
Gold Medal in 1974. In 1975, as a professional, he went to live
in West Germany, in partnership with Paul Schockemöhle. Won
the Victor Ludorum on Boomerang at the two Wembley shows
and again in 1976, when he was Europe's biggest winner on
Boomerang, who won the British Jumping Derby at Hickstead.
In 1977 he was equally successful, filling the first two places in
the British Jumping Derby, beaten by a mere tenth of a second
for the European Championship and winning the Silver Spurs
and the Victor Ludorum at the Horse of the Year show. In
1978 he was runner-up again on Carrolls Boomerang, for the
world championship in Aachen, by a mere .25 of a time fault.
He won the British Jumping Derby for the third time on
Boomerang and the Philips Industries Championship at the
Horse of the Year show. At Dublin he was again the leading
rider, to celebrate his return to living in Ireland. In 1979 he was
the leading grand prix rider, and he established an all-time
record by winning his fourth successive British Jumping Derby
at Hickstead, again on Boomerang. In 1980 he was campaigning

young horses for Carrolls Ltd, the cigarette manufacturers.

Graziano Mancinelli (Italy)
Born in 1937. Rode with the Italian junior team for four years from 1952 and joined the senior team in 1958. For many years rode for the horse-dealing firm of Fratelli Rivolta, in Milan, and was able to join the Olympic team in 1964 as the adopted son of one of the brothers. Formerly he had been considered to be professional. Rode the grey mare Rockette, by Water Serpent (the sire of Piero d'Inzeo's The Rock), and Italy won the team bronze medal. Won the European championship in 1963. Mancinelli, with the most formidable team of horses in Italy, won the Olympic individual gold medal in Munich on Ambassador, in 1972.

General Humberto Mariles (Mexico)
Born in 1913, the son of Captain Antonio Mariles of the Mexican cavalry. Grew up on his father's ranch and joined the military academy when he was thirteen. After passing out in 1931 he spent three years as an instructor, then took charge of training at the cavalry school. Mariles won the individual gold medal at the first post-war Olympic Games, held at Wembley in 1948, and on Arete he captained the victorious Mexican team. A brilliant career came to a sad end in 1966 when Mariles, involved with a drunken motorist who became abusive, pulled a gun on him and was sent to prison. Mariles died in 1973, having been arrested in Paris for drug smuggling.

Ronnie Massarella (Great Britain)
Ronnie Massarella is the manager, or *chef d'équipe*, of the British showjumping team and has been since 1970. Under his leadership it regained the Presidents Cup in 1977 and retained it in 1978 and 1979, as well as winning the World team championship in Aachen in 1978 and the European equivalent in 1979 at Rotterdam. A member of a well-respected showjumping dynasty, half Yorkshire and half Italian, Ronnie has owned several showjumpers which were ridden by David Broome but he is an inspired administrator, and because he likes people he has been thrust into the hot seat, where he has no financial

reward but spends his own money on matters which should be official business. Let us hope that this virtue brings more than its own reward. His team of amateurs won silver medals at the alternative Olympics at Rotterdam in 1980.

Mike Matz (USA)

Aged twenty-eight, from Lafayette Hill in Pennsylvania, Michael Matz has ridden with the US equestrian team since 1973. He won the individual bronze medal when the team won the gold medal in the 1975 Pan-American Games, and was on the 1976 Olympic squad. Having won the American Jumping Derby, on Jet Run, the American Gold Cup and the Valley Forge Grand Prix, he was the leading American rider at both the Washington and Royal Winter Fair, Toronto, shows in the autumn of 1977 winning the Grand Prix at the latter on Jet Run.

Paddy McMahon (Great Britain)

European champion in 1973, he made his first overseas trip to the United States with the veteran Tim II, formerly owned by Ted Williams, and joined the British team in Barcelona in 1971 with Hideaway. Has had a wide experience of riding a variety of horses round the English shows, most notably Tim II and others who won in their turn for T. Mulholland of Derby. He produced Trevor Banks' Hideaway as a young horse, and then rode for Fred Hartill of Wolverhampton, who gave him the Irish-bred Pennwood Forge Mill, a brown gelding, foaled in 1964, on whom he won the Grand Prix in Ostend on his first foreign tour. Short-listed for the Olympic team at the end of that season, he was turned down on the grounds of Forge Mill's comparative inexperience, but won the saddle of honour for his consistent performances at the Royal International. He won the 1972 Olympic trial at British Timken in August. In 1973 McMahon and Pennwood Forge Mill won the men's European title at the Wills July international meeting at Hickstead, and very shortly afterwards the King George V Cup at the Royal International Horse Show at Wembley. He has also won the Victor Ludorum at the Horse of the Year show. He now rides Golanite for Husky, having gone on his own in 1976.

Richard Meade OBE (Great Britain)

Born in 1939, only son of Mr and Mrs John O'Mahony Meade, former Joint-Masters of the Curre Hounds in Monmouthshire where they run a Connemara stud; educated at his father's preparatory school in Chepstow and at Lancing College. He was commissioned into the 11th Hussars before reading engineering at Cambridge, and is now a business consultant in London.

Richard Meade first joined the British Olympic team with his good horse Barberry at Tokyo in 1964, finishing eighth. In 1965 he was in the team that finished third for the European championship in Moscow, and in 1966 was second individually for the world championship at Burghley.

In the winning team for the European title at Punchestown in 1967, Barberry was retired with back trouble in 1968 and Richard was given the ride on Mary Gordon-Watson's Cornishman V for the Mexico Olympics, where he helped to win the team gold medal. In 1970 he took over Capt. Martin Whiteley's The Poacher, on whom he won Badminton, and then helped to win the world championship for Britain in Punchestown. At Burghley in 1971, for the last time before The Poacher was retired, they helped to win another European team title. The next year, Richard won both a team and the individual Olympic gold medal in Munich on Major Derek Allhusen's home-bred Laurieston.

In 1973 at Badminton he finished second to Lucinda Prior-Palmer and Be Fair on a last-minute ride, Barbara Hammond's Eagle Rock, who was bred by his parents. Then he took over Mrs Henry Wilkin's Wayfarer V, finishing fourth individually in the European championships in Kiev and helping to win the team bronze medals before winning at Boekelo, the Netherlands, in October. In 1974 at Burghley, on the same horse, he helped to win the team World championship silver medal. In 1975 he won at Bramham on Jacob Jones and finished third at Burghley on Tommy Buck. He did best of the British team at the 1976 Olympics, finishing fourth on Jacob Jones, put down in 1977 after an accident in the trial for the European championship team. In 1978 he finished fifth in the Kentucky world championships on Bleak Hills. He now rides Speculator and Kilcashel, but had to retire the latter from the alternative Olympics in 1980, with azoturia.

Katie Monahan (USA)
Born in 1954, Katie Monahan comes from Uppeville, Virginia.
She was second, on The Jones Boy, to Hugo Simon in the first
World Cup in Gothenburg in 1979.

Ann Moore (Great Britain)
Born in 1950, Ann is the eldest of a family of six. She won the
European junior championship on Psalm in 1968, having been
in the British junior team for three years on as many different
horses. Made her first visit to Spain with the British senior team
in 1970. Ann achieved the only British victories on the tour of
the Rome, Fontainebleau, and Aachen international shows in
1971. She was selected for the ladies' European championship
at St Gall, in Switzerland, and won the title shortly after her
twenty-first birthday.

Short-listed for the Olympic team at the end of that season,
she was first choice for the team when she won the final
Olympic trial at the Wills July meeting at Hickstead. Three days
later Psalm carried her to victory in the Queen Elizabeth II Cup.
Some six weeks afterwards, she rode him to an Olympic silver
medal in Munich. Again on Psalm, in 1973, she retained both
her European ladies' title in Vienna and was equal first on time
with Alison Dawes and Mr Banbury for the Queen Elizabeth II
Cup at the Royal International. When Psalm went lame in 1974,
shortly before the women's world championship, Ann retired.
She now plans a comeback, riding for Trevor Banks.

Captain Carlos Moratorio (Argentina)
Winner of the individual silver medal in the Olympic three-day
event in Tokyo in 1964, and of the individual world title at
Burghley in 1966. Moratorio first left his own country to ride as
its lone representative in the 1959 Pan-American Games. Won
the silver medal on Chalan in Sao Paulo in 1963, and it was
Chalan who eventually won him the world title. The horse was
subsequently sold to the United States, but his soundness was
soon in doubt and he vanished into oblivion.

Laurie Morgan (Australia)
Laurie Morgan, who rode Salad Days with the Australian
Olympic team when they won the gold medals in Rome, was a

first-class all-round sportsman with a great penchant for hunting and racing. He did not take up three-day eventing until he was over forty. A frequent and favourite competitor at Badminton, he was second on the gallant Salad Days, in 1960, only months before winning his individual gold medal. He won Badminton in 1961.

Marion Mould (Great Britain)

Marion Coakes and the little Stroller became a legend in their lifetime when they won the ladies' world championship at Hickstead in 1965, when Marion was only eighteen. A farmer's daughter from New Milton, Hampshire, Marion, the third of four children, followed her two elder brothers, John and Douglas, into the British junior team. When she graduated from the junior classes her father, Ralph Coakes, was persuaded not to sell Stroller until he had been given a season in open jumping, as he had been in the family since 1960. He soon proved his worth over bigger fences by jumping a clear round in the 1964 British Jumping Derby at Hickstead, finishing second to Seamus Hayes on Goodbye. Stroller won the Queen Elizabeth Cup for the first time in 1965 – he won again in 1971 – before winning the world title from Kathy Kusner on Untouchable from the USA. In his second season as an open horse, he helped to win three Nations Cups for Britain and the inaugural Presidents Cup. Marion was then voted Sportswoman of the Year.

In Mexico, Marion (now married to former steeplechase jockey David Mould) and Stroller jumped one of the only two clear rounds in the Olympic individual championship and eventually won the silver medal. But a bad abscess on a molar caused him not to give of his best in the team event and he was unfortunately eliminated. The course specialists at Hickstead, Marion and Stroller set up a record which will not easily be broken by winning the Wills Hickstead gold medal, for points gained in the major events during the year, for five years consecutively from 1965 to 1970. Unfortunately she was ill in 1979, but came back in 1980.

Tony Newbery (Great Britain)

The son of a farmer and cattle dealer from Alphington, near Exeter, Tony worked his way to international status via the show pony and junior jumping classes as one of the most successful child riders in the West Country. His first break came when his father bought Warwick III from the Australian rider, John Fahey, and at the age of nineteen Tony made his first trip abroad, to Aachen in 1973, where he did so well that he was selected to tour the North American circuit that autumn. His second break came the following year with the arrival of Snaffles from Ted Edgar. Brought out in Ireland by Tommy Brennan in the name of Greenwood, Snaffles brought him many international successes. In 1975 he was runner-up, to Pele, for the British Jumping Derby with one of the two clear rounds, and he won the Welsh Jumping Derby from Marion Mould's Dunlynne on the Broome family's ground. He was a member of the British Olympic team in 1976. He is married to David Coleman's daughter, Ann.

Henk Nooren (Holland)

One of the youngest Dutch showjumping riders. Henk Nooren was born in 1955. He is an ex-pupil of Hans Gunter Winkler, and with the English horse Cat's Whiskers, who came from Trevor Banks, and the German-bred Pluco, owned by the De Molshoop stable, he has won several Grand Prix including Wiesbaden in 1978. In 1977 he was in the winning Dutch team for the European championship in Vienna, and in 1978 in the team which finished second in the world championship in Aachen. He is now professional and rides for Opstalan.

Alan Oliver (Great Britain)

Born in 1932, son of Buckinghamshire farmer, Felix (Phil) Oliver. Was riding his father's 16-hand horses in open competitions as a skinny eleven-year-old boy. Had pony called Thumbs Up, by Silverdale Loyalty, bred in Cornwall, where he raced over hurdles; the pony's career started before the war with Marjorie Burgess. Alan took him over in 1946 and a year later he was the top pony in the country. Alan joined the British team in 1951 and was in training for the 1952 Olympics. In fact most of his career has been spent in England, where he has met such riders as the d'Inzeos on level terms. In 1953 he rode Galway Bay to finish equal first in the Lonsdale puissance at the RIHS with Col. Llewellyn on Foxhunter and Piero d'Inzeo on Uruguay. The latter always considered that Oliver was the one to beat in the puissance at the White City. Red Star II, Galway Bay, Planet, Red Knight, and Red Admiral made the Oliver string a force to reckon with in the early 1950s, but replacements were hard to find and Alan had a few lean years until the late 1960s, when he fought his way back to the front with Sweep III and Pitz Palu. His style has altered completely since his youth, when he affected an acrobatic, or more accurately aerobatic, position over fences. He is now making his name as a course builder with Western Fence Hire of which Major Reg Whitehead has made him a director.

Dr Vittorio Orlandi (Italy)

Born in 1940, of a family who own a big textile factory in Milan, Vittorio Orlandi was a comparative novice as an international rider when he first joined the Italian team, in the late 1960s, with the Irish horse Fulmer Feather Duster, whose first owner, Juliet Jobling-Purser, rode him in the 1970 ladies' world championship. At the Munich Olympics he rode two four-fault rounds to lead his team-mates (the two d'Inzeos and the reigning Olympic champion, Mancinelli) to a team bronze medal. The following winter he bought Raimondo d'Inzeo's Olympic horse Fiorello. At Munich in 1975 they tied first in the second leg of the men's European championship with the eventual winner, Alwin Schockemöhle, on Warwick.

Hubert Parot (France)

A member of the team which won the gold medals in Montreal in 1976, Hubert Parot, born on 23 May 1933, is married with one daughter. He is a breeder at Arbonne, Seine et Marne, near Paris, and started riding at fourteen. He was trained by his father, André Parot, and then by Noël Pelat. For several years he rode racehorses, but was forced to give up due to weight problems. After riding in three-day events he branched off to showjumping, becoming a leading national rider. In the European championship at Hickstead in 1973 he won the bronze medal, and the following year he won twenty-four international competitions. He has been the pillar of the French team for five or six years, winning puissances in Madrid, Hickstead, Lisbon and Fontainebleau, and captained it in 1979.

Nelson Pessoa (Brazil)

Born in 1935. Made his London debut in 1956. Four years later he made the decision to spend his summers in Switzerland in order to compete at the European shows, and is now permanently based in France. In 1966 he won the men's European championship on Gran Geste, but is really a derby and grand prix specialist. Has won three Hamburg and two British Jumping Derbies, plus innumerable grands prix. He has a great flair for finding horses, and for getting difficult ones going. He turned professional in 1974, riding for Moët et Chandon.

Captain Mark Phillips CVO (Great Britain)

Born in 1948, Mark was a considerable athlete when he was still at Marlborough; at the same time he rode in the Beaufort Hunt Pony Club horse trials team for five successive years, reaching the finals on three occasions.

In 1967 he rode Rock On to fourth place at Burghley. In 1968 was also fourth at Badminton, over a tough course and against really stiff opposition, and was selected as reserve for the Olympic Games in Mexico. Rode as an individual in the European championships at Haras du Pin in 1969. In Punches-town in 1970 he helped to win the world championship for Britain riding Bertie Hill's Chicago, later sold to Germany.

In 1971 and again in 1972 he won the Badminton Horse Trials on Great Ovation, a dark bay gelding by Three Cheers out of a mare by William of Valance, foaled in 1963, which he owned in partnership with his aunt, Miss Flavia Phillips. Great Ovation was in the winning European championship team at Burghley in 1971 and was first choice for the Olympic short list. Mark was subsequently a member of the winning Olympic team. He had an unlucky Badminton in 1973, when he was foiled of a possible hat-trick after Great Ovation went lame on the roads and tracks. He was kept out of the team for the European championships for want of a horse, but on Tony Hill's Maid Marion he won the Burghley three-day event and on the same mare he was going well in the United States when she had to be pulled up with tendon trouble.

In 1974 he won at Badminton for the third time, riding HM The Queen's Columbus, who was withdrawn from the world championships when he slipped a ligament while leading the field at the end of the cross-country phase. In 1975, his horses were beset by lameness, but he rode a winner at Tidworth in Favour, and finished second at Burghley on Gretna Green, borrowed from Janet Hodgson (after a brilliant performance on two strange horses, the other being Brazil). He was reserve to the British Olympic Team with Persian Holiday and Favour. In 1977 he was not selected for the European championship team, and Persian Holiday was unsound in 1978. He did very well in 1980, riding young horses for the Range Rover team.

Michael Plumb (USA)

Born in 1940. From Chesapeake City in Maryland, he was a member of the US three-day event team that won the world title in 1974, the Olympic silver medal in 1964, 1968 and 1972, and the Pan-American Games gold in 1963 and 1967. Captained all six teams, and in 1971 was classified the leading three-day event rider in the United States for the fifth time in seven years. Rode Free and Easy in the Munich Olympics, and Good Mixture in the 1974 world championships, in which he finished second individually. In 1976 he was in the winning Olympic team and won an individual silver medal on the six-year-old US Thoroughbred, Better and Better, who was second at Ledyard in 1977 behind his jockey on the Australian Olympic horse Laurenson. In 1978 he and Laurenson were eliminated at the notorious Serpent fence in the world championships; he met the same fate in the alternative Olympics two years later.

Captain Con Power (Ireland)

Con Power is the twenty-three-year-old son of a breeder and trainer in County Wexford whose breeding successes include the winner of the 1947 Grand National, Caughoo. He intended to be a jockey, but when he grew too big he joined the army instead. When he had done his year's basic training on The Curragh he went to the army equitation school at McKee Barracks in Phoenix Park, Dublin, and was selected for the world championship team to go to Burghley in 1974, but his horse went lame just when they were about to leave. He is now a most promising member of the showjumping team, and was runner-up for the leading rider's title in Rome in 1976, when he achieved several notable victories at Hickstead and on the Continent and was leading rider in Dublin. He is married to the former Margaret Latta, a member of another very famous family of horsemen and women in Co. Wexford, and they farm in Co. Meath. He was the leading rider in New York and Toronto in 1978 as well as gaining this distinction in Dublin in 1979, where he won the puissance on Rockbarton. Con Power left the army in September 1979 and now runs a training establishment with his wife in Co. Meath.

HRH The Princess Anne (Great Britain)
Princess Anne rode at Badminton for the first time in 1971, finishing fifth. Just five months later she rode Doublet at Burghley to take the individual European championship. In 1972, having been short-listed for the Olympic three-day event team, Doublet developed a 'leg' and was withdrawn from all engagements, including Badminton, for the rest of the year. Doublet, a chesnut gelding by the Argentinian-born Thoroughbred, Doubtless II, was bred by the Queen in 1963. His dam, also bred in Argentina, was Swate, a polo pony who was formerly in Prince Philip's string. The Queen gave Doublet to Princess Anne as a Christmas present in 1970.

In 1973 Princess Anne was selected to defend her European title in Kiev on Goodwill, but this former showjumper fell at the notorious second fence and was retired. HRH was twelfth in the 1974 world championships on Goodwill, but the following year they put up a magnificent performance to finish second individually for the European individual championship, in Luhmühlen, in addition to helping the British team win the silver medals. In 1976 she finished twenty-fourth in the Olympic Games after a fall. She took the following year off to have her first child, but was on the world championship short list in 1978. In 1979 she retired Goodwill after Badminton, but in 1980 appeared to have his successor in the Queen's Stevie B.

Lucinda Prior-Palmer MBE (Great Britain)
The leading lady three-day event rider in the world, the daughter of the late Major-General Errol and the Lady Doreen Prior-Palmer, Lucinda first joined the British team with her own horse, Be Fair, at Kiev in 1973, having won the Badminton

Horse Trials that year. She was then nineteen years old. Two years earlier, she and Be Fair were in the winning British team for the Junior European Championships at Wesel, West Germany. She won Badminton again in 1976 on Mrs V. Phillips' Wide Awake, and in 1977 on Mrs Hugh Straker's George, who also carried her to victory at Burghley five months later, enabling her to retain the European title. Be Fair slipped the Achilles tendon from his offside hock having gone clear across country in the 1976 Olympic Games. In 1977 she finished third on Killaire in the international three-day event at Ledyard Farm in Massachusetts, USA, and second on Village Gossip at Boekelo in the Netherlands. Second at Badminton in 1978, on Village Gossip. She rode this horse in the British world championship team in Kentucky but withdrew after the cross-country. In the spring she acquired a sponsor, Overseas Containers Ltd. In 1979 on Killaire she won her fourth Badminton setting up an all-time record. In the 1980 alternative Olympics she went from sixty-ninth to seventh place by virtue of a brilliant cross-country round. Later in the year she went to Australia and won the Melbourne Three-Day Event Advanced and Open classes on borrowed horses.

Malcolm Pyrah (Great Britain)

Son of an RAF pilot who was shot down in the Battle of Britain, Malcolm was a civil servant after leaving Hull Grammar School until, at twenty-three, he decided on a career with horses. He started with the Massarellas and saved enough money to buy three dry-cleaning shops in Hull, which are run by his half-brother. In 1973 he and his wife Judy opened their own yard in Nottinghamshire. A successful international rider with Law Court, Trevarrion, and Lucky Strike.

In 1975, when he won the Rome Grand Prix on April Love, he applied successfully to the BSJA and the FEI for reinstatement as an amateur. Not surprisingly, though, his revised status failed to be ratified by the IOC. In 1978 he helped to win the world team championship on John Massarella's Law Court, and won important competitions in St Gallen and Aachen, and in 1979 he helped to win the European team championship. In 1980 Towerlands Chainbridge and Towerlands Anglezarke joined his string for Thomas Hunnable.

Helmut Rethemeier (West Germany)

Born 1939 in Vlotho, Helmut Rethemeier is a farmer by profession. He is married with two children and has ridden since he was fourteen years old. He finished fifth individually in the European three-day event championships in Luhmühlen in 1975, and in the 1978 world championships he finished third, with a bronze medal, on Ledalco, a nine-year-old grey Holstein gelding.

Derek Ricketts (Great Britain)

Born in 1949, married to Jill Francome, sister of jockey John, in 1974. Derek Ricketts lives near the Oliver family, in Buckinghamshire, and as a pupil of Alan Oliver he first came to fame as the winner of the National Foxhunter Championship at the Horse of the Year show. Beau Supreme, who was sold to the Dutch owner Leon Melchior for a reputed £90,000 and then bought back again, was his best horse but sadly broke a leg at the Royal International Horse Show at Wembley. Now his best is Colonel and Mrs Rodney Ward's homebred former event horse Coldstream, who was in the British team for the European championships in Vienna in 1977 and in the winning world championship team in Aachen in 1978. In 1979 he helped to win the European team championship in Rotterdam and won many big prizes in 1980.

Colonel Billy Ringrose (Ireland)

Born in 1930, Billy Ringrose is the most successful rider to have been produced by the Irish Army from its McKee Barracks in Phoenix Park during recent years. Rode in his first international show in 1954, four years before he took over the best Irish Army horse since the war, Loch an Easpaig. This chesnut gelding by Knight's Crusader was foaled in 1951 in Co. Kilkenny, the nineteenth offspring of his mother, who was then aged twenty-five. For the first few days of his life he was too weak to stand without aid. The best young horse in Rotterdam in 1958, Lock an Easpaig won his first international competition in 1959, and in 1961 won in Nice, the Grand Prix in Rome, and in London, Washington, New York, and Toronto. In 1967, after jumping a clear first round in the Ostend Nations Cup, he collapsed and died during the second circuit. Col Ringrose was later *chef d'équipe* of the Irish team.

Peter Robeson (Great Britain)

Born in 1929. His father was in the British team after the war, and Peter Robeson joined the team himself in 1947 on a little home-bred mare, Craven A. Shortlisted for the 1952 Olympic team, he finally made the trip to Stockholm in 1956, riding Scorchin' for the late Hon. Dorothy Paget, and won a team bronze medal. In 1964 he rode his own horse Firecrest with the Olympic team in Tokyo and won an individual bronze after a jump-off with John Fahey of Australia on Bonvale. He won the King George V Gold Cup in 1967 and has been a consistent winner both at home and abroad on Craven A and Firecrest and, more recently, on Grebe, who was shortlisted for the Olympic team in 1972. In 1969 his training methods came under fire in a Sunday newspaper but he was exonerated by the stewards of the BSJA. He was a member of the British Olympic team in 1976, on Law Court.

Michel Roche (France)

Another French gold medallist in 1976, Michel was born on 8 September 1939, and made his debut at fifteen specialising first in the three-day event. As a member of the French team, he helped to win the Nations Cups in Ostend and Toronto in 1974, and to finish second in Rome and Rotterdam. In 1975 he was second in the championship in Rome and was the best-classified foreign rider. His best horse, Un Espoir E, was badly injured in the first qualifying competition for the French championship in 1976.

Colonel Paul Rodzianko (Russia)

In his youth a page to the Czar Nicholas of Russia, Paul Rodzianko was the only instructor still living after the war who had been taught both by James Fillis and by the Italian father of the forward seat, Federico Caprilli, who revolutionised riding over fences. After a year at the Italian cavalry school, Rodzianko returned to Russia and trained a team of Russian officers. They came to London and won the Nations Cup in 1912, 1913, and 1914, thus winning the King Edward VII Cup outright. With the outbreak of World War I Rodzianko was posted to the Austrian front and then to the Russian Embassy in Rome, where he was military attaché at the time of the revolution. He lost an estate the size of England overnight, so settled over here, joined the British Army, and later set up a training establishment in Windsor. In the early 1930s he was invited to direct the cavalry school in Dublin, where he built up the Irish Army team to become the best in the world. He served in the British Army again in World War II, and after a further period in Dublin he set up a school in England in 1955, where he instructed pupils in showjumping until his death in 1965. Rodzianko had a profound influence upon the training of showjumpers and loathed seeing horses pulled about over bad courses.

Major Lawrence Rook (Great Britain)
After leaving the Household Cavalry, Major Rook was in the first British civilian three-day event team in the Olympic Games at Helsinki when Captain Michael Naylor-Leyland fell ill. His mount was Starlight, a Devonshire-bred son of the premium stallion, Trappeur II. Nearing the end of the cross-country course, the horse fell and Rook, who was concussed, went the wrong side of a flag after landing over the last fence and sadly eliminated himself and the team. In 1953 he won Badminton on Starlight. In the 1956 Olympic Games in Stockholm he helped to win the team gold medal on Mr Ted Marsh's former champion hunter in Dublin, Wild Venture. He was the FEI technical delegate to the Mexico and Montreal Olympic Games, and was chairman of the Combined Training Committee and one of Britain's two representatives at the FEI General Assembly until October 1980.

Marcel Rozier (France)
The son of a breeder and horse-dealer at Saint-Etienne de Chalaronne in the region of Dombes, near Lyon in the Beaujolais district, Marcel Rozier was born on 22 March 1936. He has been closely connected with horses all his life, and though for some time he worked in a factory, his passion for horses never left him. He met his future father-in-law — Hubert Parot's father — when he was riding at a racecourse in the centre of France, and was introduced to equestrian sport — and also to Christiane Parot, now his wife. He started in the three-day event, then took up showjumping, and in 1964 was selected for the French Olympic team which won the silver medals in Tokyo.

Champion of France in 1970, 1971, and 1974, he won the Grand Prix of Aachen in 1971, and in 1974 the Austrian Grand Prix in Vienna with his future Olympic horse, Bayard de Maupas, on whom a year later he was fifth in the European championship in Munich, won the Derby de Bois le Roi and was second in the French championship.

Terry Rudd (USA)

Born in 1951, showjumper Terry Rudd hails from New Hope, Pennsylvania. In 1980 she won the John Player Trophy (Grand Prix) in London, on Semi-Tough.

Michael Saywell (Great Britain)

Mick Saywell, a farmer's son from Lincolnshire, learned to ride showjumpers on a succession of bad family horses. He first rode a string of horses for John Taylor, but it was not until he joined up with Trevor Banks in Yorkshire that he got his chance to become an international rider. Teamed with the half-Clydesdale Hideaway, by Blue Shah, who was bought for £70 at a Cumberland fair as an unbroken young horse, he won the Grand Prix in La Baule in 1970, went outstandingly well in the final two Olympic trials, and was an obvious choice for the British Olympic team in Munich, where he put up the most useful performance of the quartet. Having returned to John Taylor for two seasons, he rejoined Trevor Banks in 1975 and won the King George V Cup on Chain Bridge in 1976. Chain Bridge, who is by the Irish draught stallion Bahrain, won the Dublin Grand Prix in 1978 and the *Daily Mail* Cup at the Royal International, as well as the Whyte and Mackay Scotch Whisky Championship and second prize in the Calgary Grand Prix in Alberta. He now rides again for John Taylor.

Alwin Schockemöhle (West Germany)

Born in 1937, Alwin Schockemöhle, former Olympic and European champion, and the only man ever to jump a double clear round in the Olympic Games, started riding soon after the war and at seventeen became a pupil of Hans Günter Winkler at the training school at Warendorf. At Stockholm in 1956 he was reserve for both the West German Olympic showjumping and three-day event teams. Won his first international competition at Aachen in 1957, riding Bacchus, and three years later rode Ferdl in the winning Olympic team in Rome, with Fritz Thiedemann on Meteor and Winkler on Halla. German champion on three occasions, in 1965 he set up the German high jump record of 7ft 4in (2.25m) on Exakt.

In 1968 he won the Aachen Grand Prix on Donald Rex, and on the same horse (with the best score of the entire competition) led his team to win the Olympic bronze medal in Mexico. Placed in the first three in four European championships, he was generally thwarted by David Broome — second in Rome in 1963 to Mancinelli, to Broome in 1967 in Rotterdam, to Broome again at Hickstead in 1969, and to McMahon at Hickstead in 1973. He was also fourth to Broome in the men's world championship at La Baule in 1970, but was eliminated in 1974.

Won the amateur championship at Cardiff in 1974, and in 1975, with Broome out of the way as the European champion-ship was then confined to amateurs, he finally took the European title on Warwick, in Munich. Also in 1975 he was enormously successful in England, going virtually through the card at the Hickstead-Wembley CSIO with Rex the Robber, Warwick, and the young Dutch mare, Santa Monica. His greatest achievement in 1976 was to win the Olympic individual Grand Prix on Warwick Rex with the only double clear round in its history. He retired at the end of this season with insuperable back trouble but what a note on which to finish! He now has a string ridden by the twenty-two-year-old Dutchman Franke Sloothaak, who qualified for the World Cup in Amsterdam.

Paul Schockemöhle (West Germany)
Born in 1945, Paul is the younger brother of Alwin Schocke-möhle, the 1976 Olympic champion. Paul first joined the German team in 1971 and was in their Olympic team in 1976. He is now a member of all their championship teams. In 1979 he was equal first for the Grand Prix at the European champ-ionship meeting in Rotterdam, riding Deister. In 1980 he was the leading German rider with Deister and El Paso.

Hermann Schridde (Germany)
Born in 1937. A farmer from Westphalia, Schridde is another

of Hans Winkler's protegés; won the Olympic silver medal in Tokyo in 1964 riding the big chesnut Hannoverian Dozent. Also helped to win the team gold medal. In 1965 he won the men's European championship in Aachen on the same horse, and in Mexico he helped to win the Olympic bronze medal.

Lars Sederholm (Sweden)

An adopted Briton, both by marriage and by inclination, this Swedish instructor won the combined training points championship in one-day events from 1963 until 1965. Now runs a training establishment at Waterstock, near Oxford, and among the many successful riders he has coached are Graham Fletcher, Richard Walker, and Caroline Bradley.

Neal Shapiro (USA)

Born in 1948. Lives on Long Island and drives trotting horses as a hobby. Joined the United States team in 1964. On his first European tour, in 1966, he won the Grand Prix in Aachen on Jacks or Better. Sold his ex-rodeo horse, the unruly Uncle Max, to Ted Edgar on his second trip to Europe in 1968. In 1971 returned riding a horse which was the envy of all who saw him, the big bay Thoroughbred, Sloopy, who finished equal first in the Grand Prix with Marcel Rozier on the French horse, Sans Souci. He won the Olympic individual bronze medal in Munich on Sloopy and a team silver.

Hugo Simon (Austria)

Hugo Simon was born in 1942 in Germany. In 1971, in order to be able to ride in the Olympic Games, he claimed dual nationality through his Austrian grandmother and elected to ride for Austria. He competed in Munich as an individual, riding Lavendel, who finished equal fourth. A consistent winner in England with this horse and Flipper, he tied for third place in the men's world championship at Hickstead in 1974 with Frank Chapot of the United States on Main Spring. In 1975 he created a novel situation by refusing to have a dope test on one of his horses at Rotterdam after it declined to urinate. He was fined $100 in what must be regarded as a test case.

He won the first World Cup in Gothenburg in the spring of 1979 on Gladstone, the puissance in London on Sorry and the

Everest Double Glazing championship on Gladstone. He also won the Rotterdam Grand Prix on Gladstone. In 1980 he won the alternative Olympic individual gold medal in Rotterdam.

John Simpson (Canada)
John Simpson, whose elder sister Barbara was well known on the European circuit ten years earlier, enjoyed his best season in 1977, when he was twenty-seven years old. Having dominated the spring circuit in the West, he took Texas and Commander Jack to Europe for two months, winning at the Royal International, placing at Hickstead, Antwerp and Dublin in the Grand Prix and finally winning the Grand Prix of Holland at Rotterdam. On his return home he won the Spruce Meadows 'Masters' Grand Prix at Calgary. Married early in 1978, he is a rancher and owns a contracting firm.

Nick Skelton (Great Britain)
The son of a Warwickshire chemist, and pupil of Ted and Elizabeth Edgar, Nick was still a couple of weeks short of his twenty-first birthday, when, in December, 1978, he broke the British High Jump record which had stood for forty-one years. Riding the Everest Stud's grey German-bred Lastic, a Hannoverian, by Lateran, sire of Lavandel, he cleared 7ft 7^5/16 ins. Lastic has since been sold, but Nick has been very successful on Maybe with whom he won the Leading Showjumper title in 1978. He won the junior European championship in 1979 and finished seventh for the World Cup in Gothenburg. He was extremely successful at home in 1980 and helped to win the silver medals in Grand Prix des Nations in Rotterdam's alternative Olympics.

Harvey Smith (Great Britain)
Born in Yorkshire in 1938. After a career in junior classes, he won fame when he bought Farmer's Boy at York Sales in 1954 for £40. Four years later he rode him with the British team in Dublin. With his foot now on the first rung of the ladder, Harvey began to specialise in remaking horses which others had given up as a bad job. Warpaint, bought at a Leicester repository for 200 gns, was the first of them. Then there was Montana, The Frame, The Sea Hawk, O'Malley and Harvester, Madison

Time, Evan Jones, Mattie Brown, Johnny Walker, Archie, Summertime, and most recently Volvo. O'Malley, bred in Canada, lasted the longest. Leading horse in 1963 and 1974, he was then replaced by Harvester. With this enormous string spread throughout the years, Harvey has won many big prizes.

Rejected for the Olympic team in 1964, he travelled to Mexico with Madison Time in 1968. In 1972 he was on the short list for the team, omitted from the list when the final team was announced, and then ultimately reinstated. A very strong rider who likes to dominate his horses, though he rides the younger ones with considerable sympathy, he has won the John Player Trophy, the British Grand Prix, on five occasions. In 1970 he won the King George V Cup on Mattie Brown, who also won him the British Jumping Derby in 1970 and 1971. But a European title and an Olympic medal have never come his way.

His world-wide fame is due as much to his fighting spirit and his no-holds-barred approach to his sport as to his prowess as a rider. He became a professional – the first to do so – in October 1972, and early in 1973 went into partnership with Hideaway's owner, Trevor Banks. In 1974, as well as taking up all-in wrestling, he won his third British Jumping Derby at Hickstead. Later in the year he was disicplined by the BSJA stewards and suspended for three months. In 1975, he stood, unsuccessfully, for the executive committee of the BSJA, and though he was as active as ever in the show ring – but with less success than in 1974, when Salvador was leading horse – he broke new ground in issuing his first record. Its title: *True Love!* Among his best wins in 1976 was the Dublin Grand Prix on Olympic Star. In 1977 he wrote a weekly column in *The Sun* which did not exactly endear him to his fellow riders. His sons Robert and Stephen helped to win the Junior European Championship and graduated to horses.

Harvey was sponsored by Sanyo in 1978 and his string changed name in consequence. He asked not to be included in the world championship team. He won the John Player Grand Prix at the Royal International and the Radio Rentals Grand Prix at the Horse of the Year show where son Robert won *The Sunday Times* Cup and £1,400. He finished 1978 by winning the £4,000 Harris Carpets' Masters at Harwood Hall on Sanyo

San Mar, formerly Olympic Star. In 1979 he won three classes on the last day of the Royal International, but hit the headlines instead because he refused to allow his son Robert to ride in Dublin with the British team.

Melanie Smith (USA)
Born in 1950, Melanie comes from Stonington, Connecticut. She won a team gold medal at the 1979 Pan-American Games in Puerto Rico. She was the 1979 US Rider of the Year on Val de Loire and came second on the Dutch-bred seven-year-old Calypso for the 1980 World Cup in Baltimore.

Robert Smith (Great Britain)
In 1979 Robert Smith, elder son of Harvey and Irene Smith, became the youngest rider ever to win the King George V Gold Cup at Wembley's Royal International Horse Show, riding Video. The following week, he won the Grand Prix at Hickstead. His first triumph resulted in his being selected to ride with the British team in Dublin, but his father declined to make horses available to him.

As a junior, he and his brother Stephen helped to win the European championship. Robert turned professional in 1980 and signed a £80,000 contract with Simoniz, the car care firm.

Pat Koechlin Smythe (Great Britain)
Born in 1928, Pat Smythe first jumped to fame with Finality in the late 1940s but it was Tosca and Prince Hal that really established her as a leading rider. She has ridden very little since her marriage to Swiss lawyer Sam Koechlin — who rode at Badminton on several occasions — in 1963. She won the European championship four times — at Spain in 1957 on Flanagan, at Deauville in 1961 on the same horse, who retained his title a year later in Madrid; and again on Flanagan, at Hickstead, in 1963. In 1952 Tosca, a grey Irish mare, was the leading money-winner in England and defeated all the top strings of that day. In 1956, at Stockholm, she became the first woman to ride in the Olympic Games and helped, on Flanagan, to bring the team bronze medal back to Britain. Foiled in her attempts to win the Queen Elizabeth II Cup for many years, she finally triumphed in 1958 on Mr Pollard. Flanagan, who

won most of her international victories, was an Irish horse who was originally ridden round Badminton by Brigadier Lyndon Bolton and then sold to Robert Hanson.

Hartwig Steenken (West Germany)

Born in 1941. A farmer and stud-owner and perhaps the most natural horseman on the German team, Hartwig won the men's European championship at Aachen in 1971, with Britain's Harvey Smith runner-up. He won the title on his Olympic ride, Simona, a chesnut Hannoverian mare, foaled in 1958. He was an automatic selection for the 1972 Olympic team, and helped to win the gold medal in Munich. A badly fractured leg prevented him from defending his European title in 1973 at Hickstead, but he was amply compensated when he won the world championship there in 1974 on Simona. This gallant mare has now retired to stud, and in 1975 he rode Erle to finish as runner-up for the European championship in Munich. In 1977 he sustained brain damage in a car crash and died in January 1978, after six months in a coma, a sad loss to the equestrian world.

Bill Steinkraus (USA)

Born in 1925, Bill Steinkraus won the Olympic individual gold medal in Mexico, 1968, on Snowbound, riding in his fifth Olympic Games. He joined the team in 1951, rode Hollandia to a team bronze medal in Helsinki in 1952 and took over as team captain in 1955. In 1956 he won the King George V Cup, on First Boy, a feat he repeated eight years later on Sinjon. In Rome he rode Ksar d'Esprit in the Olympic team event, where his team won the silver medal.

In 1964 he brought out Snowbound, a former racehorse, and though he had to miss the team event in Tokyo as Sinjon was lame, Snowbound benefited from his first European tour and won the Grand Prix in New York the following year. In 1968 he won the Grand Prix in London before taking the gold medal in Mexico. A Thoroughbred gelding by Hail Victory out of Gay Alvena, Snowbound was foaled in 1958.

Riding Main Spring, Steinkraus had the best individual performance in Munich, with only four faults in his two rounds, which gave the US team their silver medal in the showjumping event. Steinkraus, a fine amateur musician, made the Munich Olympic Games his last, wishing to spend more time with his wife and their three growing sons. A great stylist and a most popular competitor, he is sadly missed from the international scene. He is now a CBS commentator, and president of the US team.

Colonel Douglas Stewart (Great Britain)
Col. 'Duggie' Stewart, late of the Royal Scots Greys, rode Col. Harry Llewellyn's Aherlow in the British team which won the gold medals in the 1952 Olympic Games in Helsinki. Aherlow was a brown Irish mare who later won puissance competitions on the Continent with her owner.

Christine Stückelberger (Switzerland)
Christine Stückelberger won the Olympic dressage gold medal in the 1976 Olympic Games on the bay Holstein horse Granat, which she and Georg Wahl, her trainer, with circus proprietor Freddie Knie, bought very cheaply in Bavaria. He had been sold under the hammer to go to Italy, but then started coughing and could not travel. She first competed in junior dressage in 1963. In 1968 she came out as an international rider in Aachen. She and Granat won the European championship in Kiev in 1975, the Olympic gold a year later, when she was twenty-nine years old, and finally the world championship at Goodwood in 1978, having a year earlier retained the European title in St Gallen. Wahl is a product of the Spanish Riding School of Vienna (he is an Austrian) and he and Miss Stückelberger have their training centre at Horbranz, by Lake Constance. Miss Stückelberger won the alternative Olympic gold medal at Goodwood in 1980.

Colonel Jack Talbot-Ponsonby (Great Britain)
Succeeded in winning the King George V Gold Cup at the Royal International Horse Show on three occasions between the wars, when he was stationed at the Army Equitation School at Weedon. He was a member of many a military showjumping team, and won in New York and Toronto. His best horses were Kineton, Chelsea, and Best Girl. He trained the British showjumping team for the 1952 Olympic Games, when they won the gold medal in Helsinki, and also in 1956 and 1960. Then he set

up a training establishment at his home, Todenham Manor in Gloucestershire, where he coached riders from all over the world.

A most gifted and erudite course-builder, he served both the Royal International and the Horse of the Year shows. A past master in the construction of related fences, and a believer in testing by distance rather than by over-fencing horses by building massive obstacles. He set great store by those distance problems inherent in what he termed 'disposable half-strides'. He had the ability to assess the capabilities and shortcomings of any horse. He collapsed and died out hunting in 1969 when only sixty-one.

Major James Templer (Great Britain)

In 1962 Templer and his Anglo-Arab horse M'Lord Connolly, by Connetable, were not selected for the British team for the European championships at Burghley. He then proceeded resolutely to capture the European individual title from one of the Soviet contingent, who won the team event from Ireland with Britain third, thus proving the selectors wrong. He rode his horse to victory at Badminton in 1964 and was then selected for the Tokyo Olympic team. But here M'Lord Connolly was eliminated.

Elizabeth Theurer (Austria)

In 1979, when she was only twenty-two years old, this rider from Linz won the European dressage championship at Aarhus, Denmark, beating none other than the world and Olympic champions, Christine Stückelberger and Granat. Miss Theurer was riding the grey gelding, Mon Cherie, on whom in 1980, without the approval of her federation she attended the Moscow Olympics and won a gold medal.

Fritz Thiedemann (West Germany)

Born in 1918, Fritz Thiedemann was the best advertisement ever for the jumping ability of the heavy Holstein horse. On Meteor, who won the King George V Cup in 1954, he won the individual bronze at Helsinki in 1952 and helped to win the first of three consecutive Olympic team events for Germany at Stockholm in 1956. He was still in the team with the same horse four years later in Rome, and in 1958 they won the European championship. They also won the Grand Prix at Aachen three times, and Thiedemann scored the record number of five victories in the gruelling Hamburg Jumping Derby.

Michel Vaillancourt (Canada)
Born in 1955, from Hudson, Quebec, Michel Vaillancourt won an Olympic silver medal in 1976 and a Pan-American silver team medal at the 1979 Games. In 1980, after winning the puissance in New York and Washington and helping to win the Nations Cup in Toronto, he won a team gold medal at the alternative Olympics in Rotterdam.

Tommy Wade (Ireland)
Tommy Wade was a farmer's son from Co. Tipperary. Dundrum out of a registered Connemara pony mare, was, at 15 hands 1½ins high, one of the smallest and the greatest of showjumpers. He started life pulling a milk float in the town, not far from Dublin, whose name he bore. Foaled in 1952, he was to win two international and nine national championships in Dublin. But he also won the Victor Ludorum at Wembley in 1961, and the following year took the puissance and the Guinness time championship, in addition to the Vaux Gold Tankard at the Royal Highland and the Grand Prix in Ostend and Brussels. In 1963 he won the King George V Cup and his second puissance at Wembley after which he eventually retired due to Tommy Wade's ill-health.

Richard Walker (Great Britain)
Richard became the youngest rider ever to win the Badminton Horse Trials in 1969, when he rode the Anglo-Arab Pasha to victory after all the better-fancied horses and riders had fallen by the wayside. Pasha, by an Arab sire, had previously competed in Pony Club events. Richard Walker also won the individual title in the first-ever junior European championships at Eridge in 1968, and in 1969 he helped the British senior team to win the European championship at Haras du Pin. In 1979 he won the Midland Bank Open Championship at Locko Park for the second year running, on John of Gaunt, and in 1980 he took the same horse to victory at Burghley.

John Watson (Ireland)

Born in London in 1952, John Watson, who rode Cambridge
Blue to win the silver medal in the 1978 world championships
in Lexington, Kentucky, has been riding since he was twelve
and hunts regularly with the Tipperary Foxhounds. He started
eventing in 1969 and, in 1975, competed in the European
championships in Luhmühlen and was selected for the Olympic
Games the following year, but his horse was injured while
exercising in Bromont just before the Games and could not
compete. With his wife, Julia, who comes from Wellington,
Somerset, he farms the family's 340-acre estate, where they
have a large herd of pedigree dairy shorthorns and several young
horses to make, break and sell on. In 1979 on Cambridge Blue
he helped to win the team gold medals at the European
championships in Luhmühlen.

Colonel Frank Weldon (Great Britain)

Frank Weldon, now director and course builder of the
Badminton Horse Trials and equestrian correspondent of the
Sunday Telegraph, will always be remembered for his partnership with the great Kilbarry when he commanded the King's
Troop. Together they helped to win the Olympic team gold
medal in Stockholm in 1956 when an individual bronze came
their way. Helped to win four consecutive European team
titles – in 1953 at Badminton, 1954 in Basle, 1955 at Windsor,
and 1957 in Copenhagen – and won the individual title at
Windsor. In 1956 they won Badminton.

Frank Weldon came to horse trials via the racecourse. He won
his first point-to-point in 1935, the year after he joined his
regiment at Catterick, and went on to a highly successful career
under rules which was terminated by the war. But he won the
RA Gold Cup at Sandown in 1956 and 1957 on Snowshill Jim
and was winning point-to-points up to 1959.

Kilbarry was one of the greatest horses combined training has
ever produced. A big bay of 16.3 hands, by Malbrouk out of a
mare by Heligoland, he was bred in Ireland and shown in
England until he got too strong for the ring. He was hobdayed
after a coughing epidemic in 1952 and always made a noise
thereafter, but he won a race in 1953 before his first introduc-
tion to combined training, at Stowell Park, where he won. He

was, his owner says, 'a gay, irrepressible, unpredictable fellow with a strong will of his own: he did nothing by halves.'

Now an elder statesman of the sport, Frank Weldon is an admirable technical delegate, in which capacity he served with distinction in the 1975 European championships, where he initiated dope tests and refused to allow tired horses to continue, thus avoiding accidents and serving the sport's best interests. His course-building talents are held in high regard and he ran an FEI instructional seminar at Luhmühlen prior to the championships. He is a brilliant writer on the three-day event, in *Horse and Hound*.

John Whitaker (Great Britain)
A twenty-three-year-old Yorkshire rider, son of a farmer in the Halifax area, John Whitaker has come right to the fore in the last three years with Singing Wind and Ryan's Son. He is a gifted and tactful horseman with a remarkably good eye and an exceptional pair of hands, and although he was dropped from the 1976 Olympic team when Ryan's Son stopped in the final trial he was the hero of the British alternative Olympic team in Rotterdam four years later: Ryan's Son won a team silver medal as well as an individual silver. The following week John finished second to his younger brother Michael, in the British Jumping Derby at Hickstead.

Michael Whitaker (Great Britain)
Michael Whitaker, aged twenty-two, became the youngest rider ever to win the British Jumping Derby in 1980, on Owen Gregory.

Captain Martin Whiteley (Great Britain)
Educated at Eton and returned there as a master after leaving the army. Has produced a number of excellent three-day event horses over the years. The most famous of all is The Poacher, on whom his owner won the Little Badminton event in 1965. He was in every international team from 1966 to 1971, when he was retired, and helped to win an Olympic gold medal and no fewer than four team titles — one world and three European. Whiteley rode The Poacher into fifth place in the world event at Burghley in 1966, and the following year at Punchestown was in the winning team for the European championship and

finished second individually, after a magnificent performance across country. As Capt Whiteley had back trouble, he made the horse available to the selection committee for the Olympic Games and, ridden by Sgt Ben Jones, he was in the winning team in Mexico and also in the European championship at Haras du Pin a year later. In 1970 he was ridden by Richard Meade to win Badminton, and was in the winning world team at Punchestown. Made his final appearance at Burghley in 1971, where he helped assure that the European title remained in Britain. He was then fifteen years old.

Captain Whiteley was chairman of the selection committee of the Combined Training Committee until he became a housemaster at Eton, and he remains actively concerned with the administration of the sport he served so well. He is now chairman of the Horse Trials Group, for whom he formed a supporters' club.

Sheila Willcox (Great Britain)

What Pat Smythe was to showjumping, Sheila Willcox was to combined training, until she broke her back in a fall at Tidworth which almost ended her career in 1971. She is the only rider ever to have achieved a hat-trick in successive years at Badminton, which she initiated in 1957 on High and Mighty, a dun Irish horse, by a Thoroughbred out of a Highland-cross-Arab mare. Sheila and her great horse appeared in the first three-day event at Windsor in 1955, and the following year they challenged Frank Weldon and Kilbarry so tenaciously at Badminton that the champions' margin was only 1.56 points. Kilbarry was killed early in 1957 so High and Mighty was a hot favourite for Badminton. He won, overtaking Ted Marsh on Wild Venture on the third day. He won again in 1958, finishing 47 points ahead of his nearest rival, Derek Allhusen's home-bred Laurien. He was then retired to the hunting field, having won at Turin in 1955 and taken the European title at Copenhagen in 1957. Sheila's third Badminton victory came in 1959, when she triumphed on her new horse, Airs and Graces, after a two-day duel in rain and mud with David Somerset, heir to the Duke of Beaufort, on Countryman. She is once again active in the horse world and supplies horses for dressage and eventing to the Continent.

Dorian Williams (Great Britain)
Son of the late Colonel V. D. S. Williams, whose claims to
equestrian fame are legion, Dorian has also served the horse
world in many different capacities since the end of World War
II. His informed commentaries on the public address at the
Royal International and Horse of the Year shows led to his
appointment as a BBC commentator when television first
became interested in showjumping. Then he did the same
for combined training at Badminton and Burghley. In addition
to being the most senior and popular commentator, he is also a
prolific writer on equestrian matters. He was instrumental in
starting the National Equestrian Centre (now known as the
British Equestrian Centre) at Stoneleigh, which he got off the
ground very successfully in its early years. In demand, too, as a
hunter judge, he is first and foremost a foxhunter and is a
former Joint Master of the Grafton Hounds. In 1974 he became
chairman of the British Horse Society in belated recognition of
having given so unstintingly of his time and energy for the best
part of thirty years. In 1980 he retired as Master of the
Whaddon Chase and as BBC commentator.

Ted Williams (Great Britain)
Started his showjumping career before the war riding rogue
horses for the late Percy Adcocks of Leicester — whose boast it
was that he never gave more than £20 for a horse. He thinks
that he won his first competition in 1925, as a lad of thirteen.
He has ridden jumpers throughout his life, and though he was
given an amateur licence in 1956, which enabled him to ride
with the British team and help in the winning of many vital
Nations Cups, his former professionalism always debarred him
from the Olympic Games. He has been associated with many
great horses; Huntsman, Umbo, Leicester Lad, Ann Tucker,
Tim II, Pegasus, Sunday Morning, the Australian Dumbell, the
Argentinian Discutido, and the South Americans Carnaval,
Careta, Relincho, and Rival. The greatest of them all was
Pegasus, still living in retirement on Ted's farm near Leicester.
He set up a record by being the leading money-winner in Britain
from 1955 to 1958 and again in 1960. In 1957 he toured the
American shows with the British team and won all three Grand
Prix — at Harrisburg, New York, and Toronto.

Gerd Wiltfang (West Germany)

First came to fame as the rider of the grey wonder-horse, the Hannoverian Askan, who was sold for the then record price of £56,000 in 1971 to Josef Kun (not surprisingly, he later went bankrupt). Wiltfang, whose occupation, to comply with the Olympic ruling, was then designated a 'part-time car park attendant', rode in the winning German Olympic team in 1972. Six years later, in Aachen, he won the world championship, beating Eddie Macken by .25 of a time fault, on the brilliant young horse, Roman. In 1979 he won the European championship in Rotterdam on the same horse. In 1980, Roman was the worst German horse in the alternative Olympics at Rotterdam. Gerd, thirty-three, is a baker's son from Bremen.

Hans Günter Winkler (West Germany)

Born in 1926, the son of a horse dealer from Westphalia, Hans Winkler, who succeeded to the captaincy of the German team when Thiedemann retired, jumped in his first international show in Spain in 1952. Two years later on his great mare Halla he won the world championship in Madrid from d'Oriola and the holder, Goyoaga. In 1955 he won it again in Aachen after a jump-off with Raimondo d'Inzeo, and in 1956 he won the individual gold medal at the Stockholm Olympic Games. In 1957 he won the European championships in Rotterdam. Halla jumped in her last Olympic Games in Rome in 1960, at the age of sixteen, and was retired to stud the following year.

Winkler won two King George V Cups, on Fortun and Enigk, and was in the four-cornered jump-off for the individual bronze medal in Mexico on the latter, where the team finished third. He helped to win four team gold medals, but in 1971 had the misfortune to lose his best and most promising horse, the brown Thoroughbred Jaegermeister, after an accident in Dublin. In Munich, he rode Torphy in the winning Olympic team, and rode him again to a team silver medal in Montreal.

24
International Championship Records

OLYMPIC GAMES

1900 PARIS
Prize Jumping
1 Haegeman (Belgium) (BEL)
2 Van der Poele (Belgium) (BEL)
3 De Champsavin (France) (FRA)

High Jump
1 Gardere (France) (FRA)
2 G. Trissino (Italy) ITA)

Long Jump
1 Van Longendonck (Belgium) (BEL)
2 G. Trissino (Italy) (ITA)

1908 LONDON
Polo
1 Gt Britain (H. Wilson, G. Miller, P. W. Nickalls, C. D. Miller)
2 Gt Britain (W. H. Jones, F. M. Freake, W. S. Buckmaster, Lord Wodehouse)
3 Ireland

1912 STOCKHOLM
Dressage

Team
1 Sweden
2 Germany
3 France

Individual
1 Count Carl Bonde (SWE)
  Emperor
2 Maj. G.-A. Boltenstern (SWE)
  Neptune
3 Lt. H. von Blixen-Finecke (SWE)
  Maggie

Three-Day Event

Team
1 Sweden
2 Germany
3 USA

Individual
1 Lt. Axel Nordlander (SWE) *Lady Artist*
2 Lt. von Rochow (GER) *Idealist*
3 Capt. J. Cariou (FRA) *Cocotte*

Showjumping

Team
1 Sweden
2 France
3 Germany

Individual
1 Capt. J. Cariou (FRA) *Mignon*
2 Lt. von Krocher (GER) *Dobna*
3 Baron von B. de Soye (BEL) *Clonmore*

1920 ANTWERP

Dressage

Team
1 Sweden
2 France
3 USA

Individual
1 Capt. J. Lundblad (SWE) *Uno*
2 Lt. B. Sandstrom (SWE) *Sabel*
3 Count H. von Rosen (SWE) *Running Sister*

Three-Day Event

Team
1 Sweden
2 Italy
3 Belgium

Individual
1 Count H. Morner (SWE) *Germania*
2 Lt. A. Landström (SWE) *Yrsa*
3 Maj. E. Caffaratti (ITA) *Traditore*

Showjumping

Team
1 Sweden
2 Belgium
3 Italy

Individual
1 Lt. T. Lequio (ITA) *Trebecco*
2 Maj. A. Valerio (ITA) *Cento*
3 Capt. G. Lewenhaupt (SWE) *Mon Coeur*

Figure Riding

Team
1 Belgium
2 France
3 Sweden

Individual
1 T. Bonckaert (BEL)
2 S. Field (FRA)
3 T. Finet (BEL)

Polo

Team
1 Gt Britain
2 Spain
3 USA

1924 PARIS

Dressage

Team
1 Sweden
2 France
3 Czechoslovakia

Individual
1 Gen. E. Linder (SWE) *Piccolomini*
2 B. Sandstrom (SWE) *Sabel*
3 F. Lesage (FRA) *Plunard*

Three-Day Event

Team
1 Netherlands
2 Sweden
3 Italy

Individual
1 Lt. A. van der Voort van Zijp
  (HOL) *Silver Piece*
2 Lt. F. Kirkebjerg (DEN) *Meteor*
3 Maj. S. Doak (USA) *Pathfinder*

Showjumping

Team
1 Sweden
2 Switzerland
3 Portugal

Individual
1 Lt. A. Gemuseus (SWI) *Lucette*
2 Lt. T. Lequio (ITA) *Trebecco*
3 Lt. A. Krolikiewicz (POL)
  Picador

Polo

Team
1 Argentina
2 USA
3 Gt Britain

1928 AMSTERDAM

Dressage

Team
1 Germany
2 Sweden
3 Netherlands

Individual
1 Baron C. F. von Langen (GER)
  Draufgänger
2 Cmdr. C. L. P. Marion (FRA)
  Linon
3 R. Olson (SWE) *Gunstling*

Three-Day Event

Team
1 Netherlands
2 Norway
3 Poland

Individual
1 Lt. C. F. Pahud de Mortanges
  (HOL) *Marcroix*
2 Capt. G. P. de Kruijff (HOL)
  Va-t-en
3 Maj. B. Neumann (GER) *Ilja*

Showjumping

Team
1 Spain
2 Poland
3 Sweden

Individual
1 Capt. F. Ventura (CZE) *Eliot*
2 Capt. M. L. Bertran de Balanda
  (FRA) *Papillon*
3 Maj. C. Kuhn (SWI) *Pepita*

1932 LOS ANGELES

Dressage

Team
1 France
2 Sweden
3 USA

Individual
1 Capt. F. Lesage (FRA) *Taine*
2 Cmdt. C. Marion (FRA) *Linon*
3 H. Tuttle (USA) *Olympic*

Three-Day Event
Team
1 USA
2 Netherlands Only two teams
   finished

Individual
1 Lt. C. F. Pahud de Mortanges
   (HOL) *Marcroix*
2 Lt. E. Thomson (USA) *Jenny
   Camp*
3 Lt. C. von Rosen (SWE)
   Sunnyside Maid

Showjumping

No awards as no team finished

Individual
1 Lt. T. Nishi (JAP) *Uranus*
2 Maj. H. Chamberlin (USA) *Show
   Girl*
3 Lt. C. von Rosen (SWE) *Empire*

1936 BERLIN
Dressage
Team
1 Germany
2 France
3 Sweden

Individual
1 Lt. H. Pollay (GER) *Kronos*
2 Maj. F. Gerhard (GER) *Absinth*
3 Maj. A. Podhajsky (AUT) *Nero*

Three-Day Event
Team
1 Germany
2 Poland
3 Gt Britain

Individual
1 Capt. L. Stubbendorf (GER)
   Nurmi
2 Capt. E. Thomson (USA) *Jenny
   Camp*
3 Capt. H. Lunding (DEN) *Jason*

Showjumping
Team
1 Germany
2 Netherlands
3 Portugal

Individual
1 Lt. K. Hasse (GER) *Tora*
2 Lt. H. Rang (RUM) *Delphis*
3 Capt. J. Platthy (HUN) *Selloe*

Polo
Team
1 Argentina
2 Gt Britain
3 Mexico

1948 LONDON
Dressage
Team
1 France (A. R. Jousseaume,
   Harpagon; J. Paillard,
   Sous le Ceps; M. Buret,
   St Owen)
2 USA
3 Portugal

Individual
1 Capt. H. Moser (SWI) *Hummer*
2 Col. A. R. Jousseaume (FRA)
   Harpagon
3 Capt. G. A. Boltenstern (SWE)
   Trumf

Three-Day Event

Team	Individual
1 USA (F. S. Henry, *Swing Low*; C. H. Anderson, *Reno Palisade*; E. F. Thomson, *Reno Rhythm*)	1 B. Chavallier (FRA) *Aiglonne*
2 Sweden	2 Lt. Col. F. S. Henry (USA) *Swing Low*
3 Mexico	3 Capt. J. R. Selfelt (SWE) *Claque*

Showjumping

Team	Individual
1 Mexico (H. Mariles Cortés, *Arete*; R. Valdes, *Chibucho*; R. Uriza, *Hatvey*)	1 Col. H. Mariles Cortés (MEX) *Arete*
2 Spain	2 Lt. R. Uriza (MEX) *Hatvey*
3 Gt Britain (H. M. Llewellyn, *Foxhunter*; H. M. V. Nicoll, *Kilgeddin*; A. Carr, *Monty*)	3 Chev. J. F. d'Orgeix (FRA) *Sucre de Pomme*

1952 HELSINKI

Dressage

Team	Individual
1 Sweden (G. A. Boltenstern, *Krest*; H. St. Cyr, *Master Rufus*; G. Persson, *Knaust*)	1 Maj. H. St. Cyr (SWE) *Master Rufus*
2 Switzerland	2 Mme L. Hartel (DEN) *Jubilee*
3 Germany	3 Col. A. Jousseaume (FRA) *Harpagon*

Three-Day Event

Team	Individual
1 Sweden (H. G. von Blixen-Finecke, *Jubal*; N. Stahre, *Komet*; K. Frolen, *Fair*)	1 H. G. von Blixen-Finecke (SWE) *Jubal*
2 Germany	2 G. Lefrant (FRA) *Verdun*
3 USA	3 W. Busing (GER) *Hubertus*

Showjumping

Team	Individual
1 Gt Britain (W. H. White, *Nizefela*; H. M. Llewellyn, *Foxhunter*; D. N. Stewart, *Aberlow*)	1 P. J. d'Oriola (FRA) *Ali Baba*
2 Chile	2 O. Cristi (CHIL) *Bambi*
3 USA	3 F. Thiedemann (GER) *Meteor*

1956 STOCKHOLM
Dressage
Team
1 Sweden (H. St. Cyr, *Juli XX*;
   G. G. Persson, *Knaus*; G. A.
   Boltenstern, *Krest*)
2 Germany
3 Switzerland

Individual
1 Maj. H. St Cyr (SWE) *Juli XX*
2 Mme L. Hartel (DEN) *Jubilee*
3 Mme L. Linsenhoff (GER)
   Adular

Three-Day Event
Team
1 Gt Britain (F. W. C. Weldon,
   Kilbarry; A. L. Rook, *Wild
   Venture*; A. E. Hill,
   Countryman III)
2 Germany
3 Canada

Individual
1 P. Kastenman (SWE) *Illuster*
2 A. Lutke-Westhues (GER) *Trux
   von Kamax*
3 Lt. Col. F. W. C. Weldon (GB)
   Kilbarry

Showjumping
Team
1 Germany (H. G. Winkler, *Halla*;
   F. Thiedemann, *Meteor*;
   A. Lutke-Westhues, *Ala*)
2 Italy
3 Gt Britain (W. H. White, *Nizefela*;
   Miss P. Smythe, *Flanagan*;
   P. Robeson, *Scorchin*)

Individual
1 H. G. Winkler (GER) *Halla*
2 Lt. R. d'Inzeo (ITA) *Merano*
3 Capt. P. d'Inzeo (ITA) *Uruguay*

1960 ROME
Dressage
Team
No team awards

Individual
1 S. Filatov (USSR) *Absent*
2 G. Fischer (SWI) *Wald*
3 J. Neckermann (GER) *Asbach*

Three-Day Event
Team
1 Australia (L. Morgan, *Salad
   Days*; N. Lavis, *Mirrabooka*;
   W. Roycroft, *Our Solo*)
2 Switzerland
3 France

Individual
1 L. Morgan (AUS) *Salad Days*
2 N. Lavis (AUS) *Mirrabooka*
3 A. Buhler (SWI) *Gay Spark*

Showjumping
Team
1 Germany (A. Schockemöhle,
   Ferdl; F. Thiedemann, *Meteor*;
   H. G. Winkler, *Halla*)
2 USA
3 Italy

Individual
1 R. d'Inzeo (ITA) *Posillipo*
2 P. d'Inzeo (ITA) *The Rock*
3 D. Broome (GB) *Sunsalve*

1964 TOKYO

Dressage

Team
1 Germany (H. Boldt, *Remus*;
   R. Klimke, *Dux*; J. Neckermann,
   Antoinette)
2 Switzerland
3 Russia

Individual
1 H. Chammartin (SWI)
   Woermann
2 H. Boldt (GER) *Remus*
3 S. Filatoy (USSR) *Absent*

Three-Day Event

Team
1 Italy (M. Checcoli, *Surbean*;
   P. Angioni, *King*; G. Ravano,
   Royal Love)
2 USA
3 Germany

Individual
1 M. Checcoli (ITA) *Surbean*
2 C. A. Moratorio (ARG) *Chalan*
3 F. Ligges (GER) *Donkosak*

Showjumping

Team
1 Germany (H. Schridde, *Dozent*;
   K. Jarasinski, *Torro*; H. G.
   Winkler, *Fidelitas*)
2 France
3 Italy

Individual
1 P. J. d'Oriola (FRA) *Lutteur*
2 H. Schridde (GER) *Dozent*
3 P. D. Robeson (GB) *Firecrest*

1968 MEXICO

Dressage

Team
1 Germany (J. Neckermann,
   Mariano; Mme L. Linsenhoff,
   Piaff; R. Klimke, *Dux*)
2 USSR
3 Switzerland

Individual
1 I. Kizimov (USSR) *Ikhor*
2 J. Neckermann (GER) *Mariano*
3 R. Klimke (GER) *Dux*

Three-Day Event

Team
1 Gt Britain (D. Allhusen,
   Lochinvar; R. Meade,
   Cornishman; R. S. Jones, *The
   Poacher*; Miss J. Bullen, *Our
   Nobby*)
2 USA
3 Australia

Individual
1 J. J. Guyon (FRA) *Pitou*
2 Maj. D. Allhusen (GB)
   Lochinvar
3 M. Page (USA) *Foster*

Showjumping

Team
1 Canada (T. Gayford, *Big Dee*;
   J. Day, *Canadian Club*; J. Elder,
   The Immigrant)
2 France
3 Germany

Individual
1 W. Steinkraus (USA) *Snowbound*
2 Miss M. Coakes (GB) *Stroller*
3 D. Broome (GB) *Mister Softee*

1972 MUNICH
Dressage
Team

1 USSR (Miss E. Petuchkova, *Pepel*; I. Kizimov, *Ikhor*; I. Kalita, *Tarif*)
2 Germany
3 Sweden

Individual

1 Mme L. Linsenhoff (GER) *Piaff*
2 Miss E. Petuchkova (USSR) *Pepel*
3 J. Neckermann (GER) *Venetia*

Three-Day Event
Team

1 Gt Britain (Miss M. Gordon-Watson, *Cornishman V*; Mrs B. Parker, *Cornish Gold*; R. Meade, *Laurieston*; M. Phillips, *Great Ovation*)
2 USA
3 Germany

Individual

1 R. Meade (GB) *Laurieston*
2 A. Argenton (ITA) *Woodland*
3 J. Jonsson (SWE) *Sarajevo*

Showjumping
Team

1 Germany (F. Ligges, *Robin*; G. Wiltfang, *Askan*; H. Steenken, *Simona*; H. G. Winkler, *Torphy*)
2 USA
3 Italy

Individual

1 G. Mancinelli (ITA) *Ambassador*
2 Miss A. Moore (GB) *Psalm*
3 N. Shapiro (USA) *Sloopy*

1976 MONTREAL
Dressage
Team

1 Germany (H. Boldt, *Woycek*; R. Klimke, *Mehmed*; Miss G. Grillo, *Ultimo*)
2 Switzerland
3 USA

Individual

1 Miss C. Stückelberger (SWI) *Granat*
2 H. Holdt (GER) *Woycek*
3 R. Klimke (GER) *Mehmed*

Three-Day Event
Team

1 USA (E. Coffin, *Ballycor*; M. M. Plumb, *Better & Better*; B. Davidson, *Irish Cap*; Miss M. Tauskey, *Marcus Aurelius*)
2 Germany
3 Australia

Individual

1 E. Coffin (USA) *Ballycor*
2 M. Plumb (USA) *Better & Better*
3 K. Schultz (GER) *Madrigal*

Showjumping
Team

1 France (H. Parot, *Rivage*; M. Rozier, *Bayard de Maupas*; M. Roche, *Un Espoir*; M. Roguet, *Belle de Mars*)
2 Germany
3 Belgium

Individual

1 A. Schockemöhle (GER) *Warwick Rex*
2 M. Vaillancourt (CAN) *Branch County*
3 F. Mathy (BEL) *Gai Luron*

SHOWJUMPING

MEN'S WORLD CHAMPIONSHIPS

1953 PARIS
1 F. Goyoago (SPA) *Quorum*
2 F. Thiedemann (GER) *Diamant*
3 P. J. d'Oriola (FRA) *Ali Baba*
4 P. d'Inzeo (ITA) *Uruguay*

1954 MADRID
1 H. G. Winkler (GER) *Halla*
2 P. J. d'Oriola (FRA) *Arlequin*
3 F. Goyoago (SPA) (to final as holder)
4 S. Oppes (ITA) *Pagoro*

1955 AACHEN
1 H. G. Winkler (GER) *Halla*
2 R. d'Inzeo (ITA) *Nadir*
3 R. Dallas (GB) *Bones*
4 P. J. d'Oriola (FRA) retired

1956 AACHEN
1 R. d'Inzeo (ITA) *Merano*
2 F. Goyoaga (SPA) *Fahnenkonig*
3 F. Thiedemann (GER) *Meteor*
4 C. Delia (ARG) *Discutido*

1960 VENICE
1 R. d'Inzeo (ITA) *Gowran Girl*
2 C. Delia (ARG) *Huipil*
3 D. Broome (GB) *Sunsalve*
4 W. Steinkraus (USA) *Ksar d'Esprit*

1966 BUENOS AIRES
1 P. J. d'Oriola (FRA) *Pomone*
2 A. de Bohorques (SPA) *Quizas*
3 R. d'Inzeo (ITA) *Bowjak*
4 N. Pessoa (BRA) *Huipil*

1970 LA BAULE
1 D. Broome (GB) *Beethoven*
2 G. Mancinelli (ITA) *Fidux*
3 H. Smith (GB) *Mattie Brown*
4 A. Schockemöhle (GER) *Donald Rex*

1974 HICKSTEAD
1 H. Steenken (GER) *Simona*
2 E. Macken (IRE) *Pele*
3 H. Simon (AUT) *Lavendel*
4 F. Chapot (USA) *Main Spring*

1978 AACHEN
1 G. Wiltfang (GER) *Roman*
2 E. Macken (IRE) *Boomerang*
3 M. Matz (USA) *Jet Run*
4 J. Heinz (HOL) *Pandur*

MEN'S EUROPEAN CHAMPIONSHIPS

1957 ROTTERDAM
1 H. G. Winkler (GER) *Sonnenglanz*
2 B. de Fombelle (FRA) *Bucephale*
3 S. Oppes (ITA) *Pagoro*

1959 PARIS
1 P. d'Inzeo (ITA) *Uruguay*
2 P. J. d'Oriola (FRA) *Virtuoso*
3 F. Thiedemann (GER) *Godewind*

1958 AACHEN
1 F. Thiedemann (GER) *Meteor*
2 P. d'Inzeo (ITA) *The Rock*
3 H. G. Winkler (GER) *Halla*

1961 AACHEN
1 D. Broome (GB) *Sunsalve*
2 P. d'Inzeo (ITA) *Pioneer*
3 H. G. Winkler (GER) *Romanus*

1962 LONDON
1 C. D. Barker (GB) *Mister Softee*
2 H. G. Winkler (GER) *Romanus*
   and P d'Inzeo (ITA) *The Rock*

1963 ROME
1 G. Mancinelli (ITA) *Rockette*
2 A. Schockemöhle (GER) *Freiherr*
3 H. Smith (GB) *O'Malley*

1965 AACHEN
1 H. Schridde (GER) *Dozent*
2 A. Queipo de Llano (SPA)
   Infernal
3 A. Schockemöhle (GER) *Exakt*

1966 LUCERNE
1 N. Pessoa (BRA) *Gran Geste*
2 F. Chapot (USA) *San Lucas*
3 H. Arrambide (ARG) *Chimbote*

1967 ROTTERDAM
1 D. Broome (GB) *Mister Softee*
2 H. Smith (GB) *Harvester*
3 A. Schockemöhle (GER)
   Donald Rex

1969 HICKSTEAD
1 D. Broome (GB) *Mister Softee*
2 A. Schockemöhle (GER)
   Donald Rex
3 H. G. Winkler (GER) *Enigk*

1971 AACHEN
1 H. Steenken (GER) *Simona*
2 H. Smith (GB) *Evan Jones*
3 P. Weier (SWI) *Wulf*

1973 HICKSTEAD
1 P. McMahon (GB) *Pennwood
   Forge Mill*
2 A. Schockemöhle (GER) *The
   Robber*
3 H. Parot (FRA) *Tic*

Championships now mixed, for men and women

1975 MUNICH (amateurs only)
1 A. Schockemöhle (GER) *Warwick*   1 Germany
2 H. Steenken (GER) *Erle*   2 Switzerland
3 S. Sonksen (GER) *Kwept*   3 France

1977 VIENNA (open)
1 J. Heins (HOL) *Seven Valleys*   1 Holland
2 E. Macken (IRE) *Kerrygold*   2 Great Britain
3 A. Ebben (HOL) *Jumbo Design*   3 West Germany

1979 ROTTERDAM
1 G. Wiltfang (GER) *Roman*   1 Great Britain
2 P. Schockemöhle (GER) *Deister*   2 West Germany
3 H. Simon (AUT) *Gladstone*   3 Ireland

WOMEN'S WORLD CHAMPIONSHIPS

1965 HICKSTEAD
1 Miss M. Coakes (GB) *Stroller*
2 Miss K. Kusner (USA) *Untouchable*
3 Miss A. Westwood (GB) *The
   Maverick*

1970 COPENHAGEN
1 Miss J. Lefebvre (FRA) *Rocket*
2 Mrs D. Mould (GB) *Stroller*
3 Miss A. Drummond-Hay (GB)
   Merely-a-Monarch

1974 LA BAULE
1 Mme J. Tissot (FRA) *Rocket*
2 Miss M. McEvoy (USA) *Mr Muskie*
3 Mrs B. Kerr (CAN) *Magnor*

WOMEN'S EUROPEAN CHAMPIONSHIPS

1957 SPA
1 Miss P. Smythe (GB) *Flanagan*
2 Miss G. Serventi (ITA) *Doly*
3 Mme M. d'Orgeix (FRA) *Ocean*

1958 PALERMO
1 Miss G. Serventi (ITA) *Doly*
2 Miss A. Clement (GER) *Nico*
3 Miss I. Jansen (HOL) *Adelbloom*

1959 ROTTERDAM
1 Miss A. Townsend (GB) *Bandit*
2 Miss P. Smythe (GB) *Flanagan*
3 Miss A. Clement (GER) *Nico* and
  Miss G. Serventi (ITA) *Doly*

1960 COPENHAGEN
1 Miss S. Cohen (GB) *Clare Castle*
2 Mrs W. Wofford (GB) *Hollandia*
3 Miss A. Clement (GER) *Nico*

1961 DEAUVILLE
1 Miss P. Smythe (GB) *Flanagan*
2 Miss I. Jansen (HOL) *Icare*
3 Miss M. Cancre (FRA) *Ocean*

1962 MADRID
1 Miss P. Smythe (GB) *Flanagan*
2 Mrs H. Kohler (GER) *Cremona*
3 Mrs P. de Goyoaga (SPA) *Kif Kif*

1963 HICKSTEAD
1 Miss P. Smythe (GB) *Flanagan*
2 Mrs A. Givaudan (BRA) *Huipil*
3 Miss A. Drummond-Hay (GB) *Merely-a-Monarch*

1966 GIJON
1 Miss J. Lefebvre (FRA) *Kenavo*
2 Miss M. Bachmann (SWI) *Sandro*
3 Miss L. Novo (ITA) *Oxo Bob*

1967 FONTAINEBLEAU
1 Miss K. Kusner (USA) *Untouchable*
2 Miss L. Novo (ITA) *Predestine*
3 Miss M. Bachmann (SWI) *Erbach*

1968 ROME
1 Miss A. Drummond-Hay (GB) *Merely-a-Monarch*
2 Miss G. Serventi (ITA) *Gay Monarch*
(3 Miss M. Coakes (GB) *Stroller*
(3 Miss J. Lefebvre (FRA) *Rocket*

1969 DUBLIN
1 Miss I. Kellett (IRE) *Morning Light*
2 Miss A. Drummond-Hay (GB) *Xanthos*
3 Miss A. Westwood (GB) *The Maverick*

1971 ST GALLEN
1 Miss A. Moore (GB) *Psalm*
2 Mrs M. Dawes (GB) *The Maverick*
3 Miss M. Leitenberger (AUT) *Limbarra de Porto Conte*

1973 VIENNA
1 Miss A. Moore (GB) *Psalm*
2 Miss C. Bradley (GB) *True Lass*
3 Mrs P. Weier (SWI) *Erbach*

1975 onwards
See under Men's European Championships

PRESIDENTS CUP
(World team championships based on each country's best six Nations Cup
results)

1965
1 Gt Britain, 35 points
2 Germany, 31
3 Italy, 30

1966
1 USA, 27 points
2 Spain, 26
3 France, 20

1967
1 Gt Britain, 37 points
2 Germany, 26
3 Italy, 21

1968
1 USA, 34 points
2 Gt Britain, 26
3 Italy & Germany, 25 equal

1969
1 Germany, 39 points
2 Gt Britain, 35
3 Italy, 29

1970
1 Gt Britain, 27.5 points
2 Germany, 25
3 Italy, 15

1971
1 Germany, 37 points
2 Gt Britain, 33
3 Italy, 26

1972
1 Gt Britain, 33 points
2 Germany, 32
3 Italy, 20

1973
1 Gt Britain, 34 points
2 Germany, 33
3 Switzerland, 21

1974
1 Gt Britain, 37 points
2 Germany, 33.5
3 France, 31

1975
1 Germany, 39 points
2 Gt Britain, 35
3 Italy and Belgium, 22 equal

1976
1 Germany, 32 points
2 France, 31
3 Ireland, 27

1977
1 Gt Britain, 35.5 points
2 Germany, 32
3 Ireland, 31

1978
1 Gt Britain, 38 points
2 Germany, 36
3 France, 25

1979
1 Gt Britain, 40 points
2 Germany, 33.5
3 France, 29.5

1980
1 France, 38 points
2 Gt Britain, 35
3 Switzerland, 32.5

EUROPEAN JUNIOR TEAM CHAMPIONSHIPS

1952 OSTEND	1953 ROME	1954 ROTTERDAM
1 Italy	1 France	1 Italy
2 Belgium	2 Italy	2 Germany
(only two teams)	3 Belgium	3 Netherlands

1955 BILBAO
1 Germany
2 Netherlands
3 Spain

1956 SPA
1 Gt Britain
2 France
3 Germany

1957 LONDON
1 Gt Britain
2 Italy
3 France

1958 HANOVER
1 Gt Britain
2 South Africa
3 Italy

1959 LONDON
1 Gt Britain
2 Germany
3 France

1960 VENICE
1 Gt Britain
2 Poland
3 Italy

1961 HICKSTEAD
1 Germany
2 Netherlands
3 Gt Britain

1962 BERLIN
1 Gt Britain
2 Germany
3 France

1963 ROTTERDAM
1 Gt Britain
2 Germany
3 France

1964 BUDAPEST
1 Italy
2 Gt Britain
3 Belgium

1965 SALICE TERME
1 Gt Britain
2 Italy
3 Germany

1966 COPENHAGEN
1 Italy
2 Belgium
3 Switzerland

1967 JESOLO
1 Gt Britain
2 France
3 Germany

1968 STONELEIGH
1 Gt Britain
2 France
3 Ireland
  Germany
  Denmark

1969 DINARD
1 Switzerland
2 France
3 Germany

1970 ST MORITZ
1 Gt Britain
2 Switzerland
3 Germany

1971 HICKSTEAD
1 Ireland
2 Germany
3 Switzerland

1972 CORK
1 Belgium
2 Netherlands
3 Ireland

1973 ANTWERP
1 Switzerland
2 France
3 Germany

1974 LUCERNE
1 Austria
2 Netherlands
3 Gt Britain

1975 DORNBIRN
1 Belgium
2 W. Germany,
  Poland & Gt
  Britain equal

1976 BRUSSELS
1 Switzerland
2 Ireland
3 Gt Britain

**1977 LA TOUR DE
PEILZ**
1 Gt Britain
2 Ireland & France
  equal

**1978 STANNINGTON
(NORTHUMBER-
LAND)**
1 Gt Britain
2 Ireland
3 Holland

1979 GIJON
1 Switzerland
2 Gt Britain
3 Germany

OFFICIAL FEI RECORDS
High Jump 2.47m (8 ft 1½in), set by Captain Alberto Larraguibel (Chile) on *Huaso* at Vina dé Mar, Chile, in 1949.
Long Jump 8.40m (27ft 6¾in), set by André Ferreira (S. Africa) on *Something* at Johannesburg, South Africa, in 1975.
British High Jump Record 7ft 7⁵/₁₆in, set by Nick Skelton on Everest (GB) Stud's *Lastic* at Olympia in 1978.

KING GEORGE V GOLD CUP

1911 Capt. D. d'Exe (USSR) *Picollo*
1912 Lt. Delvoie (BEL) *Murat*
1913 Lt. Baron de Meslon (FRA) *Amazone*
1914 Lt. Baron de Meslon (FRA) *Amazone*
1920 Capt. de Laissardiere (FRA) *Dignite*
1921 Lt. Col. G. Brooke (GB) *Combined Training*
1922 Maj. Count Antonelli (ITA) *Bluff*
1923 Capt. de Laissardiere (FRA) *Grey Fox*
1924 Capt. Count Borsarelli (ITA) *Don Chisciotte*
1925 Lt. Col. M. Graham (GB) *Broncho*
1926 Lt. F. H. Bontecou (USA) *Ballymacshane*
1927 Lt. X. Bizard (FRA) *Quinine*
1928 Lt. A. G. Martyr (GB) *Forty Six*
1929 Lt. Gibault (FRA) *Mandarin*
1930 Lt. J. A. Talbot-Ponsonby (GB) *Chelsea*
1931 Capt. J. Misonne (BEL) *The Parson*
1932 Lt. J. A. Talbot-Ponsonby (GB) *Chelsea*
1933 No show
1934 Lt. J. A. Talbot-Ponsonby (GB) *Best Girl*
1935 Capt. J. J. Lewis (IRE) *Tramore Boy*
1936 Comdt. J. G. O'Dwyer (IRE) *Limerick Lace*

1937 Capt. X. Bizard (FRA) *Honduras*
1938 Maj. J. C. Friedberger (GB) *Derek*
1939 Lt. A. Bettoni (ITA) *Adigrat*
1947 P. J. d'Oriola (FRA) *Marquis III*
1948 Lt. Col. H. M. Llewellyn (GB) *Foxhunter*
1949 B. Butler (GB) *Tankard*
1950 Lt. Col. H. M. Llewellyn (GB) *Foxhunter*
1951 Capt. K. Barry (IRE) *Bally-neety*
1952 Don Carlos Figueroa (SPA) *Gracieux*
1953 Lt. Col. H. M. Llewellyn (GB) *Foxhunter*
1954 F. Thiedemann (GER) *Meteor*
1955 Lt. Col. Cartasegna (ITA) *Brando*
1956 W. Steinkraus (USA) *First Boy*
1957 Capt. P. d'Inzeo (ITA) *Uruguay*
1958 H. Wiley (USA) *Master William*
1959 H. Wiley (USA) *Nautical*
1960 D. Broome (GB) *Sunsalve*
1961 Capt. P. d'Inzeo (ITA) *The Rock*
1962 Capt. P. d'Inzeo (ITA) *The Rock*
1963 T. Wade (IRE) *Dundrum*
1964 W. Steinkraus (USA) *Sinjon*
1965 H. G. Winkler (GER) *Fortun*
1966 D. Broome (GB) *Mister Softee*

1967 P. Robeson (GB) *Firecrest*
1968 H. G. Winkler (GER) *Enigk*
1969 T. Edgar (GB) *Uncle Max*
1970 H. Smith (GB) *Mattie Brown*
1971 G. Wiltfang (GER) *Askan*
1972 D. Broome (GB) *Sportsman*
1973 P. McMahon (GB) *Pennwood Forge Mill*

1974 F. Chapot (USA) *Main Spring*
1975 A. Schockemöhle (GER) *Rex the Robber*
1976 M. Saywell (GB) *Chain Bridge*
1977 D. Broome (GB) *Philco*
1978 J. McVean (AUS) *Claret*
1979 R. Smith (GB) *Video*

QUEEN ELIZABETH CUP

1949 Miss I. Kellett (IRE) *Rusty*
1950 Miss J. Palethorpe (GB) *Silver Cloud*
1951 Miss I. Kellett (IRE) *Rusty*
1952 Mrs G. Rich (GB) *Quicksilver III*
1953 Miss M. Delfosse (GB) *Fanny Rosa*
1954 Miss J. Bonnaud (FRA) *Charleston*
1955 Miss D. Palethorpe (GB) *Earlsrath Rambler*
1956 Miss D. Palethorpe (GB) *Earlsrath Rambler*
1957 Miss E. Anderson (GB) *Sunsalve*
1958 Miss P. Smythe (GB) *Mr Pollard*
1959 Miss A. Clement (GER) *Nico*
1960 Miss S. Cohen (GB) *Clare Castle*
1961 Lady S. FitzAlan-Howard (GB) *Oorskiet*
1962 Mrs B. Crago (GB) *Spring Fever*
1963 Miss J. Nash (GB) *Trigger Hill*
1964 Miss G. Makin (GB) *Jubilant*
1965 Miss M. Coakes (GB) *Stroller*
1966 Miss A. Roger-Smith (GB) *Havana Royal*
1967 Miss B. Jennaway (GB) *Grey Leg*
1968 Mrs F. Chapot (USA) *White Lightning*
1969 Mrs M. Dawes (GB) *The Maverick VII*

1970 Miss A. Drummond-Hay (GB) *Merely-a-Monarch*
1971 Mrs D. Mould (GB) *Stroller*
1972 Miss A. Moore (GB) *Psalm*
1973 Miss A. Moore (GB) *Psalm* and Mrs M. Dawes (GB) *Mr Banbury* tied
1974 Mrs J. Davenport (GB) *All Trumps*
1975 Mrs J. Davenport (GB) *Hang On*
1976 Mrs D. Mould (GB) *Elizabeth Ann*
1977 Mrs E. Edgar (GB) *Everest Wallaby*
1978 Miss C. Bradley (GB) *Marius*
1979 Mrs E. Edgar (GB) *Forever*

BRITISH JUMPING DERBY

1961 S. Hayes (IRE) *Goodbye*
1962 Miss P. Smythe (GB) *Flanagan*
1963 N. Pessoa (BRA) *Gran Geste*
1964 S. Hayes (IRE) *Goodbye*
1965 N. Pessoa (BRA) *Gran Geste*
1966 D. Broome (GB) *Mister Softee*
1967 Miss M. Coakes (GB) *Stroller*
1968 Miss A. Westwood (GB) *The Maverick VII*
1969 Miss A. Drummond-Hay (GB) *Xanthos*
1970 H. Smith (GB) *Mattie Brown*
1971 H. Smith (GB) *Mattie Brown*
1972 H. Snoek (GER) *Shirokko*
1973 Mrs M. Dawes (GB) *Mr Banbury*

1974 H. Smith (GB) *Salvador*

1975 P. Darragh (IRE) *Pele*

1976 E. Macken (IRE) *Boomerang*

1977 E. Macken (IRE) *Boomerang*

1978 E. Macken (IRE) *Boomerang*

1979 E. Macken (IRE) *Carroll's Boomerang*

1980 D. Bowen (GB) *Scorton*

THREE-DAY EVENTING

WORLD CHAMPIONSHIPS

1966 BURGHLEY

Team	Individual
1 Ireland	1 Capt. C. Moratorio (ARG) *Chalan*
2 Argentina	2 R. Meade (GB) *Barberry*
only two teams finished	3 Miss B. Freeman-Jackson (IRE) *Sam Weller*

1970 PUNCHESTOWN

Team	Individual
1 Gt Britain	1 Miss M. Gordon-Watson (GB) *Cornishman V*
2 France	2 R. Meade (GB) *The Poacher*
only two teams finished	3 J. Wofford (USA) *Kilkenny*

1974 BURGHLEY

Team	Individual
1 USA	1 B. Davidson (USA) *Irish Cap*
2 Gt Britain	2 M. Plumb (USA) *Good Mixture*
3 Germany	3 H. Thomas (GB) *Playamar*

1978 LEXINGTON

Team	Individual
1 Canada	1 B. Davidson (USA) *Might Tango*
2 Germany	2 J. Watson (IRE) *Cambridge Blue*
3 USA	3 H. Rethemeier (GER) *Ladalco*

EUROPEAN CHAMPIONSHIPS

1953 BADMINTON

Team	Individual
1 Gt Britain	1 Maj. A. L. Rook (GB) *Starlight*
no other team finished	2 Maj. F. W. C. Weldon (GB) *Kilbarry*
	3 Capt. H. Schwarzenbach (SWI) *Vae Victis*

1954 BASLE

Team	Individual
1 Gt Britain	1 A. E. Hill (GB) *Crispin*
2 Germany	2 Maj. F. W. C. Weldon (GB) *Kilbarry*
only two teams finished	3 Maj. A. L. Rook (GB) *Starlight*

1955 WINDSOR

Team
1 Gt Britain
2 Switzerland
only two teams finished

Individual
1 Maj. F. W. C. Weldon (GB)
   Kilbarry
2 Lt. Cmdr. J. Oram (GB) *Radar*
3 A. E. Hill (GB) *Countryman*

1957 COPENHAGEN

Team
1 Gt Britain
2 Germany
3 Sweden

Individual
1 Miss S. Willcox (GB) *High and Mighty*
2 A. Lutke-Westhues (GER) *Franko*
3 J. Lindgren (SWE) *Eldorado*

1959 HAREWOOD

Team
1 Germany
2 Gt Britain
3 France

Individual
1 Maj. H. Schwarzenbach (SWI)
   Burn Trout
2 Lt. Col. F. W. C. Weldon (GB)
   Samuel Johnson
3 Maj. D. Allhusen (GB) *Laurien*

1962 BURGHLEY

Team
1 USSR
2 Ireland
3 Gt Britain

Individual
1 Capt. J. Templar (GB) *M'Lord Connolly*
2 G. Gazyumov (USSR) *Granj*
3 Miss J. Wykeham-Musgrave (GB)
   Uyebrooks

1965 MOSCOW

Team
1 USSR
2 Ireland
3 Gt Britain

Individual
1 M. Babirecki (POL) *Volt*
2 L. Baklyshkin (USSR) *Ruon*
3 H. Karsten (GER) *Condora*

1967 PUNCHESTOWN

Team
1 Gt Britain
2 Ireland
3 France

Individual
1 Maj. E. A. Boylan (IRE) *Durlas Eile*
2 M. Whiteley (GB) *The Poacher*
3 Maj. D. Allhusen (GB) *Lochinvar*

1969 HARAS DU PIN

Team
1 Gt Britain
2 USSR
3 Germany

Individual
1 Miss M. Gordon-Watson (GB)
   Cornishman V
2 R. Walker (GB) *Pasha*
3 B. Messman (GER) *Wiendspeil*

1971 BURGHLEY
Team
1 Gt Britain
2 USSR
3 Ireland

Individual
1 HRH Princess Anne (GB)
   Doublet
2 Miss D. West (GB) *Baccarat*
3 S. Stevens (GB) *Classic Chips*

1973 KIEV
Team
1 Germany
2 USSR
3 Gt Britain

Individual
1 A. Evdokimov (USSR) *Jeger*
2 H. Blocker (GER) *Albrant*
3 H. Karsten (GER) *Sioux*

1975 LUHMUHLEN
Team
1 USSR
2 Gt Britain
3 Germany

Individual
1 Miss L. Prior-Palmer (GB) *Be Fair*
2 HRH Princess Anne (GB) *Goodwill*
3 P. Gornuschko (USSR) *Gvsar*

1977 BURGHLEY
Team
1 Gt Britain
2 Germany
3 Ireland

Individual
1 Miss L. Prior-Palmer (GB) *George*
2 K. Schultz (GER) *Madrigal*
3 H. Karsten (GER) *Sioux*

1979 LUHMUHLEN
Team
1 Ireland
2 Gt Britain
3 France

Individual
1 N. Haagensen (DEN) *Monaco*
2 Miss R. Bayliss (GB) *Gurgle the Greek*
3 R. Schwarz (GER) *Power Game*

EUROPEAN JUNIOR CHAMPIONSHIPS
1967 ERIDGE
Team
No team contest

Individual
1 A. Souchon (FRA) *Roi d'Asturie*
2 R. Walker (GB) *Pasha*
3 P. Giraud (FRA) *Saphir d'Eau*

1968 CRAON
Team
1 France
2 Gt Britain
3 Poland

Individual
1 R. Walker (GB) *Pasha*
2 P. Giraud (FRA) *Gallax*
3 A. Sarrant (FRA) *Palestro*

1969 EUSKIRCHEN

Team	Individual
1 USSR	1 H.-O. Bolten (GER) *Lansbub XIII*
2 France	
3 Germany	2 V. Tichkin (USSR) *Elion*
	3 Miss A. Pattinson (GB) *Sharon*

1970 HOLSTEBRO

Team	Individual
1 Germany	1 N.-O. Barkander (SWE) *Pegasus*
2 France	2 A. Fenner (GER) *Anemone*
3 Gt Britain	3 B. Wahler (GER) *Marcus IV*

1971 WESEL

Team	Individual
1 Gt Britain	1 C. Brooke (GB) *Olive Oyl*
2 France	2 F. Lault (FRA) *Un de la Cote*
3 USSR	3 S. Nikolski (USSR) *Vostorg*

1972 ERIDGE

Team	Individual
1 Gt Britain	1 B. Clements (FRA) *Quel Pich*
2 France	2 A. Hill (GB) *Maid Marion*
3 Netherlands	3 G. Heyligers (HOL) *Full-Speed*

1973 POMPADOUR

Team	Individual
1 Gt Britain	1 Miss V. Holgate (GB) *Dubonnet*
2 Italy	2 Miss S. Bailey (GB) *Red Amber*
3 Ireland	3 A. Miserocchi (ITA) *Friday*

1974 ROME

Team	Individual
1 Germany	1 Miss S. Ker (GB) *Peer Gynt*
2 Ireland	2 T. Esteve (FRA) *Urgel*
3 USSR	3 Miss J. Winter (GB) *Stainless Steel*

1975

No official championships

1976 SIEKKRUG

Team	Individual
1 Gt Britain	1 O. Depagne (FRA) *Bobineau*
2 France	2 Miss D. Saffell (GB) *Double Brandy*
3 Italy	3 Miss S. Bouet (GB) *Sea Lord V*

1977 FONTAINEBLEAU

Team	Individual
1 Ireland	1 M. Spehmann (GER) *Lorbass*
2 Germany	2 P. Cronier (FRA) *Dandy XXVI*
3 Poland	3 M. Otto (GER) *Pergola*

1978 BURGHLEY

Team		Individual	
1	Germany	1	D. Baumgart (GER) *Kurfurst*
2	France	2	R. Ehrenbrink (GER) *Huntsman*
3	Ireland	3	P. Cronier (FRA) *Danseur II*

1979 PUNCHESTOWN

Team		Individual	
1	France	1	Miss N. May (GB) *Commodore IV*
2	Gt Britain		
3	Ireland	2	J. Dermody (IRE) *Heathcliffe*
		3	McSebilleau (FRA) *Dragomiroff*

1980 ACHSELSCHWANG

Team		Individual	
1	Gt Britain	1	Miss C. Berger (GER) *Bacardi*
2	Sweden	2	Miss C. Needham (GB) *Solo*
3	France	3	R. Funder (AUT) *Dac*

BADMINTON

1949 J. Sheddon (GB) *Golden Willow*
1950 Capt. J. A. Collings (GB) *Remus*
1951 Capt. H. Schwarzenbach (SWI) *Vae Victis*
1952 Capt. M. A. Q. Darley (GB) *Emily Little*
1953 European championship
1954 Miss H. Hough (GB) *Bambi V*
1955 No competition
1956 Maj. F. W. C. Weldon (GB) *Kilbarry*
1957 Miss S. Willcox (GB) *High and Mighty*
1958 Miss S. Willcox (GB) *High and Mighty*
1959 Mrs S. Waddington (GB) *Airs and Graces*
1960 W. Roycroft (AUS) *Our Solo*
1961 L. Morgan (AUS) *Salad Days*
1962 Miss A. Drummond-Hay (GB) *Merely-a-Monarch*
1963 Cancelled
1964 Capt. J. R. Templer (GB) *M'Lord Connolly*
1965 Maj. E. A. Boylan (IRE) *Durlas Eile*

1966 Cancelled
1967 Miss C. Ross-Taylor (GB) *Jonathan*
1968 Miss J. Bullen (GB) *Our Nobby*
1969 R. Walker (GB) *Pasha*
1970 R. Meade (GB) *The Poacher*
1971 Lt. M. Phillips (GB) *Great Ovation*
1972 Lt. M. Phillips (GB) *Great Ovation*
1973 Miss L. Prior-Palmer (GB) *Be Fair*
1974 Capt. M. Phillips (GB) *Columbus*
1975 Cancelled after dressage
1976 Miss L. Prior-Palmer (GB) *Wide Awake*
1977 Miss L. Prior-Palmer (GB) *George*
1978 Mrs T. Holderness-Roddam (GB) *Warrior*
1979 Miss L. Prior-Palmer (GB) *Killaire*
1980 M. Todd (NZ) *Southern Comfort*

BURGHLEY

1961 Miss A. Drummond-Hay (GB)
Merely-a-Monarch
1962 European championship
1963 Capt. H. Freeman-Jackson
(IRE) *St Finnbarr*
1964 R. Meade (GB) *Barberry*
1965 Capt. J. J. Beale (GB) *Victoria Bridge*
1966 World championship
1967 Miss L. Sutherland (GB) *Popadom*
1968 Miss S. Willcox (GB) *Fair and Square*
1969 Miss G. Watson (GB) *Shaitan*

1970 Miss J. Bradwell (GB) *Don Camillo*
1971 European championship
1972 Miss J. Hodgson (GB) *Larkspur*
1973 Capt. M. Phillips (GB) *Maid Marion*
1974 World championship
1975 Miss A. Pattinson (GB) *Carawich*
1976 Mrs T. Holderness-Roddam (GB) *Warrior*
1977 European championship
1978 Mrs L. Clarke (GB) *Greco*
1979 A. Hoy (AUS) *Davey*
1980 R. Walker (GB) *John of Gaunt*

DRESSAGE

WORLD CHAMPIONSHIPS

1966 BERNE

Team
1 Germany
2 Switzerland
3 USSR

Individual
1 J. Neckermann (GER) *Mariano*
2 R. Klimke (GER) *Dux*
3 H. Boldt (GER) *Remus*

1970 AACHEN

Team
1 USSR
2 Germany
3 E. Germany

Individual
1 Elena Petuchkova (USSR) *Pepel*
2 Liselott Linsenhoff (GER) *Piaff*
3 I. Kisimov (USSR) *Ikor*

1974 COPENHAGEN

Team
1 Germany
2 USSR
3 Switzerland

Individual
1 R. Klimke (GER) *Mehmed*
2 Liselott Linsenhoff (GER) *Piaff*
3 Elena Petuchkova (USSR) *Pepel*

1978 GOODWOOD

Team
1 Germany
2 Switzerland
3 USSR

Individual
1 Miss C. Stückelberger (SWI) *Granat*
2 U. Schulten-Baumer (GER) *Slivowitz*
3 Mrs A. Loriston-Clarke (GB) *Dutch Courage*

EUROPEAN CHAMPIONSHIPS

1963 COPENHAGEN

Team
1 Gt Britain
2 Rumania

Individual
1 H. Chammartin (SWI)
   Wolfdietrich
2 H. Boldt (GER) *Remus*
3 H. Chammartin (SWI) *Woermann*

1965 COPENHAGEN

Team
1 Germany
2 Switzerland
3 USSR

Individual
1 H. Chammartin (SWI)
   Wolfdietrich
2 H. Boldt (GER) *Remus*
3 R. Klimke (GER) *Arcadius*

1967 AACHEN

Team
1 Germany
2 USSR
3 Switzerland

Individual
1 R. Klimke (GER) *Dux*
2 I. Kisimov (USSR) *Ikor*
3 H. Boldt (GER) *Remus*

1969 WOLFSBURGH

Team
1 Germany
2 E. Germany
3 USSR

Individual
1 Liselott Linsenhoff (GER) *Piaff*
2 I. Kisimov (USSR) *Ikor*
3 J. Neckermann (GER) *Mariano*

1971 WOLFSBURGH

Team
1 Germany
2 USSR
3 Sweden

Individual
1 Liselott Linsenhoff (GER) *Piaff*
2 J. Neckermann (GER) *Van Eick*
3 I. Kisimov (USSR) *Ikor*

1973 AACHEN

Team
1 Germany
2 USSR
3 Switzerland

Individual
1 R. Klimke (GER) *Mehmed*
2 Elena Petuchkova (USSR) *Pepel*
3 I. Kalita (USSR) *Tarif*

1975 KIEV

Team
1 Germany
2 USSR
3 Switzerland

Individual
1 Christine Stückelberger (SWI)
   Granat
2 H. Boldt (GER) *Woycek*
3 Karin Schluter (GER) *Liostro*

1977 ST GALLEN

Team
1 Germany
2 Switzerland
3 USSR

Individual
1 Christine Stückelberger (SWI)
   Granat
2 H. Boldt (GER) *Woycek*
3 U. Schulten-Baumer (GER)
   Slivowitz

1979 AARHUS

Team	Individual
1 Germany	1 Elisabeth Theurer (AUT) *Mon*
2 USSR	*Cherie*
3 Switzerland	2 Christine Stückelberger (SWI)
	Granat
	3 Harry Boldt (GER) *Woycek*

SHOWING

DUBLIN SUPREME CHAMPIONS

1946 Mrs S. G. Atkinson's *Landslide*, 7-y-o ch.g. by Baydrop, d. by Rowland
1947 N. Galway-Greer's *Mighty Fine*, 6-y-o ch.g. by Al Quaim, d. by Duke of Sparta
1948 N. Galway-Greer's *Mighty Atom*, 4-y-o ch.g. by Rockminster
1949 N. Galway-Greer's *Splendour*, 6-y-o ch.g. by Warden of the Maches, d. by Gilling Castle
1950 Waring Wills's *Wild Venture*, 5-y-o b.g. by Wild Scion, d. by Vencedor
1951 Mrs E. Glen Browne's *Sandara*, 7-y-o ch.g. by Sandyman, d. by Sarsfield
1952 Larry O'Bryne's *Babbling Stream*, by Water Serpent
1953 N. D. Mahony's *Ritz Hotel*, 5-y-o b.g. by Jamaica Inn ex Vito by Morland
1954 Matthew Parie's *What a Walk*, 4-y-o g.g. by Long Walk
1955 W. E. Wylie's *Frigorifico*, 7-y-o br.g. by Figaro ex Honoraria by Milesius
1956 T. W. Dreaper's *Man o'War*, 4-y-o br.g. by Steel Chip, d. by St Dunstan
1957 N. Galway-Greer's *Work of Art*, 6-y-o br.g. by Soldado, d. by King Cob
1958 N. Galway-Greer's *Tenerife*, 5-y-o br.g. by Soldado, d. by St Dunstan
1959 N. Galway-Greer's *Munning's Model*, 4-y-o ch-g- by Hop Bridge, d. by Bahia
1960 N. Galway-Greer's *Superb*, 5-y-o br.g. by Pennyfare
1961 Lady Helena Hilton-Green's *Last of Banogue's*, 6-y-o br.g. by Dark Artist d. by Tomahawk
1962 The Duchess of Westminster's *Badna Bay*, 4-y-o br.g. by Flamenco ex Christy Cut by Wave Top
1963 N. Galway-Greer's *Prudent Lover*, 4-y-o b.g. by Gypse, d. by Power Cut
1964 N. Galway-Greer's *Treasure Hill*, 5-y-o br.g. by Richard Louis, d. Calder Bridge by King Salmon
1965 The Hon. D. Conolly-Carew's *Ballyfine*
1966 N. Galway-Greer's *Never Forget*, 4-y-o br.g. by Blue Cliff, d. by Bahia
1967 Mrs A. L. Wood's *Urney Road*, 4-y-o b.g. by Copernicus, ex Ballyvulgan
1968 Alan Lillingston's *Josh*, 5-y-o b.g. by Josue, d. by Duke's Jester
1969 Mrs R. A. A. Latta's *Frozen Slave*, 5-y-o ch.g. by Artic Slave ex Benvoy Owl
1970 T. H. Moore's *The Yank*, 5-y-o ch.g. by Suresh, d. by Golden Years
1971 John Grennan's *Smartie*, 6-y-o b.g. by Signal Corps, d. by Knight's Wax
1972 Jack Deacon's *Slaney Valley*, 6-y-o g.g. by Bright Law, d. by Golden Years
1973 Lord Petersham's *Malcolm*, 4-y-o b.g. by Apollonius ex Dreda by Camfield
1974 Robert Irwin's *Kit-Chin*, 5-y-o b.g. by Chou Chin Chow ex Kildollagh Kitten
1975 Miss Fiona Kinnear's *Gralla*, 5-y-o ch.g. by Sunny Light, d. by Candelabra
1976 Tom Moloney's *Rainbow*, 4-y-o ch.g. by Bahrain, ex Errigal (Gralla Champion of Honour)
1977 P. P. Sweeney's *St Swithin*, 6-y-o ch.g. by Indigenous ex Boomerang
1978 M. Hickey's *Foggy Wood* 5-y-o b.g. by Woodville II ex Sibbaldia
1979 G. Chapman and Miss F. Kinnear's *Zatopec* 5-y-o ch.g. by Sunny Light ex Safe Delivery
1980 W. H. Johnston's *Golden Comet* 5-y-o ch.g. by Ozymandias ex Song

Lloyds Bank Sponsorships

Lloyds Bank In-Hand Championship
Lloyds Bank Pony Judging Study Day — in association with NPS
Lloyds Bank Young Judge of the Year — in association with
  NPS and *Pony* magazine
Lloyds Bank Young Instructor of the Year Awards — in
  association with BHS
Riding for the Disabled — Lloyds Bank Championship and
  training bursaries
Pelham Books annual *Pelham Horse Year*
BHS booklet 'Careers with Horses'
BEF consultative document 'Case for the Riding Horse'
Irish Draught Horse Society — teach-ins
British Equine Veterinary Association — congress handbook
Lloyds Bank Equestrian Year Scholarship — in association with
  Equestrian Year
Hunters' Improvement Society — booklet *Conformation of the
  Horse*
NPS leaflet *Hints for Young Judges*